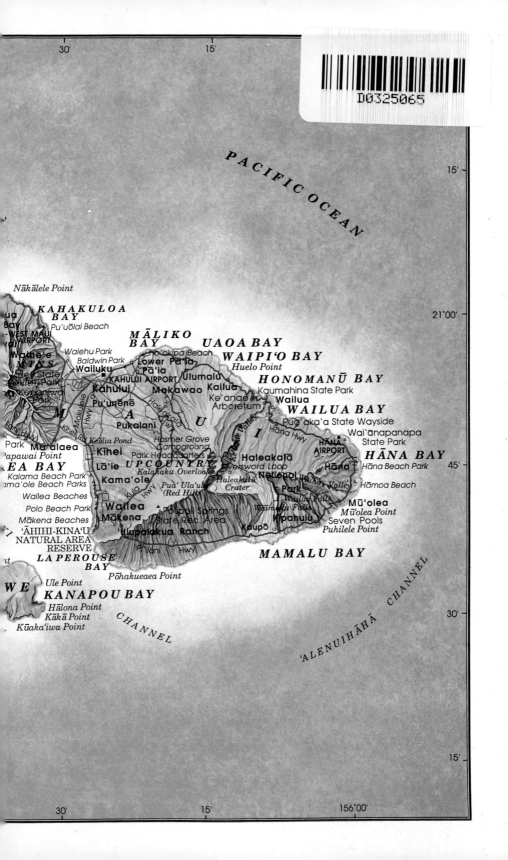

PACIFIC OCEAN

15'

21°00'

45'

30'

15'

30'

15'

156°00'

Nākālele Point

KAHAKULOA BAY
Pu'uōlai Beach

MĀLIKO BAY
UAOA BAY
WAIPI'O BAY

Ho'okipa Beach

WEST MAUI AIRPORT

Waiehu Park
Baldwin Park

Washe'e

Wai'

Lower Pa'ia
Pā'ia
Wailuku
KAHULUI AIRPORT
Ulumalu

HONOMANŪ BAY

State
Park
Tāi-ano

Kahului
Makawao
Kailua

Kaumahina State Park

Park

Pu'unēnē

Ke'anae
Arboretum
Wailua

WAILUA BAY

M A
U
I

Mokuēle Hwy

Pukalani

Pua'aka'a State Wayside
Wai'anapanapa
State Park

Kihei Rd

Keālia Pond

Hosmer Grove
Campground

HĀNA BAY

Park

Mā'alaea

Kīhei
Lā'ie

Park Headquarters

Haleakalā

HĀNA
AIRPORT

Hāna
Hāna Beach Park

Papawai Point

EA BAY

Kalahaku Overlook

Kama'ole

National

Valley

Hōmoa Beach

Kalama Beach Park
ma'ole Beach Parks

Haleakalā
Crater

Pua' Ula'ula
(Red Hill)

Park

Wailua Falls

Wailea Beaches

Kula Hwy

Polo Beach Park

Wailea
Mākena

Mākena Beaches

'ĀHIHI-KINA'U
NATURAL AREA
RESERVE

Polipoli Springs
State Rec. Area

'Ulupalakua Ranch

Kaupō

Kīpahulu

Mū'olea
Mū'olea Point
Seven Pools
Puhilele Point

Pi'ilani Hwy

MAMALU BAY

LA PEROUSE
BAY

Pōhakueaea Point

WE

Ule Point

KANAPOU BAY

Hālona Point
Kākā Point

Kūaka'iwa Point

CHANNEL

'ALENUIHĀHĀ CHANNEL

Maui

ISLAND HERITAGE
Honolulu, Hawaii

Please address orders and
editorial correspondence to:

ISLAND HERITAGE
P U B L I S H I N G

99-880 IWAENA STREET
AIEA, HAWAII 96701-3202
Phone (808) 487-7299
Email: hawaii4u@pixi.com

FOURTH EDITION, SECOND PRINTING -- 1997
Printed in Hong Kong

Produced by:
THE MADDEN CORPORATION

Published by:
ISLAND HERITAGE PUBLISHING
A Division of The Madden Corporation

Project Coordinator/1996 Editor:
HELEN AVERY DRAKE

Cartography:
ANDREA HINES

Original Cover Artwork by:
MARK A. WAGENMAN
FEDERICK WOODRUFF

TABLE OF CONTENTS

INTRODUCTION

INTRODUCTION

M aui stands out as a brilliant, spectacularly diverse jewel in the strand of beautiful islands that make up Hawai'i. From the towering grandeur of the dormant volcano, Haleakalā, to the sweeping beaches of Kā'anapali, Maui truly fulfills the daydreamer's fantasy of what an idyllic tropical paradise should be. It is here that the visitor discovers both the charming, sleepy Hawaiian village of Hāna and the fast-paced resort center of West Maui. Bustling Lahaina, the center of the whaling industry of yesteryear and the capital of the whale-watching industry of today, reflects how Maui's rich past has evolved into a different, but no less fascinating, present. Maui commands a significant place in Hawai'i's colorful and occasionally turbulent history. Here, Hawaiian chiefs played out important stages in these islands' development.

GEOGRAPHY

Maui once was two islands, each with a volcanic peak soaring above the surface of the sea like tips of icebergs. Erosion wore down the flanks of the volcanoes until they connected in an isthmus, which Mauians today refer to as the Central Valley. Maui's commercial centers of Kahului and Wailuku are here. Other distinct regions are the old whaling port of Lahaina and West Maui; Kapalua, a sleepy tropical area at the far west of the island; the tropical areas of Kīhei, Wailea and Mā'alaea along the southern coast; the Upcountry area, a place of lush pastures and cattle ranches on the slopes of Haleakalā; and, at the extreme east end, the lush, lovely Hāna.

Maui is the second largest island in Hawai'i, which consists of a string of islands in the North Pacific about a thousand miles from its nearest neighbors--the Line Islands to the south and the Marshall Islands to the southwest. Nothing but ocean lies between Hawai'i and southern California, 2390 miles (3846 km) to the east-northeast; Japan, 3850 miles (6196 km) to the west-northwest; and Alaska, 2600 miles (4184 km) to the

north. The Marquesas--from which at least some of the early Polynesian migrants came--are 2400 miles (3862 km) to the south-southeast.

The archipelago spans 1523 miles (2451 km) and includes 132 islands, reefs and shoals strewn across the Tropic of Cancer--from Kure Atoll in the northwest to underwater seamounts off the coast of the island of Hawai'i in the southeast. All are included in the state of Hawai'i except the Midway Islands, which are administered by the U. S. Navy. This southernmost part of the United States lies between latitudes 28° 15' and 18° 54'N and between longitudes 179° 25' and 154° 40'W, reaching almost as far west as Alaska's Aleutian Islands. Hawai'i's major islands share their tropical latitudes with such urban centers as Mexico City, Havana, Mecca, Calcutta, Hanoi and Hong Kong. The 158th meridian west, which passes through O'ahu's Pearl Harbor, also crosses Point Barrow on Alaska's north coast, Atiu Island in the South Pacific's Cook Islands and Cape Colbeck near the edge of Anarctica's Ross Ice Shelf.

Windsurfing at Ho'okipa Beach, the professionals' hangout

While Hawai'i's land surface adds up to only 6425 square miles (16,642 sq km - at that, still larger than Connecticut, Delaware or Rhode Island), the archipelago, including its territorial waters, covers a total of about 654,500 square miles (1,695,155 sq km)--an area considerably bigger than Alaska and more than twice the size of Texas.

Maui is one of eight main islands in the Hawaiian chain. One of the islands, Kaho'olawe, is not inhabited and, up until 1994, was used by the military for target practice. The tiny island of Ni'ihau is privately owned, and can be visited by non-residents only by invitation. The island, due to its fierce protection from outside influence, is the last stronghold of Hawaiian culture (its entire population is of at least part-Hawaiian blood), and it is the only place on the planet where Hawaiian is still spoken as the mother tongue. Scenic helicopter flights over the island may touch down for up to twenty minutes, but no contact with the residents is permitted.

That leaves the islands of Kaua'i, O'ahu, Moloka'i, Lāna'i, Maui, and Hawai'i (commonly known as 'the Big Island')--in that order, north to south and chronologically in age--for visitors to explore.

HISTORY

More than two centuries ago, King Kahekili ruled all of Maui except for the Hāna area, which fell under the de facto control of Kalaniopu'u, a powerful ruler on the island of Hawai'i to the south. In 1776, Kalaniopu'u's armies invaded Maui, but Kahekili's warriors annihilated them in a famous battle near Wailuku. Kahekili, justly famous as a mighty king in his own right, also may have been the father of Kamehameha, destined to unite all the islands in his kingdom.

In 1786, a French expedition led by Captain Jean Francois de Galaup, Comte de La Perouse, anchored in a sheltered bay south of Wailea and Mākena. The next day, La Perouse became the first non-Hawaiian to set foot on Maui. (Cook had seen Maui, but sailed by after failing to quickly find an anchorage.) Maui soon became a regular port of call.

Four years after La Perouse's arrival, Kamehameha's forces defeated the army of Kahekili, and Kamehameha, who became known as the 'Napoleon of the Pacific', brought Maui under his control. In 1793, Captain Vancouver sailed into Lahaina and confirmed La Perouse's earlier report of a fine anchorage. In less than a dozen years, Kamehameha's 'Pelelu Fleet' of canoes lingered on West Maui beaches before he sailed on to conquer O'ahu. The first whaling vessel, the *Balaena*, stopped off in Lahaina in 1819 and was a harbinger of the vast fleets to come.

Of more lasting impact, Christians built their first mission in Lahaina in 1823, and the great conversion of Maui--and Hawai'i--gained impetus. At the same time, the standard of education on the island improved, attracting the children of the rich from other islands and even the U. S. mainland.

With the decline of whaling, George Wilfong started the first sugar plantation on Maui in 1849 in Hāna. A dozen years later, James Campbell built the first great sugar mill on the island. By 1900, more than half the population on Maui was comprised of Chinese and Japanese citizens working the eleven sugar plantation fields. Through the efforts of such men as Henry Perrine Baldwin and Samuel Thomas Alexander, the sugar industry gained preeminence. Claus Spreckels had large holdings on Maui, and built an enormous irrigation ditch that brought fifty million gallons of water a day from Hā'iku (Upcountry) to the area of Pu'unēnē (Central Valley) so that sugar could prosper. Maui's center of focus shifted from Lahaina to Pā'ia, a sugar town with a nearby mill.

Not far away, near the governmental seat at Wailuku, the port of Kahului developed into the island's principal seaport; it also was headquarters for a prosperous railroad operation, with narrow-gauge passenger and freight trains under-way between Wailuku-Kahului and Spreckelsville-Pā'ia.

By 1930, transportation on Maui and between islands had improved considerably. There were some 5000 'gas-driven cars' on Maui streets and roads. Inter-Island Airways, Ltd., landed its first Sikorsky aircraft on Maui in 1929 and began regular service from the airport at Mā'alaea.

Like the rest of Hawai'i, Maui was shocked by the attack on Pearl Harbor on December 7, 1941. Maui contributed manpower to the war effort and bought more than its share of war bonds.

Post-war Maui took part in the gradual, then rapid, development of the islands. With its stunning scenery, its splendid beaches and lush pastures, and perhaps the best climate of all the islands, Maui began to attract visitors who wanted more from Hawai'i than the comparatively urban, fast-paced atmosphere of Waikīkī and the rest of O'ahu. Suddenly, Maui sparkled with a new vitality that continues today.

Watching sunset from Haleakalā

CULTURAL BACKGROUND

In anonymity and out of Asia, the ancestors of the Hawaiians began millennia ago to work their way across the vast, trackless Pacific. They journeyed from Central Asia to Southeast Asia, poised on the brink of a great adventure: the people of the land were about to become the people of the sea, and ultimately the people of 'many islands', for that is what the word Polynesia means. As they moved, they changed, altering their gods to the demands of new places, subtly reworking their myths and legends and genealogies to make them compatible with the enormous seas and the evolution of their canoes. Their mode of dress changed; their physical statures altered as they adapted to life on, and in, the water.

At some point in these long and epic voyages, the Polynesians stood offshore in the lee of a group of islands at the apex of a triangle formed by New Zealand, Tahiti and Hawai'i. Some nameless Polynesian sailor, more then eleven centuries ago, shouted excitedly to the rest of the crew and pointed out islands that would mark the crowning achievement of the long voyages. That sailor and the rest of the crew are believed today to have been from the Marquesas island group far to the southeast.

More voyages back and forth followed. One day, a new group of energetic islanders, the Polynesians from Tahiti, made the journey. In all likelihood there was war. Or perhaps it was merely the dominance of a

A laid-back afternoon on the Hāna Coast

strong, aggressive race. Whatever the cause, by about AD 1100, the people from Tahiti had surfaced as the unquestioned masters in a magnificent new home. They gave it a name: Hawai'i. Later, some would say the name had no significance, while others believed it was a variation of Hawaiki, the legendary homeland of all Polynesians.

Other newcomers made landfall here over the centuries. Seeds came in the bellies of birds; coconuts washed ashore on the beaches, and took hold. Wind-blown pollen and insects bumped up against the islands' high mountains. Natural springs and rivers formed.

The Polynesians added variety to the indigenous plants, introducing bananas, coconuts, sweet potatoes, bamboo, ginger, yams, breadfruit and candlenut (kukui) trees. They also brought dogs, chickens and pigs to Hawai'i. In time, a new civilization developed as the settlers became less Polynesian and more Hawaiian.

The life of the average Hawaiian was ordered, and he was often powerless to change it. The ali'i, the royalty, were absolute masters. A second group, the kāhuna, or priests, cast a long shadow and dealt in both the natural and supernatural worlds. As kāhuna, the priests were known to talk with the gods and interpret their powers. The ordinary men and women were maka'āinana, in many cases born to a time and place that locked them into a pattern from which they could not escape.

But it was not an altogether grim life. The maka'āinana lived in a healthy, uncrowded and stunningly beautiful archipelago where they arose to brilliant mornings and retired awash in sunsets of great beauty. They had their makahiki, or

7

Heading down Haleakalā Highway, with Upcountry pastures below

traditional games, and they revered their old people, the *kūpuna*. They cared about the family unit and about their *'ohana*, or extended family. By the time Westerners arrived here, the Hawaiian society had become complex, colorful and yet infused with this strict sense of order.

The great English explorer and navigator, Captain James Cook, found these remote North Pacific islands on January 18, 1778. European diseases and Western weapons followed, dramatically changing the lives of the Hawaiians.

The islands impressed Cook, who liaisons with his men were inevitable, but he also knew some of his sailors were infected with venereal disease.

Cook, revered as the god Lono, was killed by Hawaiians on the beach at Kealakekua, on the southernmost island, after a misunderstanding. Had he lived, he would have seen the diseases decimate the Hawaiian population from 300,000 in 1778 to fewer than 50,000 a century later. And by 1878, other forces had diminished the influence of the Hawaiians and their own land.

In Kamehameha's lifetime, Hawaiian power reached its zenith. Tough and energetic, intelligent and

Camping in Haleakalā National Park near the ocean

was surprised to find that the inhabitants spoke a variation of the languages he had heard earlier in the South Pacific. He wrote of the natives' generosity and worried over their tendency to steal; he watched with both understanding and dismay as the native girls, the *wāhine*, came aboard his two ships. He knew such implacable, Kamehameha had inherited the war god Kuka'ilimoku from his uncle, Kalaniopu'u, ranking chief at Kealakekua. He also inherited a tall frame and a tactician's approach to problem-solving. When Kamehameha saw the superior firepower of European guns and the logic of European tactics in war, he immediately appropriated English advisors and set out to buy guns. He wanted to become the person who linked the islands, each under one or more chieftains, into a true kingdom with himself as its head. By craft and treachery, by bravery and a modicum of luck, Kamehameha fulfilled his dream. A series of bloody wars and a bit of diplomacy with the king of Kaua'i brought all the islands under his rule.

Under Kamehameha, there was extensive trade and interaction with the West. When he allowed, ships from abroad filled Hawaiian harbors; but he also was careful to maintain the old ways among his people. The *kapu* system that allowed the *ali'i* to lay an edict over any person, place or thing remained in effect until Kamehameha died. If the Hawaiians did not fully understand the concept of nationhood, they certainly understood the power of authority. Kamehameha ruled as much by force of personality as by force of arms.

Upon his death on May 8, 1819, at the end of years of peace and stability, Kamehameha was buried in a secret place. It is a secret that endures. Today, no one knows the burial site of the greatest of all Hawaiians.

Almost immediately Kamehameha's influence began to dissipate. A week after the king's death, his favorite wife, Ka'ahumanu, declared Kamehameha's son, Liholiho, the next ruler; but, she added, she would rule with him. In time, she pressured Liholiho into abandoning the *kapu* system, and the inevitable change followed.

About the time Kamehameha died, word flashed around the maritime nations that there were enormous herds of whales in the Pacific. The news galvanized seamen who knew the Atlantic grounds held fewer and fewer whales, and Hawai'i assumed a new importance.

Within three years, up to sixty whaling ships at a time anchored in Honolulu Harbor alone, and the waters off Lahaina were dark with the timbers of ships. Sailors came to rely on Hawai'i's ports for women, grog and provisions. There was, they said, "no God west of the Horn," and they seemed bent on proving it. Whaling became an important industry to Hawai'i; whaling men became a prime nuisance.

Whaling meant money. Goods were transshipped, ships were repaired, and the activity attracted nonwhaling merchant vessels as well.

Whaling also bewildered and confused the *maka'āinana*, who saw the sailors indulging themselves without punishment. By now, the Hawaiians had no strong system of their own to turn to for strength, and they were finding it difficult to make sense of their lives and times.

A second group of foreigners, or *haole*, confused Hawaiians more than a little. The missionaries had arrived in 1819 with their stern visages and rigid life-styles, as well as their talk of Trinity and damnation. Between the whalers and the missionaries, battles raged over the land and souls of the native Hawaiians.

In their way, the missionaries turned out to be as tough as the oak planking of the whaling ships. Arriving first on the brig *Thaddeus* on October 23, 1819, the missionaries found the Hawaiian society in chaos following Kamehameha's death. They also found a dearth of new ideas, and moved quickly to fill the vacuum. Liholiho came to be regarded as a friend. The missionaries converted Keōpūolani, the queen mother, then

the powerful chieftess Kapi'olani.
Within two years, the missionaries
standardized the written form of
Hawaiian, printed bibles and opened
schools. They became a powerful
force in the islands, and their
descendants would become leaders
of Hawai'i society, business and
industry.

Hawai'i attracted more and more
foreigners. Americans, Britons,
French, Germans and Scots traveled
to Hawai'i, drawn to the image of a
tropical paradise, held by the
opportunities they found.

In 1859, an oil well went into
production in Pennsylvania, signal-
ing the end of the whaling industry,
as whales no longer were the only
source of the precious oil for which
they were slaughtered. War broke
out between the Union and the
Confederacy, and many whaling
ships were pressed into service as
merchantmen, decreasing markedly
the whaling fleet. Finally, in the fall
of 1871, ice caught thirty-three
whaling ships in Arctic waters north
of the Bering Strait and remorselessly
crushed the last hope of a whaling
industry.

In Hawai'i, new industries
flourished, one of them sugar.
Planters needed cheap agricultural
labor, and had to look to foreign
countries because diseases had vastly
reduced the Hawaiian population.
Plantation owners turned first to
China, then to Japan, then to Portugal, the Philippines and other places.
This marked the beginning of
Hawai'i's melting pot. Land ownership, which before Cook's arrival was
reserved only for the ali'i, became an
increasingly perplexing problem.
The Hawaiian government gave up
rights to all property except certain
lands for the king. Commoners now
were permitted to buy land, and

foreigners could lease it. The haole,
having come from civilizations that
prized land ownership, reached for as
much as they could get. The average
Hawaiian, at sea with all the attendant
bureaucracy, just got more confused.
On the one hand, he could lease or
cultivate his land, rights he never
before possessed, while on the other
hand it became easy to sell it to the
haole. The Great Mahele, the movement that began with attempts to tie
the Hawaiians closer to their land,
ended in them losing it in great
quantities.

In the 1890s, conflicts grew
between Queen Lili'uokalani, destined
to be the last Hawaiian monarch, and
a group of businessmen who objected
to the queen's push for a new constitution that would have restored much of
the Hawaiian royalty's lost powers.
On January 17, 1893, the monarchy
toppled, and the Republic of Hawai'i
formed, with a new constitution.

Five years later, on August 12,
1898, spectators jammed the area
around 'Iolani Palace in Honolulu to
hear the Hawaiian national anthem
played and watch the Hawaiian flag
slowly lowered to the ground. The
American flag was raised in its place;
the American national anthem was
played, and Sanford Ballard Dole, a
leader in the monarchy's overthrow,
was sworn in as first chief executive
officer of the Territory of Hawai'i, a
U. S. possession.

Stability and social change followed. The melting pot became more
so, and a lifestyle emerged in which
racial groups were proud of their
ancestry, but also proud of their
Americanization. It seemed there was
a little Hawaiian blood in almost
everybody. For more than four
decades, the largely agricultural
community went about its business,
attracted a few visitors, and never

The largest Buddha outside of Asia sits at the Lahaina Jodo Mission

dreamed it would be the target of a sudden attack that became the impetus for the U. S. to enter World War II.

On Sunday, December 7, 1941, Japanese aircraft swarmed in from a fleet that had crept unseen and unheard across the Pacific to a point north of the islands. The devastating raid on Pearl Harbor plunged the U. S. into the war and brought quick changes to Hawai'i. Martial law was declared, a military government installed in 'Iolani Palace, and thousands of young U. S. servicemen turned up in the islands. Some never left. Intermarriages soared. By the end of the war, the whole fabric of Hawai'i society had changed with the interweaving of the new *haole*

immigrants. The end of the war also saw the return of the young *Nisei*--the second generation Japanese--who thirsted for political power and were determined to put an end to the long rule of the entrenched Republican establishment of the day.

With their GI Bill for Education, the veterans went off to colleges and came back as lawyers, doctors, accountants and other professionals. They were politically oriented and hard-working, and they swept up with them other young men in Hawai'i fired by ambition. In 1954, in a thunderous victory, the veterans took over the top positions in Hawai'i and forced a new, political equality on the Establishment.

Attack on Pearl Harbor

In another five years, statehood marked the beginning of still another era of change. Statehood meant stability for investments; the invention of the jet meant an influx of tourists; and international publicity about America's newest state turned Hawai'i into a magnet for those seeking a new life in a paradisiacal setting. Tourism edged out agriculture as the primary source of revenue, which it remains to this day. Visitor industry revenues account for a third of all local taxes, and exceed sugar and pineapple revenues combined. More than a third of the local labor force has jobs in the visitor industry.

THE ENVIRONMENT

Fairly recently in the history of the Earth (only 25 million years ago), a series of cracks opened northwest to southeast in the ocean floor of the North Pacific. In tumultuous explosions followed by fiery rivers of magma and molten lava, land began to build up underneath the surface of the sea.

In time, the land broke the surface and lay barren and exposed to winds and the pounding sea. The rise and fall of ice caps thousands of miles away helped

13

An artist captures Lahaina Harbor's ethereal sunset tones

raise or lower the level of the sea. Still the land remained, buffeted by winds, clawed by seas which broke over the exposed shoreline. Then there was a time of quiet.

In a thundering end to the silence, the lava explosions began again. Lava flows tumbled and rolled down the sides of the mountains and, in astonishing pyrotechnics, more land was born. As the land increased, so did its diversity, as wind and waves continued to carve coves and valleys. Algae and coral polyps began to build reefs around the land. With the seeding of the land by birds, drifting coconuts and other material, the land began to turn green.

When the Polynesians arrived, they brought their own versions of how the land came to be. In one account, a mischievous Polynesian demigod called Māui fished the land up from the bottom of the ocean. A myth common to much of Polynesia held that the islands were the children of gods, usually Papa and Wakea, earth-mother and sky-father.

Today, the islands are but the tops of volcanic mountains, enormous when measured from the ocean floor up. They lie like beads on a string across the 1523 miles of ocean, and are made up almost entirely of lava.

Abundant, high-quality water and clean air bless this environmental wonderland. Plant life in Hawai'i also is a naturalist's dream. More than 2500 kinds of plants grow only in Hawai'i. Because of Hawai'i's long isolation, evolution of plant life has been rapid and diverse. Conversely, plants that are found throughout the Pacific were not present in Hawai'i until man brought them--such as the banyan, taro and figs. Most of the myriad orchids that grace Hawai'i today came from other places. There is only one native palm tree.

Because Hawai'i is so far from other land, very few animals arrived here under their own power. The hoary bat (Lasiurus) is an exception. The Hawaiian bat is smaller than its distant relatives but tough enough to fly long distances. The Hawaiian monk seal (Monachus), a species related to seals in the Caribbean and the Mediterranean, also arrived from afar. It may have been the first mammal to live in Hawai'i, and today is found nowhere else. The Polynesian rat (Rattus) stowed away aboard Polynesian voyaging canoes, and, like the Polynesians themselves, originated in Asia. The Polynesians valued the domestic dog (Canis) as pet, food source and a part of religious rituals. By all accounts, the Polynesian dog was highly dependent and unaggressive, and as new breeds of dogs came to the islands, the original version disappeared.

The presence of pigs (Sus scrofa) in the islands turned out to be a mixed blessing. They were an important food source, but when they began to run wild in the lush forests, they became a nuisance, and more. Today feral pigs are blamed for destroying much of the islands' watershed areas by digging up the forest floor and the aquifer, the natural filter through which a lot of island water flows.

Captain Cook released goats in Hawai'i, and others who came after him brought sheep, cattle and horses. These large animals were extremely destructive to Hawaiian plants. By 1900, many native plants below roughly the 1200 foot level had been eradicated, some replaced by heartier species. Today, these large animals are an asset, not a menace.

Hawai'i's isolation also gave rise to a unique bird life. Today, however, more than half the birds have

Gentle surf washes along Kīhei's sandy shores

become extinct in Hawai'i as in the entire North American continent. The birds succumbed to hunters, introduced predators, the swift mongooses brought to Hawai'i, to combat rats, and urban encroachment.

Many birds live near streams, marshes or ponds; the largest number inhabit the deep forests. Perhaps the most dramatic are the long-winged seabirds. Twenty-two different species spend their non-breeding time flying over the open ocean, scavenging for food and resting on the water, coming back to Hawai'i to breed. Millions of them nest in the sanctuary of uninhabited small islands northwest of the occupied islands of Hawai'i. Some birds that were introduced to the islands from elsewhere and thrive here include pigeons, doves, mynas, cardinals and sparrows. The state bird is the *nēnē* (Branta sandvicensis), a goose that lives high on the rugged slopes of the volcanoes. The *nēnē* has battled back from near-extinction. Many of Hawai'i's birds are found only on specific islands, such as the *'io*, or hawk (Buteo solitarius), found only on the island of Hawai'i.

Long before any land mammals came, and before plants or even birds, marine mammals swam the surrounding seas. In fact, the ancestors of some of the whales and dolphins now found in Hawaiian waters may have been here even before the islands arose from the sea. They include the humpback whales, which today are seasonal visitors, several varieties of dolphins, killer whales, sperm whales--in all, at least twenty types. Today, the most popular marine mammal is the humpback whale, important enough to Maui to deserve singling out for special attention (see "The Whales" below).

Other marine life became important to the Hawaiians, not only for food but in rituals, legends, myths and *mele* (chants). Hawaiian fishermen had their own god, Ku'ulakai, and small fishing shrines *(ko'a)* were dedicated near water to the god. The shrines often were no more than stacked rocks, but they were significant to the fishermen who offered the first of their catch at the *ko'a*.

Certain fish were considered tastier than others; fishermen often offered red and white fish to the gods. Some Hawaiian families considered certain fish, particularly sharks, to be their *'aumakua* or household god.

Each wave of newcomer brought its own fishing mystique, taste and style. Today, the fishing practices of Hawai'i's people reflect the state's multi-racial populace and preserve the islands' reputation as a top marine science center.

THE WHALES

Each year, the humpback whales come to Maui seeking waters that are about 75°F (24°C) and the shelter of the leeward shores and quiet bays. They come down from the Arctic to Hawaiian waters to breed, generally from late November to May. They cover some 2800 miles in an estimated eighty to a hundred days, and while in Hawaiian waters, they fast.

They do no arrive in herds, but flow in and out of the breeding grounds through the winter months, some staying as late as July. The newly pregnant females leave first for northern waters, followed by younger whales and then the more mature of both sexes.

Intelligence, size, gentleness--all have endeared the humpback whales to the people of Maui, who have been in the forefront of efforts to protect the whales. Not until recently did man pay much attention to the whales' sensitivity and intelligence. They have a communications system that produces sounds of haunting beauty--and specific intent. Whales also have a highly developed sense of direction and good eyesight, both in water and air (they are known to surface to look at passing ships).

Calves not only are conceived in Hawaiian waters; many are born here. Mother whales give birth in relatively shallow water of about 150 feet to discourage predators, and produce up to 130 gallons of milk a day for their offspring.

The whales' annual journey here allows the visitor to Maui a unique opportunity to see these massive ocean creatures at fairly close range--an experience possible in relatively few other places in the world.

For more information on the humpback whale and whale watching, see SPORTS. If you are interested in visiting whaling museums or stores specializing in marine mammal art and books, see the EXPLORING/SIGHT-SEEING and SHOPPING sections of this guidebook.

CLIMATE and WEATHER

Maui's pleasant climate doesn't change much throughout the year--at sea level. The temperature ranges between a daytime high near 90°F (about 30°C) in 'summer' and a nighttime low near 60°F (about 18°C) in 'winter'. There really are no distinct seasons as such. Even in 'winter' the daytime temperature is usually in the 80s. The comfort factor that this involves depends on what you're used to, where you've come from and how long you've been here. People do eventually acclimatize. Those of us who live here start to shiver and bundle up when the mercury plummets to 75°F (24°C). The coldest months are February and March and the hottest August and September.

Despite this lack of strong seasonal variation, Hawai'i is home to an extraordinary diversity of microclimates--from desert to rain forest. The temperature drops about 3°F for every thousand feet of increased altitude, a factor which has produced seasonal snow on the upper slopes of Haleakalā and the Big Island's Mauna Kea. Rainfall varies dramatically in different parts of each island. All this lush tropical foliage requires a lot of rain, yet drought in some areas of the islands is not unheard-of. The state's heaviest rains are brought by storms between October and April. Fortunately, most local rain showers are short, except in the upper reaches of valleys where the rain clouds never leave for long. The windward areas get far more rain than their leeward counterparts.

There have been only a few damaging storms in Hawai'i, the most devastating one in recent years being in September of 1992 when Hurricane Iniki (strong wind) hit the island of Kaua'i dead on with winds measuring up to 175 m.p.h., and left behind a path of destruction and property loss estimated at one billion dollars. Hurricane Iwa, active in 1982, brought gusts of 100 miles per hour to the islands, and caused an estimated $234 million in losses.

TIME and DAYLIGHT

Because of Hawai'i's tropical location, the length of daylight doesn't vary greatly from one time of the year to the next--only around three or four hours. Thus, Hawaiians have never felt any need to save it, and Hawaiian Standard Time is in effect year-round. The time differences between Hawai'i and places that do follow Daylight Savings Time vary by an hour when Daylight Savings is in effect elsewhere. Hawaiian Standard Time is five hours behind New York, four hours behind Chicago, three hours behind Denver and two hours behind San Francisco. It is also eleven hours behind London, nineteen hours behind Tokyo, twenty hours behind Sydney, and twenty-two hours behind Auckland and Suva. Add an hour to all of these when Daylight Savings is in effect elsewhere.

The popular local phrase 'Hawaiian time' simply means 'late'.

THE FLAG

The Hawai'i State flag has served Kingdom, Republic and State and was designed prior to 1816 for King Kamehameha I. Most first-time visitors to Hawai'i are intrigued to note the British Union Jack in the corner. The Union Jack honors Hawai'i's early ties with Britain. The eight horizontal stripes represent the archipelago's eight main islands. Hawai'i's State Anthem, 'Hawai'i Pono'ī', is its former national anthem and was composed by King Kalākaua.

LANGUAGE

English became the common language of Hawaiian commerce very early in the era of immigration and economic investment by Americans and other foreigners. And so it remained. The missionaries made sweeping and now irreversible changes in the Hawaiian language when they hurriedly transliterated and transcribed it for print in order to produce bibles. Subsequent efforts to suppress the native tongue were very successful. There are only a few hundred native speakers left, most of whom are either very old or from Ni'ihau. However, a strong grass roots movement to save the language has taken hold in recent years and is gaining widespread support. Virtually everyone in the islands today speaks the American variety of English, with a few local variations on the theme. Some of these should be noted because they are so common.

Perhaps the most important is the local way of giving directions. The cardinal points of the compass on an island are far less relevant than the obvious 'toward the mountain' and 'toward the sea'. A contracted form of the Hawaiian words for these directions is universally used in Hawai'i. 'Toward the upland *(uka)'* is *mauka;* 'toward the sea *(kai)* is *makai.* For the other directions, major landmarks are used.

Some people have difficulty with Hawaiian place names and street names. The Hawaiian language is beautiful and only *looks* intimidating to non-Polynesians because they are not accustomed to seeing so many vowels in a row. Basically, if you just pronounce all the letters individually, you'll be fine. In fact, you might be pronouncing Hawaiian more correctly than a lot of people who are

Mauians give their friendly 'shaka' sign

used to it. The 'glottal stop' (written ')
is the hard sound created by stopping between vowel sounds, for
example, a double 'o' is pronounced
like 'oh-oh' in English. In Hawaiian,
this is called 'okina. Just stop talking
then start again immediately. The
macron (written as a ‾ over a vowel),
called kahakō in Hawaiian, simply
means that vowel is held a little
longer – as if it were written twice,
which it occasionally is.

Consonants are pronounced the
same as in English except that 'w'
sounds like 'v' when it immediately
precedes a final single vowel and
occasionally at other times. Vowels
are pronounced as in Spanish or
Italian (ah, eh, ee, oh, oo). The vowel
combinations--ai, ae, ao, au, ei, eu, oi
and ou--are stressed on the first
member and sounded as single units,
though the second vowel in the set is
truly pronounced and not lost in the
combination. Multi-syllabic words
are almost always accented or
stressed on the next-to-last syllable.
No matter how many times you hear
the word along the tourist trail, the
very special and wonderfully soft

Hawaiian word, aloha, is NOT
correctly pronounced with the accent
on the last syllable.

You will often see Hawaiian
words written without the kahakō and
'okina. This was the custom of
English-speaking people who first
transcribed the language, and was
common practice until fairly recently.
The markings are necessary for
correct pronunciation of many
words, and for discerning between
similarly spelled words with quite
different meanings.

The other feature of local language that visitors are bound to
encounter is our own brand of
'pidgin' English. It is spiced with
words from the rich linguistic
heritage brought by people of many
lands, but, basically, it is English
with a bit of Hawaiian, and, if you
listen carefully, you'll catch on. The
idiom and the lilt are peculiar to
Hawai'i, but the pronunciation of
most words is recognizable.

Lists of commonly used Hawaiian
and pidgin English words along with
their meanings and pronunciations,
are listed at the back of this book.

IN TRANSIT

GETTING HERE

Y ou've daydreamed about your journey to Maui, and weaved scenarios in your mind about your vacation in this breathtakingly beautiful place. Now you are ready to take some of the practical steps that will make this visit as exciting and pleasurable as your dreams. Making those arrangements is easy and not all that expensive. This section spells out the options to choose from to tailor your trip to your specifications. Most people choose to travel by air rather than sea, though the latter is still possible, and most arrive during the winter season, with February at peak, and in August.

CHOOSING LOCATION

Exquisite beaches fringe the lovely island of Maui, so it is not surprising that most hotels and condominiums are on or near the beach. Here is a brief summary of the various areas of Maui to help you decide where to visit:

Kā'anapali--A man-made resort on a beach nature perfected, Kā'anapali is a world-class destination area in West Maui with resort hotels and all the attendant amenities. There are literally thousands of hotel rooms in this area, and several condominiums in nearby Lahaina, the historic old whaling town.

Kapalua--Here is another resort carved out of lava and scrub brush on the edge of a gorgeous beach. This resort area north of Kā'anapali features luxurious amenities. Between here and Kā'anapali, numerous condominiums of varying price ranges provide a beach-goer's haven.

Following Sliding Sands Trail in Haleakalā Crater on horseback

Kīhei/Wailea/Mākena--Condominiums abound along the sunny southern coast, and are located either on the beach or close by. The condominiums give way to some of Maui's most stunning hotels along pristine beaches at the resort area of Wailea. Farther south, the beautiful beaches of Mākena contribute to Maui's idyllic reputation, and are within close proximity to Wailea, as well as a short drive from Kīhei's condominiums. One of the newer first-class hotels in this area, the Maui Prince, graces a fine beach at Mākena.

Hāna--This area on the far eastern tip of Maui offers the best of both worlds: there are beautiful beaches on the shoreline, and above is an adjoining cattle ranch with Haleakalā towering in the background. Although accommodations in this area are somewhat limited, advance planning can get you a deluxe hotel room at the luxurious Hotel Hana Maui, a condominium, a private cottage, bed and breakfast lodging or even a rustic cabin.

Upcountry Maui--On the slopes of Haleakalā, nights are cool and mornings are crisp, and outstanding views abound. Here is where you'll smell the sweet fragrance of eucalyptus trees, or catch whiffs of smoke from fireplaces on winter mornings, as well as walk among hardwood forests. There are limited visitor accommodations in this area (The Kula Lodge or bed-and-breakfast inns), and if you don't mind being located away from the beach, this is a wonderful alternative.

Central Valley--The Wailuku-Kahului area has few beaches, but it does provide history and character for the visitor who prefers to be out of the tourist mainstream and into the heart of an unfamiliar place. Wailuku is the capital of the island, the seat of government, and a charming old town that is taking its restoration seriously. It is home to a number of historic sites as well as the intriguing 'Iao Valley Park and 'Iao Needle.

A walk along Wailea Beach in the mild afternoon sun

SELECTING LODGING

Hotels are the favorite of those who wish to be pampered during their stay. Most of our hotels are near the heart of the action, and are staffed by courteous, friendly, and efficient people, and offer guests a wide selection of activities from which to choose. Condominiums or private vacation homes are also plentiful and ideal for those on longer visits or those traveling with children. Bed-and-breakfast (B&B) guest rooms and cottages are available throughout the island, and are becoming increasingly popular for those preferring an intimate atmosphere and wishing to avoid crowds. For nature lovers and the budget-minded, rustic cabins and tent camping are available, but should be reserved way in advance, as they are in limited supply. For a comprehensive listing of the various types of lodging as well as local reservation services, refer to the ACCOMMODATION section of this book.

WHAT TO BRING

Visitors should pack warm-weather clothing to wear in this consistent spring and summer climate. The usual attire on Maui is casual, and apparel known elsewhere as 'summer clothing' is worn year-round in this land of perpetual spring and summer. Shorts are acceptable almost anywhere, though most businesses require customers to wear shoes (rubber thongs will usually suffice). Comfortable walking shoes are a must. Sleeveless or short-sleeved shirts are usually best for day wear, but long sleeves, or even a jacket or sweater, may be needed for cool winter evenings and air-conditioned buildings. Deluxe restaurants sometimes have a dress code requiring men to wear jackets, but not usually ties.

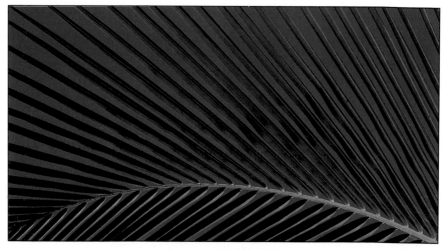

Close-up view of palm frond

PERMITS AND LICENSES

Licenses or permits are required for some activities in which visitors may choose to participate. The most common is driving. Any visitor who drives in Hawai'i must have a valid driver's license from another state or a Canadian province or a current international driver's license issued in another country. Camping permits are required for public parks that allow camping. All hunting requires a license, as does fresh-water fishing; none is required for recreational ocean fishing. Further details of these sporting licenses are discussed in the SPORTS section.

Those wishing to indulge in the romance of tropical nuptials need a license, which may be obtained from the State of Hawai'i Department of Health in Honolulu (1250 Punchbowl St., Honolulu, HI 96813 - 808-586-4545). Licenses are issued immediately after application and expire after 30 days. They are only valid in Hawai'i, and the nominal fee ($25.00) is payable in cash at the time of filing.

Numerous local companies specialize in wedding arrangements, some of which are described under "Island Weddings" in ET CETERA; others are listed under "Wedding" in the Maui Yellow Pages.

BOOKINGS

To book your air or cruise tickets, lodging, and any tours you may wish to arrange in advance, we recommend using a travel agent. You could spend days chasing specifics and comparing prices but travel agents have the information at their fingertips and they know their sources well. It costs you no more, as the agents' commission is paid by the provider, not the customer. In many cases, the agent can offer you a better deal than you could get if you booked directly. Many airlines and hotels also give priority book-ings made through agents, as they are generally less likely to be canceled.

If you plan to stay in a bed-and-breakfast accommodation or a private vacation home, there are several local reservation services available to assist you. Many of these services charge a nominal booking fee, however it can turn out to be a savings to you in the long run, reducing time, energy and money otherwise spent on long distance calls and researching on your own. For a listing of such services, refer to the ACCOMMODATION section of this book.

Airlines

Our island state is such a popular destination that, though it is accessible only by air or sea, airfares are kept low through volume and competition. There are many airlines serving the Hawaiian Islands, most landing at Honolulu International Airport, where passengers may switch to interisland aircraft to continue their journey; the additional trip usually averages twenty minutes. However, some airlines fly directly into Maui's Kahului Airport non-stop from the U.S. mainland. They are **United Airlines, American Airlines** and **Delta Airlines.**

Flight times are roughly five hours from California, nine hours from Chicago, eleven hours from New York, eight hours from Tokyo and nine and a half hours from Sydney. Domestic carriers providing service to and from the U. S. mainland are: **American Airlines, Continental, Delta, Hawaiian Airlines, Northwest Airlines, TWA** and **United Airlines.** United Airlines offers flights from San Francisco and Los Angeles directly to Kahului, Maui, and from San Francisco to Kailua-Kona on the Big Island of Hawaii. Foreign carriers currently serving Honolulu are **Air New Zealand, Canadian Airlines, China Airlines, Garuda Indonesia, Japan Air Lines, Korean Air, Philippine Airlines, Qantas** and **Singapore Airlines,** among others. Carriers providing service between the Hawaiian Islands are **Air Molokai** (521-0090), **Aloha Airlines** (800-367-5250, 244-9071), **Hawaiian Airlines**

Horseback riding in Hāna's lush pastures alongside crashing surf

(800-367-5320, 871-6132), **Mahalo** (833-5555) and **United Airlines** (800-241-6522, 242-7911). Consult your travel agent for the latest details and flight schedules.

Cruise Lines

Arriving in Hawaii by cruise ship is far more complicated now than it was decades ago when many of our visitors sailed in to our island ports. Today, most of the cruise lines that make stops at our islands--**Cunard, Royal Viking** and other European-based cruise operators--are of foreign registry and are forbidden by U. S. law from transporting American citizens from one U. S. port to another U. S. port. This law, the Jones Act, was passed in 1896. Thus, if you board a foreign vessel in New York or California, you may visit Hawai'i, but cannot make it or any other U. S. port your final destination. You may, if you board a ship in another country, make Hawai'i or another American port your final destination, but most cruise operators today do not encourage one-way traffic. Still, it is possible, and there is no more beautiful way to arrive here than by sea.

American Hawaii Cruises has two ships, the *S.S. Constitution* and the *S.S. Independence*, that cruise the Hawaiian waters departing Honolulu on a weekly basis, and docking in Kaua'i, Maui and the Big Island. The ships provide visitors with excellent service and exquisite panoramic vistas by sea, as well as a selection of land tours at each island stop-over. Reservations can be made by calling (800) 765-7000.

The cruise ship S.S. Independence on its way to Lahaina harbor.

Sight-seeing tours

Maui offers such a large assortment of tours and tour operators, that we have included only a small sampling of companies herein. Your travel agent will be able to book tours for you through the larger companies.

Many visitors, though, who prefer flexibility and spontaneity, book tours after their arrival and a bit of scouting around. Activity/ tour desks are located in or near most hotels, condominiums and shopping areas. We have listed a sampling of tour reservation services below. Additional information on specific sight-seeing and outdoor activities is provided in the GETTING AROUND and SPORTS sections.

Activity Warehouse	667-4000
Capt. Nemo's Ocean Emporium	661-5555
Hike Maui	879-5270
Keiki Tours (for kids age 5-11)	874-0117
Ocean Activities Center	879-4485
Tom Barefoot's Cashback Tours	667-5011, 871-4100

HONOLULU INTERNATIONAL AIRPORT

This is one of the busiest airports in the world, serving as gateway between East and West. Passengers arriving from the U.S. mainland or from other countries emerge from this vast complex on the ground level of the main terminal building. The airport's second level services mainland and overseas departures.

Most arriving and departing interisland flights service passengers from the recently completed interisland terminal, located next to the main terminal at the westward end of the airport. This new building is much larger than the former interisland terminal, with expanded shops, eating facilities and waiting areas, which allow for more convenient and comfortable interisland travel than was previously available.

Play--the primary objective for everyone at Kāʻanapali Beach

MAUI AIRPORTS

Maui's principal airport is Kahului, located in the Central Valley. More than a hundred flights a day in addition to helicopter traffic and the occasional private jet land there. The airport is a modern full-service complex with restaurant, lockers, information booth, car rental agencies and taxi service.

The Kapalua-West Maui Airport opened for service to commuter airlines in 1987, and has a snack shop, gift shop, porter service, and rental car agencies. Aloha Island Air and Hawaiian Airlines service this airport.

Hāna's airport is little more than a landing strip, with pickup service available for guests staying at the Hotel Hana-Maui (248-8211).

SPECIAL LEI GREETING

One of the loveliest of Hawaiian customs is giving a garland of island flowers as a gesture of *aloha* on special occasions, and a local greeting service can be contacted in advance to meet your party at the airport with colorful and fragrant leis upon your arrival to welcome you to the Valley Isle. The lei greeting services on Maui, whom you may want to call prior to your visit, are

Ali'i Leis, Flowers & Greeting Service (808-877-7088; fax: 877-0757), Trans Hawaiian Maui (808-877-7308) and Aloha Lei Greeters Maui (808-877-7040). If you prefer being "lei'd" upon your arrival at the Honolulu Airport, you can contact All Island Greeters (808-836-5631), Kenui Aloha (808-523-2825) or Leis of Hawaii (808-732-7385) in Honolulu.

Leis are Hawai'i's most colorful way of saying "aloha" and welcome

GETTING AROUND

N o single road connects all the areas that make up this wonderfully diverse island. For example, the northern seacoast area is passable in four-wheel-drive vehicles, but should not be attempted in anything else. When planning tours or simply driving and sight-seeing, it is important to remember that Maui falls easily into distinct regions: West Maui, with its exceptional climate, magnificent beaches, the old whaling town of Lahaina and the resort area of Kā'anapali, is the region most visitors know best. Kapalua, at the far western end of Maui, boasts two elegant resorts and stunning beaches. The southern shore from Mā'alaea to La Perouse Bay, which encompasses Kīhei and Wailea, features more wonderful beaches, while the 10,025-feet Haleakalā towers over East Maui, which includes the lush, green cowboy region known as 'Upcountry'. Hāna, a beautiful, sleepy seacoast area that includes a cattle ranch, holds court at the extreme eastern end of Maui, while the Central Valley features the seat of government at Wailuku and a thriving port and commercial center at Kahului.

TOURS AND RENTALS

There are a number of air and land tour companies operating on Maui, most of them very experienced in packaging tours to specific areas. Consult the Yellow Pages of the Maui telephone book for ideas. For exploring on your own, or for sudden, spur-of-the-moment sight-seeing or shopping, a rental car is preferable. It is noteworthy to mention that it is illegal to hitchhike on Maui. When driving on Maui, you will occasionally spot a person standing at the side of the road watching cars go by. It is doubtful they are simply studying Maui's traffic flow--they are most likely hitchhiking, but know not to stick out their thumb.

There are a variety of ways to get around Maui, but the best is to rent a car. There is a proliferation of car rental agencies on the island, all offering competitive rates.

Public transportation is limited to the **Gray Line Maui** (877-5507). It makes pickups at the Kahului Airport hourly between 7:00 a.m. and 5:00 p.m., ferrying passengers to Kā'anapali hotels, but is not a public bus system. From the Kapalua-West Maui Airport, Kā'anapali Resort has a free shuttle that takes passengers to and from that airport on a regular schedule.

Sample distances in both miles and driving time from Kahului Airport are as follows: Kahului--3 miles, 5 minutes; Wailuku--6 miles, 10 minutes; Kīhei--9 miles, 20 minutes; Lahaina--27 miles, 45 minutes; Kā'anapali--30 miles, 50 minutes; Haleakalā summit--37 miles, one and a half hours; Hāna--52 miles, two and a half hours; Kapalua--36 miles, one hour; Wailea--18 miles, 35 minutes.

Car rentals

More than a dozen rental companies flourish on Maui, and they offer everything from luxury cars to four-wheel drives and subcompacts. Staff at hotel desks can put you in touch with any of them, or you can take advantage of the agencies represented at Kahului and Kapalua-West Maui Airports.

Rental agencies caution against driving on the northeast coast, or on the road past Seven Pools near Hāna because the roads can be difficult for standard-drive vehicles. A driver's license and major credit card are required.

Whatever you select from Maui's wide choices, reserving a car in advance is a good idea, as cars can be scarce at peak visitor times. Nationally known agencies at or near Kahului Airport include: **Avis Rent A Car** (871-7575), **Budget Rent-A-Car** (871-8811), **Dollar Rent A Car** (877-2731), **Hertz Rent A Car** (877-5167), and **National Car Rental** (877-8851). **Word of Mouth Rent A Used Car** (877-2436) offers late model cars at reasonable rates. **Maui Rent A Jeep** (877-6626) offers a discount for senior citizens.

Driving tips

Maui's posted speed limits are realistically set. Major highways generally are good quality, but back country roads tend to be narrow and twisting. Traffic slowdowns from heavy construction or sugarcane and pineapple trucks that crawl down two-lane roads occur often, and motorists must exercise both caution

and patience. Most urban centers are relatively easy to drive in, but Lahaina town can be traffic-clogged at times, and parking is at a premium. While driving generally is a good experience, there are times to remember the local phrase, 'ain't no beeg t'ing, brah', meaning, 'it's no big deal; take it easy'.

Bicycles, mopeds and motorcycles

It's possible to see Maui on a bicycle if you are both experienced and careful. Long-distance bicycling can be tedious in East Maui, where Haleakalā rises more than 10,000 feet in forty miles. On the other hand, a paved bicycle path from Kā'anapali to Lahaina only three miles away makes bicycling in that area a pleasure. Bicycles may be rented in West Maui at **Cruiser Bob's Rent-A-Bike** (579-8444) and **West Maui Cycles** (669-1169), or in Kīhei at **Kukui Activity Center** (875-1151), and **South Maui Bicycles** (874-0068).

Mopeds may be rented in West Maui at **A&B Moped Rental** (669-0027) and in Kīhei at **Maui Mopeds & Scooters** (874-6798) or **Kukui Activity Center** (875-1151).

Motorcycle enthusiasts can tour Maui on a Harley Davidson for half or full days (solo or in an escorted group), by renting a bike from **Island Riders**. There are two Maui stores, in Lahaina (661-9966) and Kīhei (874-0311). Riders must be at least 21 years old, with a valid motorcycle license or permit, plus a major credit card.

Companies offering bicycling tours from the summit of Haleakalā down through the lush region of Upcountry Maui have proliferated in recent years. **Cruiser Bob's** (579-8444) is Maui's original downhill bike tour, having been in business since 1983. Escort vans transport bikes and cyclists up to Haleakalā's summit, from which they coast down 38 miles, a drop of 10,000 feet. Bikes are equipped with special brakes and participants are issued protective gear and rain jackets. The trip includes breakfast going up, lunch coming down, and pickup service in Lahaina. Similar packages are offered by **Maui Downhill** (871-2155), **Maui Mountain Cruisers** (871-6014), and **Makawao Mountain Bike** (572-2200).

Chris' Bike Adventures (871-BIKE) also offers a number of mountain bike tours, including a Haleakalā Wine Trek, combination day-long boat/bike tours of the islands of Lāna'i or Moloka'i, a "Wilder Side of Haleakalā" tour, and one along the northwest coast of Maui. **Mountain Riders Bike Tours** (242-9739) offers a Haleakalā downhill trip, as well as an Upcountry wine tour and a South Maui coastal tour.

Land tours

There are a number of sightseeing tour companies operating on Maui, some of them highly specialized, others prepared to show visitors the best of Maui. For a complete listing, see Tours in the Maui Yellow Pages. **Arthur's Limousine Service** (871-5555) goes to Hāna and Haleakalā in classic Lincoln and Cadillac stretch limousines. They also offer Japanese speaking drivers and tour guides. **Barefoot's Cashback Tours** (661-8889) can arrange all kinds of tours, from sunset sails to off-island adventures to wild boar hunts, with a 10% discount off regular prices for cash purchases, a 7% discount for credit card purchases. **Gray Line Maui** (877-5507), one of Maui's largest tour operators, provides airport transportation as well as tours. **Roberts Hawaii Tours** (871-6226) has large tour buses and vans for land tours of Maui, and can also arrange day trips to other islands. **Trans Hawaiian Maui** (877-7308) offers Hāna and Haleakalā Sunrise tours, in vans, stretchouts and limousines, and has guides who speak a number of foreign languages.

Temptation Tours (877-8888) offers an assortment of luxurious upscale tours of Hāna and Upcountry, from full-day excursions to Hāna to a Haleakalā sunrise tour, with a visit to the Hawaii Protea Cooperative in Kula, one of Hawai'i's major suppliers of tropical flowers. **Ekahi Tours** (877-9775) lets visitors see the Hāna area and the lush Ke'anae Peninsula up close, and also escorts tours to Haleakalā at sunrise.

For visitors making the Hāna drive on their own, **Hana Cassette Guide** (572-0550) features informational tapes about Hāna, Haleakalā and 'Īao Valley. **Best of Maui** (871-1555) offers cassette tours of Hāna, Upcountry and Seven Pools, and their package includes a free videotape, audiotape player, guidebooks, flower or bird identification card and a full color map.

Bike tours wind down Haleakalā Highway

Taxis and Shuttles

Maui has about two dozen taxi companies, and rides tend to be pricey. In West Maui, there are: **Alii Cab Co.** (661-3688); **Kaanapali Taxi** (661-5285); **Classy Taxi** (661-3044); and **Kapalua Executive Cab Service** (667-7770). In East Maui, there are: **Jake's Taxi** (877-6139); **La Bella Taxi** (242-8011); **Yellow Cab of Maui** (877-7000), which services the Kahului Airport; and in Kīhei, **Kihei Taxi** (879-3000), **Wailea Taxi & Tours** (874-5000) and **Royal Sedan & Taxi Service** (874-6900).

The **Kaanapali-Lahaina Shuttle** runs regularly (on the half-hour) between the Royal Lahaina Resort at Kā'anapali and Lahaina's Wharf Cinema Shops and Restaurants, operating from 8:00 a.m. until 10:25 p.m., for a nominal fee. The **Kaanapali Shuttle** runs from 7:00 a.m. to 11:00 p.m. and is free of charge. Inquire at your hotel or condominium for current schedule information and the location of the pickup point nearest you, or call 661-3271.

Limousines

Maui has several limousine services, most operating twenty-four hours a day. **Arthur's Limousine Service** (871-5555, 800-345-4667) operates stretch Lincolns and Cadillacs all over the island, and even boasts a '64 Rolls Royce Princess. Chauffeurs wear uniforms and caps, roll out a red carpet for every client, and have been known to fill the car with helium balloons and release them through the sun roof in celebration of weddings or other festive events. Each of Arthur's limousines contains a complimentary bar. Japanese speaking drivers and tour guides are available upon request. In the Kapalua area, there is **Kapalua Executive Limousine Service** (669-2300), with island-wide tours and airport service. **Wailea Limousine Service** (875-4114) has a well-deserved reputation for service and style. Other companies are listed in Maui's Yellow Pages under "Limousine Service".

Air Tours

Flights aboard small airplanes and helicopters afford visitors a view of Maui from a wonderfully different perspective. Prices vary depending on the length of flights. Some flights not only include airborne tours of Maui, but also cross over to the nearby islands of Lāna'i and/or Moloka'i, or even go on for a day to O'ahu or the Big Island. Many offer passengers complimentary videos of each flight. Hotel activity desks generally have up-to-date information on rates and routes, or the tour firms themselves can be telephoned directly. Prices change frequently.

Most helicopter services operate out of Kahului Airport. **Alexair Helicopters** (877-4354) provides a menu of ten aerial tours of West Maui and entire-island flights, with flight durations from twenty minutes to two and a half hours. They recommend making reservations two to five days in advance for their tours. Charter and rental service to other islands are also available. **Hawaii Helicopters Inc.** (877-3900) specializes in East Maui tours of Ke'anae, Hāna and Haleakalā (45 minutes), but also offers a 60-minute West Maui-Moloka'i tour and 60- and 90-minute circle-island tours. Four cameras are mounted both inside and outside the helicopter, and a videotape of your specific tour is provided as your complimentary gift. **Cardinal Helicopters** (877-2400) offers four tours: West Maui, Hāna/Haleakalā, full island and Hāna Safari, with reasonable rates which include a complimentary videotape.

Family owned and operated **Blue Hawaiian Helicopters** (871-8844) has more than twenty years experience in the business, with excellent military-trained pilots. Many major motion picture companies have employed the services of this operator for their aerial shooting needs, including the movie *Jurassic Park*, filmed on Kauai in 1992. Top-of-the-line stereo head-sets cancel all outside noise so that passengers may clearly hear the pilot's narration and accompanying compact disc music.

Sunshine Helicopters (871-0711) features both tours and charter services. **Temptation Tours** (878-2911 or 877-8888) offers a helicopter ride one way to or from Hāna, and a van sight-seeing tour on the opposite leg of the trip. Each tour is limited to six people, and includes a gourmet picnic lunch served at one of Hāna's beautiful black sand beaches.

Big Island Air (808-303-8868) offers twin-engine aircraft tours of the Big Island from Maui, with the highlight being Kilauea Volcano, including flying over Maui's coastlines, waterfalls and Hāna. Tours depart from both Kahului and Kapalua. **Paragon Air** (244-3356), Hawaii's oldest fixed-wing air charter, provides air tours that can be coupled with ground tours. Tour packages offered are: the Kalaupapa-Moloka'i Tour, the Big Island Volcano Tour, Hāna Air Safari and the Private Golf Tour. Private charters are also available.

For the adventuresome visitor, open cockpit biplane tours are offered by **Biplane Barnstormers** (878-2860) out of Kahului Airport (see photo below). Five scenic tours are available, for one or two passengers, as well as custom tours and aerobatic flights.

Flying over Maui in a biplane is a unique way of seeing the island

Air tour without leaving the ground

The newest air tour adventure on Maui is offered by **Incredible Journeys!** (661-0092), located in the lobby of the Hyatt Regency Maui in Kā'anapali. After an informative "pre-flight" briefing, a maximum of seven passengers climb into a comfortable cockpit, don earphones, buckle up and experience an incredibly realistic 20-minute "helicopter" tour over Maui without ever leaving the ground. After "lift-off" at the Kahului Airport (the seats actually vibrate), passengers visit Maui's most beautiful scenic areas, including the crater of Haleakalā, the West Maui mountains, Molokini, Kā'anapali Beach, and more. The "flight" has a pre-recorded narration describing what's being seen, accompanied by upbeat music, and spectacular photography. The rising and falling of the scenery, which is projected on three sides thus allowing a 180° panoramic view, is so realistic that a few people may experience varying degrees of motion discomfort. During the pre-flight briefing, passengers are provided elastic "sea-bands" for each wrist to help ensure a comfortable experience, however, those prone to motion sickness may want to consider taking additional measures on their own before the "flight" to ensure maximum enjoyment. Tours run from 9:00 a.m. to 9:00 p.m. daily; the price is $34.95 for adults, $24.95 for children under 12. Reservations are recommended.

Water tours

Some fine sailing, snorkeling, scuba diving and fishing expeditions in Maui waters can be arranged for those who enjoy sailing, getting face-to-face with sea creatures, or fishing the deep blue. For details on fishing charters, sailing hires and other water sports and activities, see SPORTS.

Extended Cruises

American Hawaii Cruises (800-765-7000) runs seven-day cruises around the Hawaiian Islands aboard their two historic, 30,000-ton sister ships, *SS Constitution* and *SS Independence*, built in 1951. The *SS Constitution* was re-christened in 1982 by Her Royal Highness Princess Grace of Monaco, who sailed aboard the ship in 1956 with her wedding party. The *SS Independence* was completely refurbished in 1994 and the *SS Constitution* was refurbished in 1995.

Originating in Honolulu, the ships make similar rounds visiting the islands of Hawai'i, Kaua'i and Maui, with ports of call at Hilo and Kona, Nāwiliwili, and Lahaina, where they cross paths. Land excursions are arranged for passengers at each stopover. Shipboard accommodations--cabins, staterooms and suites--range in size, location and price and determine the overall cruise fare. This is a wonderful way to see the islands in all their natural beauty, while at the same time learning about their history and customs.

EXPLORING

Sight-seeing
Historical sites
Museums
Beaches & parks

The lower pools of 'Ohe'o Gulch

SIGHT-SEEING

Visitors to Maui could hurry around this lovely island in a day or two, but that would be a waste, and most of their time would be spent driving in the car. There is simply too much to see to rush. Like the other islands, Maui enjoys not only great scenic beauty, but a colorful history. Sights you will want to see often combine beauty and nostalgia, evoking a more gracious time.

Maui residents advise that the best way to see the island is to divide your time among the distinct parts of the island. For example, it's possible in a day-long tour to see the summit of Haleakalā, visit Kula and the Upcountry cowboy town of Makawao, and include the sprawling 'Ulupalakua Ranch. Most of the Kapalua area can be seen in a day, while allowing for a leisurely lunch and perhaps some beach time. This requires planning, and to that end we have divided this section into sight-seeing districts comparable to the various regions of Maui: Lahaina/Kā'anapali, Kapalua, Kīhei/Wailea, Hāna, Upcountry Maui and Wailuku-Kahului.

LAHAINA/KĀ'ANAPALI

Twenty-three miles from Kahului Airport, or a short six miles from the commuter airport of Kapalua-West Maui, the area of Lahaina and Kā'anapali thrives as a resort region that has heavy overtones of its colorful past. In many ways, this is Maui's heart. The great Kamehameha made this his seat of government after the conquest of Maui in a famous battle near 'Īao Needle, on the other side of the mountains. The missionaries settled here in the mid-1800s, launching their efforts to convert the Hawaiians to Christianity. It also was the magnet for whaling ships, with as many as 400 ships anchoring off Lahaina.

Kamehameha III was a resident of the area when he proclaimed new laws and Hawai'i's first official constitution. A great Hawaiian intellectual, David Malo, studied and worked in Lahaina, and is buried in the hills behind the town. Lahaina's magnificent views of other islands, its beaches, and its fine climate (although the name in Hawaiian means 'merciless sun') have long attracted

visitors. Today, tourism is the life-blood of the region.

Approaching Lahaina on Highway 30 from Kahului is a fine way to get into the mood of the area; the drive goes around a lava coastline and affords views of the islands of Kaho'olawe and Lāna'i, the islet of Molokini, and, in the distance, the island of Moloka'i. There are several scenic points, and during the whale-watching season, from late November to May, these areas are crowded with cars.

Here also are small, roadside parks with good ocean views-- **Pāpalaua, Ukumehame, Launiupoko** and **Puamana.** They offer a chance to stop, stretch, feel the sun, and enjoy the view. The road winds past **Olowalu,** a community of a few homes, a general store and an excellent French restaurant, Chez Paul (see DINING). It is the site of a famous massacre-- in a trading dispute, the captain of the *Eleanora* turned his ship's guns on Hawaiians in canoes alongside his ship. More than a hundred Hawaiians died in the cannonade, and more than 200 were wounded, many to die in the next few days. That was in 1790, but the massacre is remembered still. Among other consequences, the massacre led to the capture of Isaac Davis and John Young and their ultimate designation as advisors to the ambitious Kamehameha. Young was to become a close friend and was with Kamehameha when the monarch died.

From Olowalu to Lahaina, the road continues to curve between the sea and sugarcane fields, and finally leads on into the town itself. Some long-time residents look on Lahaina as a classic example of survival: the town has gone from fishing village, to whaling capital of the Pacific, to supplier of goods and staples to the sugar plantations, and finally to the hub of visitor activities on Maui.

Some old flavor remains in Lahaina--the narrow streets, the buildings hunched against each other, the smell of the sea and the view across the harbor to other islands. The number of visitors walking the streets today at least rivals the crowds of a century ago when Hawaiians, whalers, missionaries and beachcombers all gathered at Lahaina.

Lahaina itself is a National Historic Landmark, and is also protected as a Maui County Historic District. The **Lahaina Restoration Foundation** (661-3262) works hard at seeing interesting old buildings and landmarks refurbished and restored. In 1890 the old seawall, where residents and visitors gathered to watch sunsets, was rebuilt. The **Wo Hing Temple**, built in 1912, has been renovated, and the historic Pioneer Inn has undergone extensive refurbishing recently. Most of the two-mile stretch of Front Street, the focal point of Lahaina, retains its old look and feel despite the modern veneer. For those who want to see Lahaina in a leisurely manner, walk down this street and a few streets beyond, to see the town both as it is and was. Here are some of the major attractions:

In the heart of the town is a ninety-three-foot replica of a 19th century brig, *The Carthaginian*; inside is a well-designed, interesting

A replica of a nineteenth century brig, The Carthaginian is a floating whaling museum.

exhibit of whales and whaling. *The Carthaginian* is moored at the dock at the end of Papelekane Street and is open from 10:00 a.m. to 4:30 p.m. Admission fees are: $3.00 for adults, and $2.00 for senior citizens. Children may enter the exhibit free of charge.

Immediately behind The *Carthaginian* is the **Pioneer Inn,** built in 1901. It served as West Maui's major hotel until the 1950s. It was renovated in 1964, and, as of this writing, has completed another refurbishing. Breakfast on the *lānai* was a favorite of the *kama'āina* (long-time resident) for several generations.

The **Hauola Stone,** believed to be a site where early Hawaiians practiced medical arts, is north of *The Carthaginian.*

Near the Hauola Stone is the **Brick**

courthouse destroyed by a gale the year before.

Next to the courthouse is the site of the **Old Fort,** built in the 1830s and used mostly as a prison. The reconstructed fort replaced the one downtown in the late 1850s; its coral blocks helped make the new prison.

At the end of Wharf Street is a site remembered, not especially fondly, as the place where the government managed a market where Hawaiians traded with whaling men. The site was known as **Rotten Row.**

On Front Street between Dickenson Street and Papelekane Street are three important historical sites. The **Masters' Reading Room** was built in 1834 by missionaries and ships' officers. Made from blocks of coral, the building is one of the oldest Western structures on Maui, and

The bright green and white-trimmed Pioneer Inn, Lahaina's longtime landmark

Palace, ordered built by Kamehameha the Great as a residence. It is believed to be the first Western-style building constructed in Hawai'i.

Walk south from *The Carthaginian* down Wharf Street to get to the **Old Lahaina Courthouse,** built in 1859 from the stones of a previous

today is headquarters of the Lahaina Restoration Foundation. The **oldest coral stone house** in the islands is nearby; it was the **home of William Richards,** the first protestant missionary to Lahaina. These two structures flank the **Baldwin Home Museum.**

The Reverend Dwight Baldwin,

his wife Charlotte and their eight children lived in the Baldwin Home from 1836 to 1868. The New England style house contains some of the original furnishings. Daily tours of the home are given between 10:00 a.m. and 4:30 p.m.; admission is $3.00 for adults, $2.00 for senior citizens, and children are free of charge.

Across the street and down by Hotel Street is one of Lahaina's more visible landmarks, a **Banyan Tree** that was planted in 1873 to commemorate the 50th anniversary of the arrival of Lahaina's missionaries. Today, the tree covers a square--more than half an acre--and is so big its various trunks are propped up in places. It is a convenient meeting place for people, and a bandstand for mynah birds that gather in the early evening to serenade anyone who will listen.

At the corner of Front and Shaw Streets is **Malu'uluoLele Park,** a site which seems unremarkable today, but once was a significant part of Lahaina. It contained a pond and a

small island where Maui chiefs lived and died. Once it held a mausoleum, but the remains were moved and the pond filled in. Leveling the ground obliterated the physical evidence of its history, but old-timers today remember tales from their childhood about spirits lingering in the area.

The first stone church built in the isands, about 1830, is located on Waine'e Street. It was destroyed several times, and its name changed from Waine'e Church to **Waiola Church** (water of life). Nearby is the **Waine'e Cemetery,** filled with gravestones from the 19th century; it is the burial site of Keōpūolani, a queen of Kamehameha the Great.

Also on Waine'e Street, which intersects with Shaw Street, is the **Hongwanji Mission,** a Buddhist meeting place since 1910. The original small building was replaced in 1927 with the present building, which continues to be an important site for West Maui's Buddhist community.

A few steps down Waine'e Street

Sitting on the dock of Lahaina Harbor, watching the boats go by

from the Buddhist mission is the **homesite of David Malo,** the Hawaiian intellectual who embraced many of the new *haole* teachings, and then feared they would diminish the importance of ancient Hawaiian ways and ultimately fought against them.

On the opposite corner is **Hale Pa'ahao,** the old prison, made of the blocks from the Old Fort on Front Street. Built in the 1850s primarily to get rampaging sailors off the street, the prison held inmates whose offenses ranged from murder to riding a horse on Sundays.

Another Buddhist structure, the **Shingon Temple,** is located north on Luakini Street, which is parallel to Waine'e Street. It was built by and for the Japanese laborers who came to Maui near the turn of the century to work in plantation fields.

Luakini Street is significant also because it was the route of the tragic Princess Nāhi'ena'ena's funeral procession. She died at age twenty-one, a victim of the conflicts in 1837 that pitted the old Hawaiian ways against the new thought brought by the missionaries.

Nāhi'ena'ena had been in love with her brother since they were children together in Lahaina, but now her brother was King Kamehameha III, and the focus of divergent opinions on Hawai'i and its future. Hawaiian tradition would allow Nāhi'ena'ena to marry her brother and bear royal children. To the Hawaiians, this was the natural and logical way of perpetuating a dynasty and ensuring stability throughout the land. To the new *haole* missionaries, it was an anathema. The king was torn between these viewpoints; Nāhi'ena'ena was shattererd and became dissolute and wretched. Before her twenty-second birthday, the young princess died. Long after her death, the king could be found sitting quietly by her graveside.

The story of Nāhi'ena'ena and Kamehameha III became the classic tale of cultures in conflict, and all

43

The imposing two-ton Buddha seems to dwarf the mountains beyond

people of Hawai'i, whatever their beliefs, mourned. The princess' first funeral was in Honolulu, where the king led a procession of great chiefs behind a simple cart draped in black silk; at the church, the service was conducted by one of the most famous missionaries, Hiram Bingham. Kamehameha III then fitted out a ship and sent his sister's body home to Lahaina, where a roadway was cut through groves of breadfruit and *kou*. The cortege with its black-draped coffin moved along a road layered with sand, grass and mats. The lament of the common people could be heard along the route. Nāhi'ena-'ena was entombed in a mausoleum and remembered forever by her people. Today, that route is Luakini Street.

you pass the still-functioning **Pioneer Mill**, built in 1860. **Lahainaluna High School** is the oldest school west of the Rockies, opened in 1831 by missionaries. In its heyday, the school accepted pupils from other parts of Hawai'i as well as California. An adjunct of the schools was **Hale Pa'i Printing House.** It, too, is historic--it published Hawai'i's first newspaper and made Lahaina famous. Hale Pa'i was restored in 1982, and features an exhibit of the early printing press. It is operated by Lahaina Restoration Foundation, and you may call their office (661-3262) for the current hours of operation. Admission is free of charge, and donations are accepted.

Visitors to Hale Pa'i who also want to look around the school are asked to sign in at the vice principal's office.

The Sugarcane Train carries passengers between Lahaina and Kā'anapali

That road ends at Lahainaluna Street, a major entryway into the town itself and along which Lahainaluna High School and Hale Pa'i are located across the highway and 1.5 miles up in the hills. To reach them,

Visitors who are aware of David Malo's contribution to Hawai'i sometimes ask to see his gravesite; he is buried on **Mt. Ball**, above the school and near the giant 'L' visible from Lahaina.

Kā'anapali's sandy beach is still the most popular attraction of the Resort

Back in town and past Lahaina-luna Street, visitors still exploring Front Street will come across the **Lahaina Jodo Mission** near Māla Wharf. The Mission contains a Japanese cultural park, with pagodas, temples and a bell tower. The site commemorates the first Japanese immigrants, and in 1968 the centennial of their arrival was celebrated with the dedication of the largest Buddha outside of Asia. The buildings are closed to the public, but visitors may stroll around outside and enjoy the air of serenity.

One of the newer and most popular attractions in Lahaina is **The Hawaii Experience Omni Theater** (661-8314) at 824 Front Street, with a domed screen over three stories high, showing an exciting and informative film featuring breathtaking photography of Hawaii's scenic wonders. The 40-minute movie, "Hawaii: Islands of the Gods", is presented daily on the hour from 10:00 a.m to 10:00 p.m. Seating is planetarium-style, designed with clear views of the 180° screen from every seat. The cost is $6.95 for adults, $3.95 for children between ages 4 and 12.

Three miles outside of Lahaina, on Route 30, is the resort area of Kā'anapali, reachable by car, bicycle (there is a bicycle lane) or on foot. One way of getting there is on the **Lahaina-Kaanapali & Pacific Railroad;** old-timers remark that "the name is longer than the train". Also called the 'Sugarcane Train', it is a colorful string of three passenger cars pulled by the steam engine 'Anaka' and backed up by a second engine 'Myrtle', both rebuilt to turn-of-the-century specifications. The train chugs between Lahaina and Kā'anapali across a 400-foot-long trestle and beside a championship golf course. They are the most beautiful miles any

train could cover. Stations at either end of the track are built in Victorian style, as befitting the Hawaiian monarchy era theme. Passenger cars are fitted with wooden seats; the locomotive's cab is trimmed in mahogany. There are six daily departures from three stations, running every hour and twenty minutes, between 9:00 a.m. and 5:30 p.m. No reservations are needed, and tickets may be purchased at hotels or at tour activities desks, or at the train stations themselves, where jitneys take passengers to and from pickup points in Lahaina and Kā'anapali. Roundtrip fares are: $12.00 for adults, $6.00 for children; children two years old and younger ride for free. Schedules and fares vary from time to time, so it is best to call for current information (661-0089) or inquire at your hotel.

The **Lahaina Express,** provided compliments of Hilo Hatties and The Wharf Cinema Center, is a free shuttle running on the half-hour between Lahaina and Kā'anapali Resort, from 8:00 a.m. to 10:00 p.m. daily. Shuttle stops in Lahaina are located at the Wharf Cinema Center and at Hilo Hatties.

For those who wish to drive on their own to Lahaina, there are a number of conveniently located parking lots just one or two blocks off Front Street, with hourly rates. For those who don't mind walking a few blocks, a public lot is available free of charge (three hours maximum), situated at the far end of Front Street, between the Banyan Tree and 505 Front Street. It is best to arrive early in the morning, if possible, as free parking spaces are at a premium during peak times. Lahaina Center offers paid parking, which is free with validation of a purchase from one of their stores, restaurants or movie theaters. Lahaina Shopping Center has free parking, but, again, parking places are often elusive.

Kā'anapali itself is something of a miracle--an incredibly lush and comfortable resort area carved from lava, farmland and scrub brush by one of Hawai'i's oldest companies, Amfac. A string of world-class hotels provides luxurious rooms and suites, while surrounding them are tennis courts, golf courses and a long stretch of dazzling beach. In the center of the hotel complexes is Whalers Village, an eight-acre site containing art galleries, whaling artifacts, restaurants, and shops. **The Whale Center of the Pacific** (661-5992), on the third floor, has what has been called the largest collection of whaling memorabilia in the world, including a replica of the whaling bark, *Sunbeam*, whaleship log books, maps and scrimshaw collection. Its hours are 9:30 a.m. until 10:00 p.m. daily. Directly across from this museum is **Hale Kohola** ("house of the whale" - 661-9918), open daily from 10:00 a.m. to 6:00 p.m., which contains interesting whale exhibits featuring humpback whales, and also has a gift shop. Two videos run continuously throughout the day in their small theater, one entitled "Dolphins and Orcas", by Bob Talbot, cinematographer for "Free Willy", and the other entitled "Humpback Whales of Hawaii". Both museums are free of charge, however any donations are greatly appreciated.

An interesting part of Kā'anapali is **Black Rock** (Pu'u Keka'a), a volcanic formation eroded by the sea that was considered a holy place by early Hawaiians. They thought it was one of the places where spirits of the dead left the earth for the spirit world. It also was the place where Maui's most famous king, Kahekili, liked to climb and then leap into the sea. Today, Black Rock has been integrated into the design of the Sheraton-Maui. It is also an ideal spot for snorkeling, as the colorful reef fish are abundant and accustomed to visitors.

The Pioneer Inn's wooden sailor is almost as famous as the hotel itself

KAPALUA

Highway 30 passes Kā'anapali and heads up to Maui's northwest coast, leading to the resort area of Kapalua and the Nāpili Bay region, an old favorite of many Maui residents.

There is a cutoff from the main highway down to a secondary road, once the principal highway, that leads past restaurants, condominiums and private homes. *Makai* (seaward) of the highway, the shoreline alternates between rocks worn smooth by the tides and small, sandy beaches. Just to the north is Kapalua, 750 acres of meticulous landscaping, golf courses, tennis courts and pools, all rises from the sea, giving beach goers a good look at its coves and deep valleys.

Beyond Kapalua, a winding road goes up and down the cliffside past deeply carved bays and Nākālele Point. At one point, at Honokōhau, there are taro fields. On down the road is a large, famous boulder known as the **Bellstone.** When someone strikes one side of the rock, and you listen on the other side, a clear, bell-like sound rings out. Don't be too surprised, though, if you don't hear it. Not everyone does.

The road continues to Kahakuloa, a small, remote town where the

Honokōhau Bay

part of a massive elaborate resort complex, with two luxury class hotels--the Kapalua Bay Hotel and the Ritz-Carlton Kapalua--as its focal points.

Kapalua also is famous for its beaches, favorites of local residents who sometimes drive from as far away as Upcountry just to bask in the sun. The area also offers a visual bonus: just across a stretch of blue water, the green island of Moloka'i villagers like to keep to themselves. Most houses are unpretentious wooden homes. There are two churches, Protestant and Catholic.

Kahakuloa is the most isolated village on Maui, and the road to it from the Central Valley side has only recently been paved. Car rental companies used to frown on taking rental cars on that stretch of the road, due to its rugged unpaved condition, but that is now a thing of the past.

Dramatic cliffs near Maui's northernmost tip

An aerial perspective of sunlit Wailea Beach

KĪHEI/WAILEA

Maui's southern coast is dry and sunny--a magnet for young beach goers. It also attracted a number of developers over the years who looked at the area's beaches and climate, and forecast a need for housing. The result is a string of condominiums leading from near Māʻalaea, a major boat harbor, on through the Kīhei sector and into Wailea, a glossy resort area with a number of fine hotels and restaurants. Beyond Wailea lies Mākena, a network of excellent beaches off the beaten path.

To get to Māʻalaea from Kahului Airport, travel on Highway 380 across the isthmus to Highway 30; proceed on 30 and watch for the signs for Māʻalaea; the turnoff intersects the main highway on the makai (seaward) side. This area is the site of a small boat harbor with a number of charter boats, as well as condominiums and a few restaurants.

Back on Highway 30 to Highway 31, a well-marked secondary road leads into Kīhei, an area with a growing number of good restaurants and row after row of condominiums. Here too are several popular beach parks--**Maipoinaʻoeiaʻu,** at the upper end of Kihei, across from the Maui Lu Resort, and **Kalama** and **Kamaʻole Beach Parks** in the heart of Kīhei. Many visitors claim this area has the best combination of beaches, weather and views on Maui, and perhaps in all of Hawaiʻi. With the addition of new shopping centers and shops, Kīhei is a self-contained spot that caters to a variety of tastes and budgets. From Kīhei's beaches there are excellent views of Haleakalā, the sweep of coastline and the West Maui Mountains off in the distance, as well as excellent whale-watching vantage points.

At the other end of Kīhei is a 1500-acre complex of fine hotels, restaurants and shops, with excellent golf courses, tennis courts and

Taking an afternoon stroll in Kīhei

activities such as scuba diving, snorkeling, and windsurfing. This is Wailea, Alexander and Baldwin's jewel-like resort set against the arid lava flows of southeast Maui. The area has grown over the last five years, with the addition of several new luxury hotels and restaurants.

One of the area's great features is the string of five excellent beaches, one after the other. Maui's beaches lie like a sandy lei around the island, but here in Wailea they seem to sparkle.

Just down the road, past the Polo Beach Resort, is Mākena, an area formerly wild and pristine, which in recent years has undergone development resulting in the building of the luxurious Maui Prince Hotel and Makena Surf condominiums and townhouses, as well as two championship golf courses. It is an area of superb beaches, but no amenities. Years ago the area was a semi-permanent campsite for transients, and attained a certain notoriety. One of the beaches, Oneuli (residents call it 'Little Beach' or 'Little Mākena') still has a reputation as a nude beach and is subject to occasional police sweeps. Oneloa ('Big Beach' to residents) lies on the other side of the distinctive Pu'u Ōla'i, a 360-foot cinder cone; Big Beach offers not only good swimming but an excellent place to watch sunset. In the **'Āhihi-Kīna'u Natural Area Reserve,** unusual marine life abounds in the tidal pools offshore.

South of this natural reserve site is La Perouse Bay, marking the spot where, in May of 1786, the French explorer Comte de La Perouse became the first Westerner to set foot on Maui. La Perouse sailed away from Maui in search of new adventures and disappeared at sea. Today the bay named for this Frenchman is reachable by four-wheel-drive vehicle, as the road is rough. The ancient Hoapili ('King's') Trail leads from La Perouse Bay on south along Maui's rugged coastline. Snorkeling is good here, but currents can be strong, so caution is advised.

Learning how to body board at Kā'anapali

HANA

To approach Hāna is to turn back the calendar to a place that time forgot, existing in one century while wearing the face of another. Even in Maui, itself a special place, Hāna stands apart, a virtual heaven-on-earth.

Part of its charm lies in its isolation. Although there is a small airstrip served by a commuter airline, access is limited, and most people rent a car and drive here via the only road--the Hāna Highway. Carved from the hillside in 1927, and generally following an old trail, the road has by some counts more than 600 curves, plus fifty-four one-lane bridges, and driving is an exhilarating and somewhat challenging experience.

Just the effort in getting to Hāna makes it a special place. The drive can take about two and a half to three hours from Kahului, depending on how often you stop to enjoy the lush scenery. The many scenic lookouts and rushing waterfalls along the way are well worth a leisurely pace.

On Highway 36, **H. A. Baldwin Park** is a good place for camping, swimming and surfing. Just beyond is Pā'ia, Maui's most important town at the peak of the sugar era, and now an important windsurfing hub because it is near Ho'okipa Beach, a mecca for the popular sport, attracting windsurfers from all over the world each year. Pā'ia's old-town flavor is a mixture of history, the surfing mystique and a laid-back lifestyle.

In the heart of Pā'ia is the **Mantokuji Buddhist Temple.** Down the road is **Twin Falls,** a swimming hole formed by two mountain streams. It is reachable by following a sign posted just under two miles beyond Kākipi Gulch.

Past Twin Falls is the village of **Huelo,** and shortly after that a second small town, **Kailua.** These are the quiet, sleepy places that add to the aura of peace and contentment along the northeast coast. As the

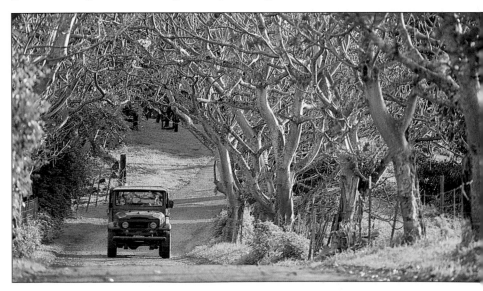

road winds past them, the incredibly lush foliage cloaks the roadside. You'll want to drink in the beauty of the streams and waterfalls along the way.

Past Kailua are **Kaumahina State Park** and Honomanū Bay down below. At **Honomanū Park,** there is a lovely black sand beach, although the park has no amenities and the swimming can be treacherous. A short distance on down the highway is the **Ke'anae Valley Lookout,** where you can admire views of Wailua in one direction and Ke'anae Valley and up to Ko'olau Gap in the other.

Before heading down a narrow paved road (look for the 17 mile marker) to **Ke'anae Peninsula,** stop at the **Ke'anae Arboretum,** located on the

area is home to hoards of hungry mosquitoes, so if you have mosquito repellent, it is advisable to spray some on before you tour the grounds.

Down on the peninsula, modern taro farms look much like their older counterparts. Many of the area's residents are Hawaiians who hold on to their old ways.

The next stop is Wailua, remarkable for its well-known **Coral Miracle Church.** The church's real name is actually **St. Gabriel's Church.** When parishioners set out to build a church in 1870, they found sand and coral washed ashore, which they used as building materials.

Past Wailua is **Nāhiku,** a rainswept area three miles down from the highway, and once the location of

St. Gabriel's Church, Wailua

right side of the road just around the bend from the YMCA's **Camp Ke'anae** (see ACCOMMODATION). The Arboretum features reconstructed old taro patches and some sixty varieties of taro, the Hawaiian staple from which *poi* is made. Here also are many other types of native Hawaiian plants. Take note that this

a rubber plantation. The turn-off is identifiable only by a collection of mailboxes and a narrow paved road leading *makai* (seaward). At the turn of the century, Nāhiku was believed to be the only place in America where rubber was grown commercially. Today, there are still a few rubber trees in evidence. Two good swimming holes are located here, one reached from the landing at the end of the road, one via a path on the right after the village's two churches.

Back on the main road and continuing towards Hāna, watch for **Hāna Gardenland** (248-7340) on the right side of the road; it is open daily from 9:00 a.m. to 5:00 p.m. and has no entry fee. This tropical plant nursery offers shipping of its beautiful plants to virtually anywhere you wish, and also has a casual open-air cafe, which serves a nice selection of reasonably priced breakfast and lunch fare. You can also order food to go, with thirty minutes' advance notice.

A short way past Hāna Gardenland, look for a turnoff on the left,

Just past the airport turnoff is a side road that leads to **Wai'ānapanapa State Park,** a dramatic seacoast area of great natural beauty. Trails lead through the **Wai'ānapanapa** and **Waimao Caves.** Like most other Hawaiian areas, Wai'ānapanapa has both legend and fact, and they occasionally meld. Wai'ānapanapa Cave is partially filled with water, which turns red in the spring. Folklore has it that a jealous husband traced his wife, a princess (Popoalaea), to the cave and killed her; others blame the color on tiny red shrimp. Some people on Maui who find spiritual power in certain sites claim that Wai'ānapanapa is a place of great spirituality. Reasonably priced cabins with electricity,

Ancient ruins of a Hawaiian village in the vast Haleakalā National Park

Ulaino Road, which leads down to a massive old *heiau*, situated on private land. The **Pi'ilanihale Heiau** is said to be the largest in the islands, with huge walls, more than fifty feet in height, still intact. Returning to the main road, you are less than a mile away from Hāna's airport; the turnoff is clearly marked.

bedding, water and kitchens are available in the park for limited stays, and normally must be reserved far in advance (see ACCOMMODATION). Tent camping is also permitted

Beyond the caves, along the shoreline, a natural blowhole and a high arch distinguish the point. Nearby Honokalani black sand beach fringes

One of the deep caves at Wai'ānapanapa State Park

the small bay, where swimming is good when the water is calm.

From the black sand beach, it's possible to follow a trail along the seacoast that was part of King's Highway, a 16th century construction project spearheaded by Chief Pi'ilani. Today, it takes about two hours to cover the three miles into Hāna.

About a mile before the town of Hāna is **Helani Gardens** (248-8274), a seventy-acre nursery started in 1970 and opened to the public in 1975. The lower acreage is manicured and trimmed; the upper sixty-five acres are left wild for those who like to wander among a variety of exotic plants. One section contains a large treehouse built mostly by the founder of the gardens, complete with windows, electricity and plumbing. Having recently come under new ownership, the gardens are closed, as of this writing. Visitors should call for current information regarding hours of operation and entry fees.

In Hāna town, the pace is easy and the sights are heart-warming. The town's population is mostly Hawaiian, with a sprinkling of celebrities who have found the town's quiet ways to their liking. The homes and the few shops huddle in the arm of **Kau'uiki Head,** a volcanic outcropping. Rising above the town on a *pu'u* (hill) is a large cross, memorial to Paul Fagan, who founded the Hāna Ranch and the area's landmark, the **Hotel Hāna-Maui.** The panoramic view of Hāna from the cross is spectacular.

Stop and relax in this lovely town. This is the place where, for years when you telephoned the police department, you got a recorded message: "...if this is an emergency, leave your name and number and we'll call you back." This is also the town where Sunday services at

Wānalua Church are conducted both in Hawaiian and English.

Hale Waiwai O Hāna, a museum near the turnoff to Hāna Bay, chronicles the colorful and sometimes turbulent past of Hāna. This was the birthplace of Ka'ahumanu, who became a favorite (and strong-willed) wife of Kamehameha I, whose armies crushed the Maui armies in a battle that raged near Ka'uiki Head. Hāna evolved into a plantation town, but sugar began to diminish as an area industry in the 1940s, and many people left Hāna for employment elsewhere. San Francisco industrialist Paul Fagan bought 14,000 acres and converted them into a cattle ranch; he also built the lovely **Hotel Hana-Maui.**

The museum is housed in the **Hāna Cultural Center** (Uakea Road - 248-8622), open daily from 10:00 a.m. to 4:00 p.m. Admission is free, however a small donation is suggested. There is a park with public tennis courts near the center of town, and down along the bay an old pier affords a good look back at Hāna. From the pier, a trail goes off to the right and onto Ka'uiki Head (not an easy walk) and to a site where a plaque marks Ka'ahumanu's birthplace.

Hasegawa General Store, a longtime Hāna landmark, burned down in the summer of 1990, but has opened in a new location just across the street from the Chevron station, in a weathered green building that was formerly the Old Hāna Theater. It still brims with groceries, staple items and souvenirs. Hasegawa's was celebrated some years ago in a song by Paul Weston's band that was a national hit. The **Hana Ranch Store** is the other market in town, offering food and sundries, as well as souvenirs and postcards. If you want to see

57

what's going on in town, take a look at the community bulletin boards just outside the entrances to these stores, with notices advertising everything from vacation rentals to massage therapists.

Past Hāna town, the sense of isolation continues. The road follows the coastline, marked by waterfalls and small bridges over cool streams. This is Highway 31 and leads into Kīpahulu, a part of Haleakalā National Park. En route, you pass the turn-off to **Hāmoa Beach,** a lovely white sand beach, part of which belongs to the Hotel Hāna-Maui. The beach has an outdoor shower and a restroom designated for public use. The other facilities are for hotel guests only.

Wailua and **Kanahualiʻi Falls** are seven miles outside of Hāna. A trail leads down to a rocky beach where a settlement was wiped out on the morning of April 1, 1946 by a *tsunami* (tidal wave) generated by an earthquake in Alaska. Above the road is a concrete cross honoring one Helio, a Hawaiian Catholic who lived during the 1840s and converted hundreds of people to Catholicism.

Now inside the National Park, visitors always admire **'Oheʻo Gulch,** an area where twenty-four pools topple one into another and finally into the sea. This is known, erroneously, as Seven Sacred Pools or **Seven Pools.** A path on the left bank of the Palikea Stream leads down to fine swimming and picnicking areas. On the other side and some distance above are taro farms maintained by the Cultural Center in Hāna. There are free tours of this area conducted by National Park Rangers (call 248-7375 for schedules and information).

A trail takes visitors who want to walk up Waimoku Falls Trail to **Makahiku Falls,** a half-mile hike, and then another mile and a half on to

Waimoku Falls (see "Hiking" under SPORTS).

At Kīpahulu Ranch, the paved road ends. Famed aviator Charles A. Lindbergh is buried on the *makai* side of the road in the churchyard of **Palapala Hoʻomau Church.** Lindbergh spent much of his later years in Hāna and helped restore the church. A year before his death in 1974, he picked this as his burial site.

Most car rental companies ban renters from driving in the area beyond Kīpahulu. It is a gravel road linking Kīpahulu with the small town of **Kaupō,** eight miles away, and is sometimes flooded during heavy rains. This route can best be navigated by a four-wheel-drive vehicle. A word of caution: it is a good idea to check with Park Rangers and/or residents of the area before making the long drive around the Hāna Coast towards 'Ulupalakua.

The Kaupō General Store is the heart of tiny Kaupō, and is not only the town's supplier but its post office as well. The town also contains **Kuialoha Church,** built in 1859 and since restored. On a hill above the road are the remains of a *heiau;* a second, larger one lies at the head of the Kaupō Gap behind the small school.

Although the road along this coastline is bumpy, narrow and difficult to navigate at times, the journey is exciting, and along the way are great views of unmatched beauty. Past the old Nu'u Landing and at the end of a dry creekbed, there are caves and petroglyphs. In the distance, you will see Molokini Island, and beyond it the island of Kaho'olawe.

At 'Ulupalakua, visitors enter the Upcountry area. From the ranch region the road winds back down through Kula and you are suddenly a world away from remote Hāna.

The ever-changing and timeless beauty of the Hāna Coast

UPCOUNTRY MAUI

For most visitors, Upcountry is a different--and unexpected--world. It reminds many travelers of Wyoming in that it is cool, green and dotted with cattle ranches. The mood is decidedly Western, with cows, horses, four-wheel-drive vehicles, cowboy hats, rail fences, pine forests and temperatures much cooler than at Maui's lower elevations.

On the slopes of Haleakalā, pheasant and francolin can be seen against the green grasses. A wide variety of flowers grow here, including the exotic protea, a South African plant that is hardy, varied and colorful, and proving to be a lucrative export for Maui growers. Protea is sold at roadside stands off Highways 377 and 378. The famous Kula onion grows here as well. Jacaranda and towering eucalyptus trees line some back roads, and from almost everywhere above the 1500-foot level, there are magnificent vistas of the ocean, West Maui Mountains, and valley below.

Highways 37, 377 and 378 lead to Haleakalā, and wind through Upcountry. Off Highway 37 is Makawao Avenue, leading to the unpretentious cowboy town of Makawao, which somehow continues to change, and yet, in some ways, stays the same. You may pass horses as well as cars along the town's main route, Baldwin Avenue.

Highway 37 melds into 370, leading to **'Ulupalakua Ranch** and a

Ideal for grazing cows, cool, green pastures line Haleakala's slopes.

small visitor center where it is possible to buy wines grown on the ranch. The ranch owner, C. Pardee Erdman, and a young wine-maker from California, Emil Tedeschi, combined their talents to produce Hawai'i's first commercial wine. The 2000-foot elevation and the Carnelian grape made the wine produced by **Tedeschi Vineyards, Ltd.,** a commercial and aesthetic success. The ranch road winds to a tasting room where the wines and other local products are displayed and sold.

The drive to 'Ulupalakua from the Central Valley area should take an hour and a half or so, without rushing. It goes past pristine Keōkea Park, a good place to picnic. It also goes past a famous octagonal church

more than 700 plants (the protea among them), rest areas and a picnic table. On another site in Kula, the **University of Hawai'i College of Tropical Agriculture** operates a twenty-acre Experimental Station where important research takes place--and lovely roses grow. The site is off Highway 37 on Copp Road, south of Kula Elementary School.

Above Makawao on Highway 39 is the small community of Olinda, with its rolling green hills, fragrant eucalyptus trees, and expansive views of the West Maui Mountains and central valley.

Downhill from Makawao, Baldwin Avenue leads into the town of Pā'ia, site of a sugar mill and fast becoming known around the world

Upcountry's clouds are as much a part of the scenery as pastures

in Kula, **the Church of the Holy Ghost.** This 1897 Catholic church on a hillside above Waiakoa has a large altar that had to be shipped in sections around Cape Horn.

Not far away, off Highway 377, is the **Kula Botanical Gardens,** with

as headquarters for Maui's burgeoning windsurfing industry. For those with a four-wheel-drive vehicle and an urge to get off the beaten path, there is the 10.5-mile trip on Waipoli Road from Highway 377 to **Polipoli Springs State Recreation Area.** The

Moody skies accompany the ascending Haleakalā Highway

road can be driven in a rental car, however, it is bumpy and rutted in places, not to mention narrow, making driving conditions hazardous at times, especially if the clouds roll in and impair visibility. In wet weather, it is advisable to travel the road only in a four-wheel-drive vehicle. Once there, you are in the middle of a hardwood forest. If you climb another thousand feet on foot, you can stand atop a volcanic cinder cone and enjoy an astonishing view of neighboring islands. There is a single cabin in the area that can be reserved through the State Parks office in Wailuku (243-5354).

Dominating the Maui scene is spectacular Haleakalā, a volcano 33 miles long and 10,023 feet high. The 300. Hikers and campers in the crater can--and often do--get sunburned and rained on in the same day. Before your visit, check current weather conditions by calling 871-5054.

The most direct way to Haleakalā is to drive on Highway 37 from Kahului, then eventually veer left onto Highway 377. You will come to another left turn, onto Highway 379 for the last few miles to the **Visitor Center of Haleakalā National Park**, on the western rim of the summit, usually open from sunrise until 3:00 p.m. From there, the road takes visitors on a series of switchback turns in increasingly frigid temperatures to the 10,023-foot summit. There is no public transportation to Haleakalā, and visitors must use

The desolate terrain of Haleakalā Crater

circumference is 21 miles; the area of the crater is 19 square miles. The crater itself is 7.5 miles long, 2.5 miles wide. The national park area surrounding the volcano is 42.6 square miles. One end of the crater gets less than thirty inches of rain a year, while the other end gets more than rental cars, taxis or travel via an escorted sight-seeing excursion to visit the area. There is a small admission fee to the park, and no charge for senior citizens age 62 and older.

The views are spectacular. The road winds through ranchlands, and with each turn offers a view of the land below, of West Maui's mountains (usually peeking through a cloud cover, particularly in the afternoon). In the distance are islands--inhabited Moloka'i and Lānai, the island of Kaho'olawe, and the islet of Molokini. Some hundred miles to the south are the tops of the volcanic massifs of Mauna Loa and Mauna Kea on the Big Island of Hawai'i.

Four overlooks permit excellent views of the crater itself. They are: **Leleiwi,** at the 9000-foot level; **Kala-haku,** two miles below the summit; the **National Park Visitor Center** near the summit; and the **Red Hill Visitor Center,** Pu'u 'Ula'ula, the top of the mountain.

At the summit is a cluster of white, somewhat futuristic buildings and domes. This is **Science City,** home of a communications station, University of Hawai'i observatories, radar installations, television relay stations and a satellite tracking station. It is from this area that laser beams have been aimed at satellites as part of the Strategic Defensive Initiative, better known as 'Star Wars'. The site is off-limits to visitors.

One fourth of a mile above the park entrance, a paved road leads to the **Hosmer Grove Campground** and picnic area, a half-mile from the highway. The area contains a shelter against inclement weather, and in-cludes tables and charcoal pits. Charcoal pits are also located in an open site just below the road. There are tent sites, running water and parking. There is no charge for camping here, but permits are necess-ary from Park Headquarters (572-9306), or may be obtained by writing P. O. Box 369, Makawao, Hawaii 96768. For recorded Park informa-tion, call 572-7749.

Park Headquarters, at the 7000-foot level and just a mile inside the

Sunset viewers on the summit of Red Hill, Pu'u 'Ula'ula

park entrance, is a good place to start your visit in this area. The headquarters' hours are 7:30 a.m. to 4:00 p.m. Inside the building is a wealth of information on Haleakalā, including maps, photographs, a slide presentation and friendly Park Rangers who can answer any question about this unique site. Here is where hiking and camping permits are issued.

Those are the facts of Haleakalā; but like the islands themselves, more than facts are necessary for a real understanding of this incredible mountain. For example, on some late afternoons at Leleiwi Overlook, your shadow is thrown against the clouds, frequently encircled by a rainbow. Local people call it the 'Spectre of the Brocken'. Stop to enjoy the variety of trees along the trail at Hosmer Grove Campground; some are from India, Japan and Australia. Many people make the effort to witness sunrise on Haleakalā--a spectacular sight when it's clear--but sunsets are just as rewarding.

To see the sun drop behind the West Maui Mountains and watch the sky invent new colors is a never-to-be-forgotten experience. A thrilling part of the Haleakalā sunrise experience is viewing the crater from the summit, and watching the sun break over the cinder cones that jut up from the crater floor. To the east, the Big Island forms out of the darkness, then the sun soars well above the horizon, changing the whole spectrum of colors. To view dawn at Haleakalā means enduring a two-and-a-half- to three-hour drive for those staying at West Maui resorts. It is a good idea to call Maui's weather/recreation forecast (871-5054) before starting up. Warm clothing is never out of place at the summit, which can be 25° to 30° (F) colder than Maui's lower elevations. In winter, it is possible to encounter snow, and occasionally

Making the pilgrimage to Haleakalā Crater before sunrise

snow forces the temporary closing of the road.

Inside the crater, there is a desert-like atmosphere. There are lichens, pili grass, clover, evening primrose, *'ōhelo, māmane,* tarweed, *'ōhi'a* and the rare silversword plant *(Argyroxiphium sandwicense).* The beautiful silversword is a well-known member of the same family as sunflowers, asters, and chrysanthemums. The plant grows for as many as twenty years and gets as high as eight feet, with between one hundred and five hundred flower heads.

Outside the crater, on the slopes of the volcano, the *nēnē* bird, nearly extinct at one point, is fighting its way back. Thoughtful visitors admire these birds but do not disturb them or disrupt their activities. Generally there are tame *nēnē* around Park Headquarters who are accustomed to visitors snapping photos.

Persons with high blood pressure or a heart condition should remember to move slowly in the thin air of upper Haleakalā; such persons are advised not to hike or drive alone.

Haleakalā is justly called 'The House of the Sun', but legends vary on how the demigod Māui, for whom the island is named, accomplished the

feat that earned the massive volcano its name.

Legend has it that Māui, the son of Hina, slowed the sun in its passage to give his mother more time to dry *tapa* (bark cloth); the sun had simply been passing overhead too quickly. Māui accomplished this from his stance on the summit of Haleakalā, but exactly how depends on what legend you want to believe.

One says that Māui fashioned a giant net--he was a fisherman of renown--and caught the sun as it was streaking overhead. Another legend uses the lariat theory: The prankster caught the sun by its legs as, one by one, the sunlight fell in shafts of light into the crater. He then tied the legs to an *'ōhi'a* tree and forced a promise from the sun that it would travel much more slowly across the sky, giving Hina--and women everywhere--more time to accomplish their tasks.

Two additional adventures are possible in Haleakalā--hiking or riding horses into the crater. Inside the crater are three cabins, called Paliku, Holua and Kapalaoa, which can accommodate parties of up to twelve people, and are rented via the Park Service (see ACCOMMODATION).

Dormant cinder cones located within the massive Haleakala Crater.

Central Maui was formed by the gradual joining of lava flows from Haleakalā and the West Maui Mountains. This broad isthmus is the site of thousands of acres of sugar cane, which is harvested by first burning it. The sight of dark smoke rising from the fields startles some visitors, especially the view of the fires at night, but the practice is accepted and widely used. Occasionally, the debris of the burning cane, black flakes often referred to as 'Hawaiian snow', drifts over a town or residential area, forcing residents to close their windows until it passes.

Within the area are two of Maui's major towns, and its commercial heart. Kahului, where the main airport is located, is also a deep-water port. Three miles towards the mountains is Wailuku, Maui's capitol and seat of government. It is still a charming, old-fashioned town with twisting streets and old wooden structures, as well as unique shops and a few noteworthy restaurants.

Kahului is Maui's supply center--it contains the shops and stores where staples are sold. When Maui residents 'go to town' for gas, groceries, clothing, furniture or building materials, they are likely talking about Kahului. Much of what they buy is contained in three shopping malls, all in a row along the main thoroughfare, Ka'ahumanu Avenue, named for a favorite wife of Kamehameha I. As you move towards Wailuku, they are the Maui Mall, Kahului Shopping Center and Kaahumanu Center. All have a variety of shops, restaurants and ample parking.

There are several places of interest as you head towards Wailuku from the airport. The first is adjacent to the airport itself--**Kanahā Beach Park,** reachable via Alahao Street just off the baseyard road to the Department of Water Supply. The park has restrooms, parking space, large shade trees, and a view across Kahului Harbor. The park generally is uncrowded and overlooked by most visitors. Between the airport and town is **Kanahā Pond,** a protected wildlife refuge and home of the migratory Hawaiian stilt, or *ae'o*. Kanahā Pond formerly was a royal fishpond and now is one of the few places in Hawai'i where the stilt can breed and feed unmolested.

The harbor near the edge of town has become important to Maui as a place where goods are received, and to the Japanese fishermen as a fueling base for their boats. Here also is the state's first bulk sugar plant. Next to the harbor is a small park, **Hoaloha Park,** a good place to picnic off the beaten path.

Take the Waiehu Beach Road in the center of town to **Haleki'i,** a partially restored *heiau*, or Hawaiian temple, just outside of Kahului. It can be reached by turning off Waiehu Beach Road onto Kūhiō Place, which is just past a bridge over 'Īao stream. Haleki'i was in use during the reign of Maui's famous King Kahekili in the late 1700s. An on-site diagram explains the layout of the walls and terraces. A path leads from the site toward the mountains, and ends in a second temple about a hundred yards away. The second site, **Pihana,** dates from 1779 and was a sacrificial temple. From the Haleki'i site, there is an especially good panoramic view of Kahului Harbor.

Wailuku is an easy place to explore on foot. The same Ka'ahumanu Avenue that runs through the center of Kahului melds directly

67

into Wailuku's Main Street. That goes on to become 'Iao Valley Road and leads directly into 'Iao Valley. If you park near the town's only 'high rise', the nine-story **Kalana O Maui** (County Office Building), you can see most things of interest just by strolling around.

Across High Street from the County Office Building area is the **Wailuku Library,** which is home to a fine Hawaiiana collection. Just a few steps down from the library is **Ka'ahumanu Church,** a Congregational Church built in 1876 and now a Wailuku landmark. The church was the third built by Maui's first Christian congregation. It replaced an earlier building dating from 1832, which had replaced the grass-thatched original where Queen Ka'ahumanu used to attend services.

An interesting way to sample the flavor of Maui is to attend the church service held at 9:00 a.m. on Sundays.

While the service is in English, the invocation and hymns are in Hawaiian. These powerful voices not only sing praises, they link the present with the past. The church itself is closed during the week, but visitors generally can find the caretaker by walking around to the back of the church. Justly proud of the church, the caretaker usually gives visitors a good-natured, off-hours tour.

If you continue down High Street, which becomes Highway 30, for three miles, you will come to the town of Waikapū. This is the site of the **Maui Tropical Plantation,** fifty acres of beautifully kept agricultural park. Open 9:00 a.m. to 5:00 p.m. with free admission, the park exhibits Hawaiian plants such as ferns, orchids, bougainvillea, and pineapple, and trees such as coffee, macadamia nut, papaya, avocado, and starfruit, in a nicely landscaped setting. A forty-minute "Tropical Express" narrated

Swards of green sugar cane border Mokulele Highway in the Central Valley

tram ride ($8.00/adult, $3.00/child) through the park runs from 10:00 a.m. to 4:00 p.m., departing every thirty minutes. (The tour is discounted for Hawai'i residents: $5.00/adult and $1.00/child.) The tram stops periodically for photo-taking opportunities, as well as a coconut husking demonstration. Interesting walk-through exhibits detail the history of macadamia nuts, irrigation, coffee and sugar in Hawai'i. Their large marketplace has one of the widest range of Hawaiian food products (fresh and packaged) you'll find on Maui, at reasonable prices. There is also a tropical restaurant, which offers a special "Hawaiian Country Barbecue" certain nights of the week, with live country music. For more information or to make dinner reservations, call 242-8605.

At the intersection of High Street and Main Street, the road winds on into 'Iao Valley, a three-mile drive alongside 'Iao Stream. Just off to the left as you leave High Street is the **Bailey House Museum,** consisting of two buildings: the home built by Edward Bailey in 1841 when he was head of the Wailuku Female Seminary, and the kitchen-dining room of the school, built in 1838. Also known as the Old Bailey House, the home is made of twenty-inch-thick stone walls covered with plaster and goat hair, and sandalwood beams carved by hand.

Bailey was the principal of the school until 1849, when the school closed and he was forced into other employment. As a painter, he left a perception of his times that are valuable today. His paintings hang in the Museum. The complex is **Maui Historical Society Museum,** which houses important traditional Hawaiian artifacts, from tapa cloth to tools to furniture. In back of the building is

a canoe shed and other exhibits. The Bailey House Museum is open daily from 9:00 a.m to 3:30 p.m. There is a small admission charge, and conducted tours can be arranged (244-3326).

Two miles along the same road from Wailuku is a Maui County park known as **Kepaniwai Heritage Gardens,** where there are picnic tables with the 'Iao Stream flowing nearby. There is a formal garden with structures representing the peoples of Hawai'i, such as the Portuguese outdoor oven, the Chinese moon gate, the Japanese tea house and the Hawaiian grass-woven house. The Gardens are open daily and there is no admission charge. This area also provides excellent backdrops for photographs, or just a comfortable place for a respite from sight-seeing.

The area was not so comfortable for Maui warriors in 1790, when the forces of Kamehameha I clashed in a bloody battle with the men from Maui. Seemingly invincible, Kamehameha's army defeated the Mauians in a battle that gave the place its name--Kepaniwai, or 'damning of the waters', indicating that the Wailuku Stream was blocked by the bodies of the defeated Maui fighters. Today, however, the area is a place of gentleness and peace.

At the end of the road is **'Iao Valley State Park.** 'Iao is a multi-faceted Hawaiian word bound up in the concept of light and supremacy. The park contains its own grandeur. Soaring green mountains and strands of clouds give the park a certain majesty. Near the center of it all is the 2250-foot **'Iao Needle,** a sharp-rising and heavily eroded peak that forms a dramatic centerpiece for the park. Trails lead up to the top of a ridge for a closer view of the Needle, and down to the stream through a variety of exotic foliage. It is easy to see why Mark Twain called this area "The Yosemite of the Pacific."

Look for another attraction in the valley. Before reaching the park area, in a part of the valley known as **Pali 'Ele'ele** (dark gorge), there is a sweeping curve where visitors often stand and gaze at boulders on a distant ridge. The boulders are said to form a likeness of the late President John F. Kennedy. This phenomenon, like beauty, is in the eye of the beholder. Some people see the resemblance; others can stand looking at the boulders for a long time and never discern the profile hidden amongst the dark boulders.

Iao Needle, deep in the West Maui Mountains, is a Maui landmark.

Wailua Falls, Hāna

BEACHES

A lei of sandy beaches encircles Maui, as good as or better than any in Hawai'i, and among the best in the world. Maui's splendid shores delight the eye--waves curling up on the curving sand, or smooth rocks smashed and rolled by breaking waves whose booming sound is heard far inland. The beaches beckon residents and visitors alike to the old, restless ocean. They also hold tales of Maui's past. The great Kamehameha I's war canoes rendezvoused at the beaches before sailing onward in waves of conquest that brought all the islands under his control. The first European to set foot on Hawai'i did so on a Maui beach (La Perouse in 1786). As a rule, the tides off Maui do not fluctuate as sharply as they do off some of the other islands, but the sea still must be approached with respect and caution. Only then will visitors derive safety and pleasure from the eighty or so beaches that fringe Maui.

WARNINGS

Heed all warning signs posted at beaches. Lifeguards are a rare sight on Maui beaches, and residents and visitors alike must exercise common sense on a beach outing. Recorded information on current surf conditions around the island is available at 244-8934, code 1521, a service provided by GTE Hawaiian Tel, or 871-5054. Some other hazards are listed here, not to discourage ocean enthusiasts, but to diminish the dangers and enhance your holiday fun.

Many visitors spoil their vacations by spending too much time in the sun the first day or two. The sun in Hawai'i is much harsher than in more northerly (or quite southerly) climes, primarily due to the thinner ozone layer and direct angle of the sun at this latitude. A sunblock with an SPF of 30 or greater is recommended for all skin tones. Limit your sun exposure the first few days so as not to overdo it. You can increase your sun exposure in gradual increments as you develop a tan. Remember to take along some bottled water to cool yourself off and prevent dehydration.

One of the gravest potential dangers of the deep is the caprice of waves. 'Typical' wave action varies with the local shoreline and the season. On Maui's north shore, the sheer size of the winter surf is dangerous. The surf on the eastern and western shorelines can also be high in winter. In summer, high seasonal surf can occur off the south shore.

Shorebreaks are places on or near the shore, where incoming ocean swells cross abruptly from a deep to a shallow bottom and the waves break with enormous downward force. Though they are dangerous for swimmers, these beaches are popular as they provide excellent conditions for body surfing. It is well, though, to know how to deal with them. Neck and back injuries can be sustained, and turning your back on or trying to jump over or through a large incoming wave invites trouble. The force of the waves can pound you against the bottom, knock your breath away and incoming wave and can sweep a person off his or her feet and cause you to lose your sense of direction. The trick is to take a deep breath and dive *under* the wave.

Another potential danger at such beaches is the backwash, water which has been washed onto the shore and must run back again to the sea. On steep beaches, or after the arrival of particularly voluminous waves, the force of this water can be almost as powerful as the incoming wave and can sweep a person off his or her feet and out to deeper water.

This water rushing back to the sea sometimes gets trapped by other incoming waves and can build to a considerable volume. When this happens, the only way it can move is sideward, creating a rip current that runs along the beach until it finds a deeper bottom. If you find yourself caught in a rip, the best course of action is to flow along with it until its force diminishes. Don't exhaust yourself trying to swim against it. It's easier and safer to walk back along the beach to the place where you started than to fight the water. Some rip currents flow straight out to sea through channels in the reef. If you are caught in one of these, swim to the side of it and get out. This type of rip is far more dangerous.

Sometimes this backed-up water cannot find an outlet and must flow back out *under* the incoming wave. This creates the condition known as undertow. An undertow is a brief phenomenon, lasting only until the wave has passed. For a person pulled down in an undertow, a few seconds under water can seem much longer. Remain calm and come up for air on the other side of the wave.

Another potentially dangerous wave action is the collision of deep ocean swells with rock ledges. It is never safe to venture out to the edge of rocks where surf is breaking. Freak waves can wash over the rocks without warning and many unsuspecting people have been swept away by such waves.

Underwater ledges, too, can present some danger from the surprise of

Patterns of early risers' footprints, Kāanapali Beach

a sudden dropping away of the bottom. Very shallow water can become very deep without notice, so non-swimmers should always keep away from such areas.

RATINGS

We have rated Maui's beaches according to our interpretation of the following criteria: water safety, bottom configuration (sand, rock, coral), cleanliness/maintenance of beach area, and type and quality of facilities (restrooms, showers, picnic tables, barbecue pits, parking). This is naturally arbitrary and not everyone will agree with the ratings because people look for different qualities when searching for the beach they want to frequent. Maui is blessed with a variety of beaches. Some such as Nāpili, Fleming's or Oneloa, afford great views. Others, such as the beaches at Mākena, are far enough off the beaten track to remain relatively uncrowded. Hāmoa Beach, at Hāna, is a little jewel-like beach that is every person's dream of a tropical paradise, while the stretch of sand at Kā'anapali is long, wide and unblemished.

Our rating indicators are as follows:

Superb	☆☆☆☆
Excellent	☆☆☆
Good	☆☆
Fair	☆

Additionally, there are symbols denoting beaches that are especially good for board surfing ●, body-surfing ● (includes body boarding), windsurfing ●, snorkeling ●, and swimming ●. Scuba diving areas are listed in SPORTS, since a beach is not needed for this activity.

The ratings and descriptions of beaches are arranged beginning with the beaches in West Maui and move in a counterclockwise direction around the island.

Note: "L" in heading of beach description designates a lifeguard on duty.

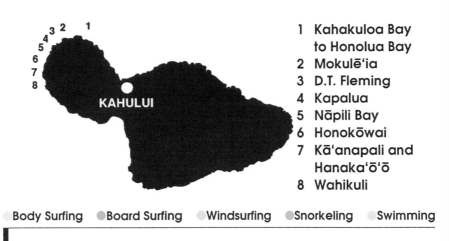

1 Kahakuloa Bay
   to Honolua Bay
2 Mokuleʻia
3 D.T. Fleming
4 Kapalua
5 Nāpili Bay
6 Honokōwai
7 Kāʻanapali and
   Hanakaʻōʻō
8 Wahikuli

Body Surfing   Board Surfing   Windsurfing   Snorkeling   Swimming

LAHAINA/KĀʻAANAPALI

1 Kahakuloa Bay to Honolua Bay ☆☆☆☆ (scenic/historic significance)

The lovely shoreline along this northwest end of Maui holds an important spot in the hearts of Hawaiians. This is where the Polynesian voyaging canoe *Hōkūleʻa* left for its epic journey across the Pacific. Drive along the coastline, and admire the dramatic sea cliffs. Water enthusiasts, however, would be wise to go elsewhere. The ocean is difficult to reach and certainly too hazardous to go into unless you are a strong swimmer. Maui surfers go to several spots along this coast to perfect their skills, but visitors likely would be happier at areas with easier access and fewer hazards.

On May 1, 1976, the Polynesian voyaging canoe *Hōkūleʻa*, a replica of an old Polynesian sea-going, double-hulled canoe, left from Honolua Bay to sail in the wake of the ancient voyagers. The purpose was to prove that Polynesian pride was well-earned in ocean journeys that eclipsed anything being achieved in the Europe of that time. A month after it sailed, the *Hōkūleʻa* reached the island of Mataiwa, 168 miles north of Tahiti, then sailed on into Papeete to a tumultuous welcome.

2 Mokuleʻia (Slaughterhouse) ☆

After passing D. T. Fleming Beach Park, along Highway 30, you will see cars parked along the road and a sign for the Mokuleʻia-Honolua Marine Reserve. A steep dirt and rock trail lead down from the road to a white sandy beach below. The bay is a good spot for snorkeling and swimming during summer months when calm conditions prevail. No offshore fishing is allowed, since this is designated as a Marine Life Conservation District. The winter's big waves make this beach a favorite with bodysurfers, but ocean conditions make it too hazardous for other water sports. Locals call this beach 'Slaughterhouse' after Honolulu Ranch built a slaughterhouse on the site, which was torn down in the '60s.

● Body Surfing   ● Board Surfing   ● Windsurfing   ● Snorkeling   ● Swimming

3 D. T. Fleming Beach Park ★★★★   L

Most water sports are possible at this scenic beach, but caution is advised. The beach can be hazardous in some conditions, and an eye should be kept on the incoming swells. There is some confusion about the name of this beach park--some people think it refers to the beach at Kapalua, sometimes known as Fleming's Beach. The park honors community leader D. T. Fleming (1881-1955), who was born in Scotland but adopted Maui as his home, and was involved in many facets of community life here. The park includes restrooms, paved parking and public access. There is a lifeguard stationed at this beach.

4 Kapalua ★★★★

Perhaps the most stunningly beautiful of all Maui beaches, Kapalua Beach, has been a Maui favorite for years. Located past the Napili Kai Beach Club, you will see a public right-of-way leading to a small parking area. Formerly known as Fleming's Beach, this curving, white sand beach is sheltered by two rocky lava arms with clear, calm waters ideal for safe snorkeling and swimming, and an excellent view of Moloka'i. Palm trees provide nice shady areas for relaxing out of the sun. Access to the beach is at the south end. Facilities include public showers and restrooms. This is definitely one of the top beaches on the island!

Taking the kids for a swim in Kīhei's calm surf

5 Nāpili Bay ☆☆☆☆

A long, curving beach rims this beautiful bay that is sheltered by rocky out-croppings. This picturesque beach affords a splendid view of Moloka'i, which looms large and seemingly close. Winter months can bring larger surf and good conditions for board surfing, and generally the swimming is excellent, except during high waves. There are two public right-of-ways to the beach, one just past the Napili Shores, and the second at the Napili Sunset on Hui Street. Parking is along the street. There are no public facilities.

6 Honokōwai Beach Park ☆☆☆

Located off of the Lower Honoapiilani Highway, this narrow white sand beach features a good spot for children to play in the water. Past the rocks on the beach lies a good area for snorkeling, but it is only fair for swimming. The park includes an off-street parking area, restrooms, barbecues, picnic tables and showers.

7 Kā'anapali and Hanaka'ō'ō ☆☆☆☆

The wide, clean, curving beaches of Kā'anapali are among the most photographed in the world. Nearby, Hanaka'ō'ō, called 'Sand Box Beach' by residents, is narrow at the south end but broadens as it rounds to the attractive area around Hanaka'ō'ō Point. Both offer excellent conditions for water lovers. Swimmers, snorkelers and surfers enjoy Hanaka'ō'ō, and Kā'anapali is good for swimming and beginner windsurfing.

Sugar cane once covered most of Kā'anapali, and a boat landing for shipping the cane was near the Black Rock area. The Kā'anapali Resort has made the beach, and Maui, famous.

No fringing reef protects this area, but inshore waters usually are calm, nevertheless, an infrequent storm can cause high waves along the beach. Public access to Hanaka'ō'ō goes through private property here, but many visitors come up the beach from Kā'anapali. Access to Kā'anapali is via a public right of way at the north end of the beach.

8 Wahikuli State Wayside Park ☆☆☆

Breathtaking views and excellent swimming and snorkeling make this one of West Maui's most attractive beach parks. The park's lovely sandy beach and its convenience regularly draw a crowd. There are good facilities, including restrooms, showers, pavilions, grills and picnic tables.

EXPLORING/Beaches

77

Body Surfing Board Surfing Windsurfing Snorkeling Swimming

9 Lahaina ☆☆

Snorkeling, scuba diving and surfing are popular at this beach, which begins at the end of the boat harbor and continues along Front Street. A shallow and very rocky bottom between the reef and the beach discourages most swimmers.

An unforgettable Wailea Beach sunset

9 Lahaina
10 Puamana and
   Launiupoko
11 Kulanaokala'i
   and Awalua
12 Olowalu
13 Ukumehame
14 Pāpalaua

●Body Surfing ●Board Surfing ●Windsurfing ●Snorkeling ●Swimming

10 Puamana Park/Launiupoko State Wayside Park ☆☆☆

These convenient parks, located near mile marker 19 and 18 respectively, have a pleasant atmosphere and large trees, perfect for a relaxing beachside picnic. Both beaches have pockets of sand and rock. A word of warning: sharks have been sited in the shallow waters off of Launiupoko, and swimming is discouraged. The parks include paved parking lots, barbecue grills, showers, restrooms and picnic tables.

11 Kulanaokala'i and Awalua ☆☆

The picturesque view of other islands from these beaches and the easy swimming offshore make this a popular area with visitors. A low spit of sand called 'Cut Mountain' divides the beaches. These are unimproved yet attractive beaches, with easy access but without amenities. The Hawaiian word, Kulanaokala'i, translates beautifully: 'to stand firmly in the calmness of the sea'. Located near mile marker 16.

12 Olowalu ☆

This excellent spot for snorkeling and scuba diving also holds an important place in Maui's history. The beach is the site of a famous massacre (see SIGHT-SEEING); today, visitors can combine a walk among petroglyphs and the remains of a *heiau* with snorkeling. The swimming is only fair because of the shallow reef offshore. There are no amenities, and parking is roadside. Located near mile marker 14.

13 Ukumehame Beach Park ☆☆

This narrow roadside park, located near mile marker 12, is a popular spot among local fisherman, as well as a good place to swim. Near the shore, the ocean is shallow and the bottom has patches of sand and rock. There is public access and a small paved parking area.

EXPLORING/Beaches

●Body Surfing   ●Board Surfing   ●Windsurfing   ●Snorkeling   ●Swimming

14 Pāpalaua State Wayside Park ☆☆

A long, narrow beach fronts this roadside park and provides a wonderful vantage point for viewing the island of Kaho'olawe. The offshore ocean bottom is rocky and shallow. The beach has public access, barbecue grills, picnic tables and portable comfort stations. Good swimming and picnic site. Look for a sign at mile marker 11.

KĪHEI/WAILEA

15 Mā'alaea ☆☆

To the left of this beach is a bird sanctuary, and to the right a boat harbor. Not an especially good swimming beach, Mā'alaea offers at least two good surfing areas. At times, a strong wind makes this area uncomfortable for picnickers, but attractive to windsurfers. Maps may show a variety of names for this beach, but they are simply old shoreline names. Fitness buffs know it as a place where they can jog on hard-packed sand, but again, the strong winds here can act as a deterrent. There are no public facilities, but there is public access located past the Makana A Kai condominiums, on Hauoli Street.

16 Maipoina'oeia'u Beach Park ☆☆☆☆

The name in Hawaiian means 'do not forget me' and the park is dedicated to "all those who sacrificed their lives to preserve our freedom for all humanity." Consequently, the park is known as 'Veterans Park', and sometimes as 'Memorial Park'. The beach, located in front of the Maui Lu Resort, is a continuation of the long ribbon of sand that extends along the southwest coast. There is a fine, sandy bottom offshore with only a sprinkling of rocks. Facilities include a small paved parking lot, showers, picnic tables and restrooms.

17 Kalama Beach Park ☆☆☆☆

This park is as much a playground as a haven for water-lovers and the athletically inclined. The park is huge (36 acres), with a dozen pavilions along with restrooms, showers, picnic tables, grills, tennis courts, a soccer field, volleyball courts, and more. Offshore, the bottom is rocky with pockets of sand, but off to the right is about a four-mile stretch of sandy beach.

15 Māʻalaea
16 Maipoinaʻoeiaʻu
17 Kalama
18 Kamaʻole I, II, III
19 Wailea
20 Polo
21 Mākena
22 La Perouse Bay

Body Surfing　　Board Surfing　　Windsurfing　　Snorkeling　　Swimming

18　Kama'ole Beach Parks I, II & III ☆☆☆☆

These three separate parks are simply unbeatable for good swimming,
sandy beaches, brilliant views and a fine climate. These are among the best
beaches in Hawai'i. The only time swimming is not safe is during the occasional storms that come up from the south-southwest, known as Kona storms.
Facilities are excellent, with paved parking, public access that is clearly
marked, showers, grills, picnic tables and restrooms.

19　Wailea ☆☆☆☆

Conjure up the ideal shore, one with wide, white sand beaches with
graceful curves and offshore views of other islands, and you'll be close to the
image of Wailea. The broad expanse of sand and unbeatable climate make
these very attractive spots for sun worshippers and water lovers. There is
marked public access to the four beaches--**Keawakapu, Mōkapu, Ulua, and
Wailea**. Public facilities consist of showers at Keawakapu and restrooms and
showers at both Mōkapu and Ulua. These beaches lay in front of some of
Maui's most deluxe resorts--the Grand Wailea, Four Seasons, Maui Inter-
Continental, Stouffer Wailea Beach and the Kea Lani Resort--with lush
landscaping enhancing the picturesque setting.

20　Polo ☆☆☆

Long and wide, Polo Beach is located past the Kea Lani Resort and next to
the Polo Beach condominium complex. Swimmers and snorkelers, however,
should watch for storms or high surf, which can cause strong currents and a
dangerous backwash. The beach has a small park and a paved parking area,
showers and restrooms.

● Body Surfing   ● Board Surfing   Windsurfing   ● Snorkeling   ● Swimming

21 Mākena ☆☆☆☆

These sweeping beaches with beautiful stretches of sand, plenty of room and panoramic views of Molokini and Kaho'olawe lie more or less adjacent to each other. The beaches of **Po'olenalena, Malu'aka, Oneuli, Pu'uōla'i** and **Oneloa** (commonly called **Big Beach**) have good swimming and snorkeling. Board surfing at Pu'uōla'i and Oneloa is popular, as is bodysurfing at all but Oneuli. There is a dark sand beach, a rocky offshore bottom and steep drop-off at Oneuli. Pu'uōla'i is a pretty, secluded spot known locally as **"Little Beach"**, and can be reached by hiking up and over "Red Hill", a rocky cinder cone situated at the western end of Big Beach. Although officially illegal, nude bathing is part of this beach's popularity. These beaches are reached via the same road that leads back through Wailea and Kihei. It is best to visit these beaches in the morning, as it is not unusual for the skies to cloud over around 11:00 a.m.

82

22 La Perouse Bay ☆☆

Fishermen more than swimmers come to this public beach, where the first non-Hawaiian set foot on Maui. Captain Jean Francois de Galaup, Comte de La Perouse, came ashore on May 30, 1786. La Perouse was one of France's fine navigators and explorers, but when he sailed on into the Pacific, his vessel disappeared with all hands, and his fate remains a mystery of the sea. Here at the bay named for him, a series of small beaches lie between rocky outcroppings, and there are many tide pools. Waters can become rough during storms or heavy surf. There is public access, but no facilities at this rocky beach.

Beyond La Perouse Bay, the coastline is rugged and dramatic. In general, the beaches of this area are small, remote and lacking in both facilities and public access. Continuing past the pavement violates most car rental contracts. Visitors who are able to make their way down to these areas would be wise to admire them without getting into the water. Additionally, there are many scenic shoreline areas before reaching the Nu'u Landing, including the many small inlets that are visible as the road winds down toward the coast from 'Ulupalakua, and the dark sand beach of Huakini Bay.

HĀNA

23 Seven Pools Park ☆☆☆☆ *(for its natural beauty)*

The beach itself is dangerous, but the series of beautiful pools below the highway are stunning. There are more than seven pools--actually twenty-four in all. Swimmers should beware of flash flooding during heavy rainfall. The bridge over 'Ohe'o Stream allows views up and down the Kīpahulu Valley. Hiking and camping in the area are possible, but remember: no ocean swimming here, because of the strong currents and the prevalence of sharks. The area has many legends, but for years was erroneously called sacred; today it is a favorite stopping place for visitors.

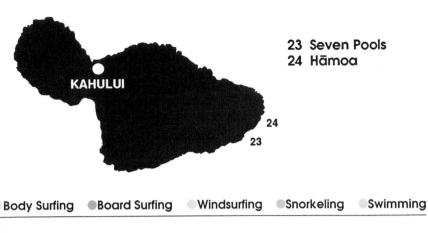

23 Seven Pools
24 Hāmoa

KAHULUI

24

23

Body Surfing   Board Surfing   Windsurfing   Snorkeling   Swimming

24 Hāmoa Beach ☆☆☆☆   L

This jewel-like setting evokes the idyllic tropical paradise, with its high cliffs and sheer beauty. The good running surf makes this a popular swimming and bodysurfing beach. Breaking surf comes straight in to the beach and often creates some strong currents near the shore. At times there is a lifeguard provided by the Hotel Hana-Maui, whose guests frequent the beach. There is public access via a stairway descending from the road. The Hotel Hana-Maui owns the private restroom facilities and covered picnic pavilion situated at the back of the beach, and they are available for use by hotel guests, however, one restroom is designated for public use. A beachside rinsing shower may also be used by non-guests.

'Ohe'o Gulch, commonly referred to as Seven Pools

●Body Surfing   ●Board Surfing   ●Windsurfing   ●Snorkeling   ●Swimming

25   Hāna Beach Park ☆☆☆

A favorite of residents and tourists alike, this large, pleasant beach park features good swimming and snorkeling, but some fearsome currents out past the sheltered bay. Nevertheless, the area is safe and generally calm, with shorebreaks and gentle winds. The sand is brown and clean. The park includes a pavilion, picnic tables, restrooms and showers, paved parking and a boat ramp.

26   Wai'ānapanapa State Park ☆☆☆☆

This large, scenic and historic park is a good spot for picnicking and swimming, when the water is calm and if you are a strong swimmer. Wai'ānapanapa must be approached with some caution because of strong rip currents and a beach unprotected by any reef. Further along at Pa'iloa, sunbathers and explorers will enjoy the black sand beach. It is easy to spend long hours in this area because of the ancient legends associated with it (see Hāna under SIGHT-SEEING), and visitors should plan to bring a lunch and stay awhile. The park has excellent facilities, from paved parking to restrooms and picnic areas.

Wai'ānapanapa's coarse black sand beach

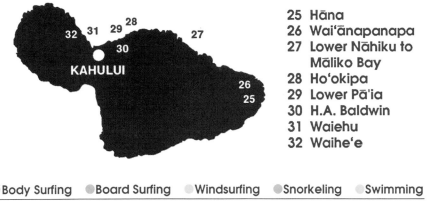

25 Hāna
26 Wai'ānapanapa
27 Lower Nāhiku to
   Māliko Bay
28 Ho'okipa
29 Lower Pā'ia
30 H.A. Baldwin
31 Waiehu
32 Waihe'e

● Body Surfing ● Board Surfing ● Windsurfing ● Snorkeling ● Swimming

WAILUKU - KAHULUI

27 Lower Nāhiku to Māliko Bay ☆

The coves and inlets along this fascinating but difficult coastline are not good for swimming or other water sports. Board surfing and snorkeling are possible, but public access is difficult to find. There are other places where the water is murky from stream runoff, and still other places where calm ocean means fishing or just strolling along the shoreline. In at least one spot, the county of Maui has posted 'Keep Out' signs because rental cars frequently get stuck. Still, the coastline itself is engaging.

Ho'okipa Beach attracts expert windsurfers from around the world

EXPLORING/Beaches

●Body Surfing　●Board Surfing　●Windsurfing　●Snorkeling　●Swimming

28　Ho'okipa Beach Park ★★★★

This convenient park alongside Hāna Highway is a mecca for windsurfers from all over the world. Although it is not a great place to swim, it is the best spot for experienced windsurfing, and can be good for surfing as well. Ho'okipa is the home of Maui surfing dating back to the 1930s. This park's high rating comes from its reputation as a challenging, world class windsurfing site. There are pavilions, showers, grills, restrooms, picnic tables and a paved parking lot.

29　Lower Pā'ia Park ★

This is a temperamental area, with good swimming when waters are calm, but poor otherwise. There are shorebreaks for bodysurfing and offshore breaks for board surfing, but these can be quirky. Windsurfers frequent the area. To the right of the park is a rocky point from which local children jump into the water. There are restrooms, picnic areas, a softball field and basketball courts.

30　H. A. Baldwin Park ★★★★

Bodysurfers flock to this long sandy beach that probably is the most used beach park in this corner of Maui. The surf breaks along the shore, and occasionally offshore as well, attracting surfers, especially windsurfers. There are excellent facilities: picnic tables, pavilions, grills, restrooms, showers, plus playing fields suitable for soccer and baseball, and plenty of parking. The park is named for Harry A. Baldwin, a delegate to Congress and community leader. Tent camping is allowed here, with a county permit.

31　Waiehu Beach Park ★

On clear days, there is no better place to get a good view of Haleakalā than from this beach park. While the swimming here is poor, the park is a wonderful out-of-the-way spot for a picnic and for viewing the ocean. Parts of this beach are heavily used by local fishermen. The park is next to the Waiehu Municipal Golf Course, and once contained a wharf that was destroyed in the tsunami (tidal wave) of 1946. The park includes a pavilion, restrooms, showers, grill and picnic tables.

32　Waihe'e Beach Park ★★

An impressive reef creates a good swimming area off this beach park, however, swimmers must watch for strong currents where the reef ends. Residents come to this beach to gather *limu* (seaweed). There are restrooms, picnic areas and a paved parking lot. Access via Halewaiu Rd.

SPORTS

Scuba Diving
Windsurfing
Golfing
Hiking
Whale Watching

SPORTS & RECREATION

Maui's climate and terrain combine to make this an outdoor enthusiast's paradise, perfect for the many traditional sports savored for centuries by Hawaiians, as well as more modern-day pursuits. A variety of recreational activities awaits the visitor--some, such as whale watching, can be enjoyed in few other places on earth. You may wish to try one of the sports so synonymous with Hawai'i--like surfing or windsurfing--or something more universal, like golfing. Whatever your athletic interests may be, the conditions and setting are ideal.

To enjoy your Maui recreational experience, use the proper equipment, pay attention to the common-sense rules of safety, and get the necessary permits. Also, be on guard in the water, as Maui has few lifeguards along the beaches. The few you will see are employed by the hotels in the area. Maui has no official water rescue units. The people who are likely to assist in water emergencies are volunteers. Swimming, surfing and snorkeling areas are listed under BEACHES.

SCUBA DIVING and SNORKELING

Another world awaits exploration along Maui's shores. Good scuba diving and snorkeling are possible year-round at many spots off Maui for beginning and advanced divers.

Among favorite diving areas are: Wai'ānapanapa State Park, Hāna Bay and Nu'u Landing along the Hāna Coast; Mākena Beach, Hāloa Point, Wailea and Ulua Beaches, and McGregor Point along the southwest coast; Olowalu and Black Rock in West Maui; and Kapalua Bay, D. T. Fleming Beach Park, Honolua Bay and Hononana Bay at Kapalua.

Take a tank dive for an even deeper look at Maui's undersea environment. Certified divers may rent equipment and go out on their own, or may arrange a chartered excursion. Those unfamiliar with local conditions are encouraged to take an escort, as this sport is potentially dangerous, even for trained divers. Introductory classes are available for those seeking certification.

Dives take place wherever conditions are best at the time; this generally means the north shore in summer and the south shore in winter, as this is the prevailing pattern of calm waters. Depths range from twenty to a hundred and fifty feet, with most areas falling into the middle of that spectrum. An excellent island-by-island guidebook is available which the local diving community considers the ultimate resource for diving Hawaii's waters, called *Hawaii Below: Favorites, Tips and Secrets of the Diving Pros* by Rod Canham. Serious divers may want to pick up a copy.

One of the most popular dive spots in Hawai'i is Molokini Island, a crescent-shaped top of an eroded volcano, a quick boat ride away from Maui. Exploring its surrounding waters is an experience that many divers repeat as often as possible. Taking any ocean creatures from this marine conservation district is prohibited. As a result, the area is brimming with ocean life, from eels to turtles, from whitetip reef sharks to manta rays.

Diving the back side of the island instead of the bay affords a truly spectacular underwater view of the volcano's sharp decline and hints at the depth of surrounding waters. Remember, however, that the back side of Molokini also has strong currents, so extreme caution is advised.

There are a number of shops on Maui that rent scuba and snorkeling equipment and have diving maps. Some of the diving charter companies and retailers also organize whale-watching cruises and photographic tours. Most of them also certify new divers after the required courses, which generally last five days.

Among dive shops in Lahaina are:

Capt. Nemo's (661-5555); Central Pacific Divers (661-7647); Dive Maui (667-2080); Extended Horizons (667-0611); Hawaiian Reef Divers (667-7647); and Lahaina Divers (667-7496). Kihei shops include: ProDive Maui (875-4004); Dive & Sea Center (874-1952); Ed Robinson's Diving Adventures (879-3584); Makena Coast Charters (874-1273); Molokini Divers (879-0055); and Mike Severns Diving (879-6596).

Maui Dive Shop operates out of Lahaina (661-5388/-0722/-5117), Kahana (669-3800), Kihei (879-1919/-1533/-3388), Wailea (879-3166) and Kahului (871-2111) and carries beach and water sports accessories of every description.

SURFING

While many Polynesians enjoyed riding the surf in their outrigger canoes, Hawaiians alone developed the art of riding boards specifically designed for play atop the rolling waves. It is not surprising that they invented the sport of surfing, since these island-based people lived constantly within reach of the sea and its changing waves.

In modern times, this ancient sport has been refined and extended

"Howzit brah" -- the typical pidgin English greeting

beyond anything its inventors ever imagined. Its popularity has spread around the globe, and professional surfers demonstrate their skill and daring while vying for six-figure purses. The manufacture of surfing equipment also developed as well as, in recent years, the new variant: windsurfing. The areas best suited to surfing and windsurfing are noted in the BEACHES section.

Board surfing

This is the original. No one knows how long ago it developed, but Hawaiian petroglyphs dating back to about the eighth or ninth century show people board surfing, and as early as the fifteenth century, Hawaiians had so refined the sport that contests between champions were held, for what even we would consider to be high stakes. Ancient Hawaiians gambled with unbridled enthusiasm at every opportunity, wagering their property, their wives, even their lives on the outcome of a single game.

Many famous surfing exploits were passed down through the voluminous oral history of these people. Their name for what we call surfing was *he'enalu*, which can be loosely translated as 'wave sliding' but which, like everything else in the Hawaiian language, is rich with a range of subtlety and poetic nuance that says much more. The best surfing breaks were reserved for use by the ruling chiefs and violators of this *kapu* could be punished by death.

Surfing, like all things Hawaiian, declined dramatically during the first century or so of European immigration to the islands, but surfing, both on boards and in canoes, began to be promoted again in Hawai'i early this century. Surfing's international fame began to spread with demonstrations in Atlantic City and Australia that were given by surfing champion and Olympic gold medal swimmer Duke Kahanamoku.

The original boards were eighteen-foot, hundred-and-fifty-pound monoliths, often made of koa wood. This began to change in the mid-1940s with the development of hollow boards and ones built of such lightweight materials as balsa and redwood, then fiberglass and synthetic foam. The evolution of surfboards has also seen a wide variety of lengths, widths and thickness, and these variations on the theme have been found to excel in varying conditions so that, today, top surfers keep collections of several boards from which to choose.

The activities desks at the major hotels are good resources for renting surfboards, as well as at **Hawaiian Island Windsurfing** (871-4981), **Hi-Tech Surf Sports** (877-2111) and **Second Wind Sail & Surf** (877-7467) in Kahului, or **Local Motion,** with three stores on Maui: in Lahaina (661-7873 and 669-7873) and Kihei (661-7873). For private surfing instruction, contact one of the following: **Andrea Thomas Surfing School** (875-0625), **Nancy C. Emerson School of Surfing** (244-7873), **Alan Cadiz's HST** (871-5423) or **West Maui Surfing Academy** (661-7337).

Bodysurfing

This is a cross between board surfing and swimming and stems from the same principle as board riding, except that the body replaces the board as the vehicle. The ancient Hawaiians called this activity *kaha nalu* or *pae* or *paepo'o*. There are two basic techniques for accomplishing this feat: keeping the body straight with the arms pinned against the sides while riding the shoulder of the wave just ahead of the breaking water, and the alternative of keeping one or both arms straight out in front for greater maneuverability. The former technique seems to work best in offshore breaks while the latter seems best in the large, shallow shorebreaks.

Most expert bodysurfers use both, sometimes while riding the same wave. Though purists decry it, virtually all bodysurfers also use fins to increase propulsion and enhance their ability to catch a wave.

Paipo boarding

The term *paipo* is a post-World War II corruption of the Hawaiian word *paepo'o*, and essentially is a 'belly board'. This type of wave-riding board is short and thin--three or four feet long and only a quarter to half an inch thick--either flat or with a slightly concave surface to fit the body. They are mostly homemade and mostly used by Hawaiians. Their use requires skill and they have been largely superseded in popularity by the now well-known 'Boogie (TM) board'.

Body boarding

The body board, developed from the paipo board described above, was invented in Hawai'i in the early 1970s by Tom Morey, and is made of flexible foam. The 'boards' are a couple of feet wide, about four feet long and around three inches thick, and, like their parent paipo, are ridden prone. The latest development along this line is a high performance body board (now termed 'turbo-board') that was invented by Russ Brown in 1983. Considered the Porsche of body boards, it is stiffer and faster than the standard model. These inexpensive water toys have become ubiquitous in Hawai'i, and are readily available for rent or for sale all over the island.

Sand sliding

This too is an ancient pastime that has been given a modern tool. The original idea was to throw oneself onto the sand at the precise moment when a receding wave had left just a thin sheet of water on which the body would then slide. Precise timing was (and is) essential, as too early a leap results in a mere sinking to the sand and too late a one ends in an abrupt abrasive halt.

Bare-body sand sliding is seldom seen anymore, but paipo boards and the more recent body boards are also used in this fashion. Nowadays the hot trend is the 'skimboard', a short foam 'board' about three quarters of an inch thick that is thrown onto the receding wave then jumped upon.

Skilled standing riders have developed some fancy skateboard-like maneuvers on this type of board, and contests have been held on O'ahu.

WINDSURFING

Windsurfing is a marriage of surfing and sailing that is even more complicated than it appears because it requires techniques and styles that are being improved all the time. This modern variation of the ancient sport of surfing was conceived in 1970 by Californian Hoyle Schweitzer and executed by his friend, Jim Drake. The popularity of this new sport spread like wildfire and today a circuit of amateur and professional contests is already well established.

On Maui, windsurfing has grown in quantum leaps, and Ho'okipa Beach, on the island's north coast, has become an internationally recognized site of world windsurfing championships. Windsurfing contributes millions of dollars annually to Maui's economy.

Windsurfing schools include: **Kaanapali Windsurfing School** (667-1964), **Maui Windsurf Co.** (877-4816), **Maui Windsurfari** (871-7766), **Second**

Colorful sails are almost always on display at Ho'okipa

Wind (877-7467), **Windsurfing West Maui** (871-8733), **Hawaiian Island Windsurfing** (871-4981), **Alan Cadiz's HST** (871-JIBE), **Nancy C. Emerson School of Surfing** (244-7873), **New Waves Windsurfing School** (875-4045) and **Windrigger Maui** (871-7753). Most also rent sailboards, as do the **Ocean Activities Center** (879-4485) and the **Maui Sailing Center** (879-5935) in Kihei.

PARASAILING

Some people prefer to rise above it all--up to 200 feet--in a parasail. Power boats tow the parasails and the wind does the rest. The result is a stunning and different view of Maui. **West Maui Para-Sail** (661-4060) and **Lahaina Para-Sail** (661-4887) are two of the older companies around, both operating out of Lahaina. **Island Watersports** (667-0536) also operates from Lahaina. **UFO Parasailing** (661-7836), and **Parasail Kaanapali** (669-6555) are located in Kā'anapali.

Parasailing high above West Maui waters

SPORTS & RECREATION

TENNIS

Maui has more than eighty tennis courts available for public use, and the island's fine climate means the courts get plenty of use all year long. Some courts are lighted for evening play. Listed here are free public courts and resort or commercial courts available to the public for a fee. Resort courts open to the public offer additional facilities to guests, and racquet rentals are available.

Public courts in the Lahaina/Kā'anapali area include: **Lahaina Civic Center** (1840 Honoapiilani Hwy.), five lighted courts, and **Malu'uluoLele Park** (Front and Shaw Sts.), four lighted courts. There are four lighted courts at **Kalama Park** (Kīhei Rd.) and six unlighted courts next to the **Maui Sunset** (Waipulani Rd.) in Kīhei. In Hāna, you'll find two lighted courts at **Hāna Ball Park** next to Hotel Hana-Maui. In Upcountry, the **Eddie Tam Center** in Makawao and the **Community Center** in Pukalani both have two lighted courts. In the Wailuku-Kahului area, courts include: The **Kahului Community Center** (Onehee and Uhu Sts.), two lighted courts; the **Community Center** in Wailuku (Wells and Market Sts.), seven lighted courts; **Maui Community College** (Kaahumanu and Wakea Ave.), two unlighted courts; and **Wailuku War Memorial** (1580 Kaahumanu Ave.), four lighted courts.

Resort and commercial courts in the Kapalua area include: **Kapalua Tennis Club** (100 Kapalua Dr., 669-5677), ten Plexipave courts, four of which are lighted; **Village Tennis Center** (1 Ritz-Carlton Drive, 665-0112), ten courts, five of which are lighted. In Lahaina/Kā'anapali, courts are located at: **Maui Marriott Resort** (100 Nohea Kai Dr., 667-1200) with five courts, three of which are lighted; **Royal Lahaina Tennis Ranch** (2780 Keka'a Dr., 661-3611), with eleven courts, six of which are lighted; and the **Hyatt Regency Maui** (200 Nohea Kai Dr., 661-1234). The Sheraton-Maui has three lighted courts, however, the hotel closed in January 1995 for extensive renovation. In Kīhei/Wailea, courts are found at: **Makena Tennis Club** (5415 Makena Alanui, 879-8777), with six courts, two of which are lighted; and **Wailea Tennis Club** (131 Wailea Iki Pl., 879-1958), nicknamed "Wimbledon West", has fourteen courts, including eleven Plexipave, three lighted and three grass, plus pro shop, lessons and rentals. Wailea Tennis Club offers three- and five-day tennis packages at their Wimbledon West Tennis Academy for serious tennis enthusiasts.

Hourly rates for resort courts range anywhere from $7.50 to $18 per person for non-guests, and some offer reasonable all-day rates.

GOLFING

From duffer to professional, there's no playing golf like the experience of playing golf on Maui or neighboring Lāna'i. The courses are different from each other in design and difficulty, but they share vivid scenery and beautiful climate.

The courses listed here are open to the public; green fees are competitive with courses elsewhere, but rates can vary considerably from summer to winter, with low season considered from May through November, and high season December through April.

Kaanapali Golf Courses (661-3691) helped bring championship golf to Maui when they were first opened. The two courses have excellent views of the ocean and the West Maui Mountains. The North Course is a Robert Trent Jones Jr. design; at one point, the ocean is a water hazard, and Kā'anapali Beach is a sand trap. This is an 18-hole, par 72 (forward tees par 73) course. The South Course was designed by Arthur Jack Snyder and is 18 holes, par 72. The fourth hole sometimes offers a distraction as the Sugarcane Train chugs by. The courses feature a pro shop, rentals, storage, lessons and a restaurant.

Kapalua Golf Club (669-8044) must be ranked among the most beautiful in Hawai'i. There are two courses. The Bay Course, an Arnold Palmer design, is 18 holes, par 72, and has two ocean holes. The Village Course, designed by Arnold Palmer and Ed Seay, is 18 holes, par 71. This course offers panoramic views; the 18th green is bordered by a lake. They also have fine amenities, including two pro shops, club rentals and storage, golf lessons, restaurants and bar, putting greens and a driving range.

Wailea Golf Club (875-5111) boasts incredible weather and sweeping views. There are three courses. The Blue Course is a 6,859-yard, 18-hole, par 72 course designed by Arthur Jack Snyder. The 7,070-yard Gold Course, was designed by Robert Trent Jones Jr. The Emerald Course opened in December 1994, and is an 18-hole, par 72 course, designed by Robert Trent Jones Jr.

The stunning clifftop 12th hole at "The Challenge at Manele", Lana'i

On the Blue Course, golfers encounter four lakes, 74 bunkers, wide fairways and a fair number of hills. On the rugged Gold Course, golfers find tricky greens and hazards that include ancient lava rock walls, one lake and 93 bunkers. The Emerald Course offers lush blooming vegetation and excellent views of Haleakalā and the ocean, with a double green shared by the 10th and 17th holes. This course shares with the Gold a training facility with separate chipping and putting areas, practice bunker and challenging driving range. The Gold and Emerald Clubhouse has received an award for its design excellence. Wailea golf packages are available for visitors staying at Wailea resort hotels or condominiums.

Makena Golf Club (879-3344), located next to the Maui Prince Hotel, has two 18-hole, par 72, courses, the North Course and South Course. Both were designed by Robert Trent Jones Jr., and offer sweeping views of Haleakalā and the sea. Amenities include a pro shop, club rentals and two practice putting greens.

The beautifully landscaped **Silversword Golf Club** (874-0777) located on Pi'ilani Highway in Kīhei is a challenging 6800-yard, 18-hole, par 71 course with good rates. The driving range, pro shop, restaurant and bar add to the course's appeal.

Pukalani Country Club (572-1314) affords a vista of the Central Valley and West Maui Mountains, and sometimes has strong winds. It is 18 holes, par 72. There is a restaurant, a pro shop and club rentals.

Waiehu Municipal Golf Course (243-7400) near Wailuku is a fairly difficult 18-hole, par 72 course. The front nine were designed in 1929, the back nine in 1968. There is a pro shop, club and cart rentals.

Maui Country Club (877-0616) in Pā'ia is open to the public only on Mondays. The course has plenty of trees and sometimes gusty winds. It is an 18-hole, par 74 course.

Sandalwood Golf Course (242-4653) is one of Maui's newest courses, located at 2500 Honoapiilani Highway in Waikapu, between Kīhei and Wailuku. Designed by Nelson Wright, this is a hilly par-72 course, with an attractive clubhouse, restaurant, chipping green, three putting greens and practice range.

The **Grand Waikapu Country Club** (244-7888) is a private club located above Sandalwood Golf Course in Waikapu. Its spectacular 74,788 square-foot tri-level clubhouse is a Frank Lloyd Wright design, offering panoramic views of the Central Valley below, with the blue ocean beyond. Golf and spa packages are available to non-members. The ladies' spa has showers, sauna, jacuzzi, television, lounge and juice bar. The men's facility has a Japanese style sauna (furo), showers and lounge. The top floor features Monroe's, a large circular dining room used for private functions, and a pro shop. The Grill is a casual Marilyn Monroe-themed restaurant located on the lower level, with an outside terrace for those who enjoy dining al fresco. The story goes that this particular Frank Lloyd Wright design was chosen by the late Marilyn Monroe and Arthur Miller for their country home in Connecticut, but the house was never built, as they subsequently divorced. Even if you don't plan to play golf here, it is worth a tour.

The neighboring island of Lana'i offers golfers two challenging 18-hole courses. **The Experience at Koele** (565-4600), a design collaboration between Greg Norman and Ted Robinson, which opened in May 1991, is built on a lush 163-acre, 2000-foot plateau. It is an 18-hole, par 72 course that winds through a lovely natural setting of pine, koa and eucalyptus trees. The signature hole, number 8, plays from a 250-foot elevated tee, bordered by a lake, set amongst mist-shrouded trees and lush greenery. Seven lakes, rushing streams and picturesque waterfalls accent the course's beauty. In 1991, it was named "Best New Golf Course" by Fortune Magazine and ranked in the "Top Ten New Resort Courses" of 1991 by Golf Magazine.

The Challenge at Manele (565-2222) opened on Christmas Day 1993, and is situated in a dramatic shoreline setting surrounding The Manele Bay Hotel. A Jack Nicklaus design, every hole of this links-style, 18-hole, par 72 course offers expansive vistas of Hulopo'e Bay. The ocean is a water hazard on three holes. Its signature hole, number 12, is situated atop a cliff rising 150 feet above the ocean and requires a 200-yard tee shot over the water. Both courses may be played by non-guests of the hotels.

HIKING

At least two dozen trails lead hikers into Maui's beautiful and varied wilderness, those in Haleakalā being the most popular. Trails elsewhere are as short as a half-mile and as long as ten to twelve miles, and appeal to different levels of stamina, skill and experience. Besides referring to books about hiking in Hawai'i in RECOM-

MENDED READING, several local organizations regularly schedule group hiking activities, and welcome visitors to join their excursions as well as provide tips for making your hike pleasant and safe. The most logical procedure for would-be hikers is to inquire with County, State or National Park officials for information.

Hiking up in the clouds at Haleakalā Crater

A number of other sources of hiking information is available to visitors. The **Hawai'i Geographic Society** (P. O. Box 1698, Honolulu, Hawai'i 96806, 808-538-3952) offers books, maps and other publications and requests written inquiries from Hawai'i-bound hikers. The **Sierra Club, Hawai'i Chapter** (P. O. Box 2577, Honolulu, Hawai'i 96803 - 808-538-6616) will, for a small fee, send an information packet describing state trails and trip-planning information. The Sierra Club offers numerous day hikes throughout the islands and welcomes visitors to join them. **Hike Maui** (P. O. Box 330969, Kahului, HI 96732 - 808-879-5270) conducts half-day and full-day hikes for a fee that includes pickup, transportation, equipment and lunch. The **Hawai'i State Department of Land and Natural Resources, Forestry and Wildlife Division** (1151 Punchbowl St., Rm. 325, Honolulu, Hawai'i 96813 - 808-587-0166) has free trail maps. Highly recommended is the inexpensive guidebook *Hiking Maui* by Robert Smith (Wilderness Press), which provides extensive descriptions of the route, highlights, rating of difficulty, driving instructions, distance and average hiking time on all the island's hiking trails.

Planning and taking safety precautions is especially important when hiking in Haleakalā, which can be difficult if hikers are not equipped properly. Weather conditions in the crater can sometimes change not merely day-by-day, but hour-by-hour (see SIGHT-SEEING).

Crater Bound (P. O. Box 265, Kula, HI 96790 - 808-878-1743), an Upcountry wilderness guide business, offers guided Haleakalā morning hikes, leaving Kula Lodge at 8:00 a.m. and returning before lunchtime. Overnight escorted trips inside the crater for three days and two nights are also available, with gear carried in by pack animals, allowing hikers to walk freely, unencumbered by heavy camping gear. A packing service is also provided for those who wish to hike the crater on their own.

For relatively easy outings, hikers should go along **Halemau'u Trail** from the highway, not quite a mile to the rim of the crater, which affords a good view; or down **Sliding Sands Trail.** More difficult, but exciting, is the eight-mile hike down Halemau'u Trail to the **Hōlua cabin,** a trek that takes roughly a half day for an experienced hiker. Good hikers should allow at least eight hours for another expedition: down Sliding Sands Trail to the crater floor, across **Kamoao Pele Trail** to Halemau'u Trail, and back to the highway via Hōlua and the Halemau'u Trail.

There are longer hikes, more demanding and more rewarding. One is the hike down Sliding Sands Trail, which includes an overnight stay at Hōlua cabin campground. Another is a hike to Palikū campground for an overnight stay and a return via the Halemau'u Trail.

There are points of interest along the way in the crater. One is the **Bottomless Pit** of the Halemau'u Trail, a ten-foot-wide yawning well that, bottomless or not, is clogged with debris sixty to seventy feet down. Be careful approaching the edge.

The **Bubble Cave** is another point of interest and is not far from the Kapalaoa cabin; it is a large, collapsed bubble made by gases from molten lava in an eruption. The lush, green area around the Palikū cabin sharply contrasts with the desert-like crater floor. **Silversword Loop** off Halemau'u Trail has a number of places that may look like piles of stone, but are the remains of sacred sites constructed by the Hawaiians, and should not be disturbed.

The silversword, a rare plant that dots the crater, is found in few other places on Earth, and long has been identified with Haleakalā. It is a fragile plant and its roots can be easily damaged if stepped on.

The Park Service asks that all hikers register at the head of each trail when heading into the crater. This is a sensible procedure designed to protect hikers in the event of emergencies.

Another hike begins at the summit and ends some five hours later and nearly 4000 feet down on the outside of Haleakalā. **Skyline Trail** starts at the south end of the Science City complex near the park boundary, leads across a rugged landscape that has a compensating tremendous view, then drops down into scrub trees. Halfway down the trail is a marker pointing to **Haleakalā Ridge Trail**. A third of a mile in that direction the **Polipoli Trail** branches off and leads to **Polipoli Springs Recreational Area**. This tough but rewarding hike ends in the midst of magnificent hardwood trees.

It is important to remember that, no matter how warm it may seem at sea level, the temperatures get markedly cooler (as much as 30°) in the higher elevations of Haleakalā, whether inside the crater or out. Warm clothing and rain gear are necessary. If you intend to cook at the campgrounds inside the crater, it is necessary to bring in a lightweight cook stove. Open wood fires are not permitted.

Below Polipoli, there are a number of connected trails--**Redwood,**

Boundary, Polipoli, Tie and **Plum. Waiohuli Trail,** tying up with Boundary Trail, leads to an overlook with a view of Kēōkea, a small Kula community, and on to Kīhei on Maui's southwest coast. **Waiakoa Trail** begins at the Kula Forest Reserve and winds seven miles up Haleakalā and comes back through a series of dramatic switchbacks. This network of trails offers spectacular views, and close-ups of the wide variety of Maui flora.

Back in the Central Valley, the beautiful park area of 'Īao Valley near Wailuku is crisscrossed by trails demanding different levels of expertise. There are easy walks for the family, and more demanding hikes. All offer close-up views of the profuse plants and flowers. No permission is necessary to hike any of these well-marked trails.

One 'Īao Valley trail begins behind the lookout shelter and winds through the bluff and back to the parking lot; this is **Tableland Trail,** about two hours and two miles long, and relatively strenuous. Equally challenging, but rewarding, is the three-mile **Po'ohahoahoa Stream hike,** which should be taken only by the most physically fit and experienced hikers.

In the southwestern area of Maui, a six-mile trek on the **King's Highway Trail** through the 1790 lava flow is a popular hike. It begins at La Perouse Bay and goes south and inland, ending eventually on private prop- erty. Around the coast and back in the Hāna area, the **Wai'ānapanapa Trail** begins at the park and follows the old King's Highway path over a trail that is well-defined, but not gentle.

Horseback riding, an alternative to hiking the Crater

HORSEBACK RIDING

Some of the most spectacular riding trails in the world cross Maui pastures, woodlands and lava flows. Excursions range from pleasant and uncomplicated rides to overnight expeditions into Haleakalā Crater.

Riding a horse along a sandy beach or past an old Hawaiian *heiau*, into the crater or along a high meadow, is a great experience on Maui. There are stables on Maui that offer lessons to novices, in preparation for later rides that may be extended and more challenging. **Maukalani Riding School** (572-0606) and **Piiholo Riding Club** (572-0606) provide equestrian instruction, and are located in a cool Upcountry location. The stables listed here are arranged by area, and are specifically geared to handle riding excursions.

East Maui--**Pony Express Tours** (667-2200) of Kula can manage overnight or day-long crater trips, providing equipment and food as well as a guide. The cost of their Haleakalā Crater day trips ranges from $120 to $140 per person,

depending on length of tour. Two-hour *paniolo* (cowboy) rides across Haleakalā Ranch are also available at a cost of $60 per person. **Thompson Ranch Riding Stables** (878-1910) in Kula has been in business since 1902 and offers a variety of half-day, full-day or overnight riding excursions for the whole family through Haleakalā Crater as well as the picturesque Upcountry area. In the Ha'iku area near Pāia, **Adventures on Horseback** (242-7445 or 572-6211) has an exceptional "waterfall adventure ride" limited in size to groups of six. The horses are extremely well-trained and cared for, making the escorted riding experience enjoyable even for less experienced riders. The tour crosses two-hundred-foot high oceanside cliffs and rolling green pastureland, winding through a lush rainforest, where participants are served a picnic lunch and may enjoy a swim in a refreshing natural pool. Although expensive ($170 per person), the experience is a unique and memorable one.

On the Hāna Coast, the **Hāna Ranch** (248-7238) conducts guided riding tours of the sprawling Hāna Ranch. Although Hotel Hana-Maui guests are given priority booking, non-guests may ride on a "space available" basis. A 25-minute drive past Hāna, in the Kīpahulu District of Haleakalā National Forest, takes you to **'Ohe'o Stables** (667-2222), which offers a three-hour ride through the mountains above 'Ohe'o Gulch (aka Seven Pools). The tour runs from 11:30 a.m. to 2:30 p.m. and takes riders by Waimoku Falls. The price of the three-hour ride is $95 per person, and children under the age of 12 are subject to approval.

Southeast Maui--**Makena Stables** (879-0244) in Mākena offers one ride a day, either a three- or four-hour ride, or a Winery Ride (5 1/2 hours) with a personalized tour of Tedeschi Winery at Upcountry's 'Ulupalakua Ranch. Excursion times vary according to season, and refreshments are included on all rides. The minimum age requirement is twelve years old. The stables are closed on Sunday.

West Maui--Napili's **Ironwood Ranch Riding Stables** (669-4991) offers a wide variety of riding tours, from a three-hour mountain ride with a catered picnic lunch ($135/person) to a two and one-half hour trip through a pineapple plantation and into the West Maui Mountains ($110/ person), with refreshments included. For more experienced riders, a West Maui Mountains "Ironwood Odyssey" excursion, two hours long, takes riders through lush tropical valleys ($125/person). The minimum age for riders is twelve. For advanced rides, eighteen is the minimum age, and there is a 200-pound weight limit. Transportation to and from Kā'anapali and Kapalua is available upon request.

North Maui--**Seahorse Ranch** (244-9862), in northeast Maui, is a 45-minute drive from Kīhei or 75-minute drive from Kapalua, and offers rides through picturesque mountains and valleys. Three-hour escorted trips include a picnic lunch and beverages, and are limited to eight riders. The cost is $95 per person, and other specialty rides are available. **Mendes Ranch** (871-5222), a working cattle ranch, offers a "Paniolo Horseback Adventure" and barbecue for a cost of $130 per person. A combination helicopter/horseback excursion is also offered, which includes a 30-minute helicopter tour of West Maui, for $219 per person. The ranch is open daily except on Sunday, and riders may choose Western or Hawaiian saddles.

HUNTING

Maui has considerable state land where hunting is permitted to those with licenses. Feral pigs, goats, pheasant and francolin are the game. Hunters should go in person to the proper state office and pick up both hunting regulations and maps of the proscribed areas. Maps of public hunting areas are available from the Division of Land and Natural Resources, Division of Forestry (54 High Street, Wailuku, HI 96793 - 243-5352, or 587-0166 on O'ahu). All hunting requires a valid State of Hawai'i Hunting License; non-resident hunting licenses cost $95.00 and may be purchased from licensed agents at sporting goods stores such as Honsport (877-3954) at Kahului's Kaahumanu Center, or from the

Division of Conservation and Resources Enforcement (1151 Punchbowl Street, Rm. 330, Honolulu, 96813 - 587-0077). For the most recent hunting statistics state-wide, call the Hunting Seasons Hotline (808-587-0171) for a recorded message.

Most of the hunting area is in East Maui. Hunting seasons generally last from November through January, but it is best to check with the Forestry Division. Persons who bring firearms into Hawai'i must register them with local police within twenty-four hours or face a penalty. If guns are rented or purchased here, they also must be registered with the police.

Hunting on private land is next to impossible on Maui unless you are acquainted with persons who own property on which they will allow you to hunt. In that eventuality, other state regulations, such as registration of guns, may still apply and it is a good idea to discuss the proposed hunting with the state's

Division of Forestry and Wildlife.

Hunting Adventures of Maui (572-8214), located in Ha'ikū, escorts a maximum group of three persons on hunting expeditions on 100,000 acres of privately owned ranchland, providing all of the equipment, transportation, meat storage and packaging, food and beverages. Among the types of game hunted are wild boar and Spanish goat. Participants are picked up at the Kahului Airport.

If you want to work on improving your shooting skills, you can call **Papaka Sporting Clays** (879-5649). Located on a small volcanic crater on 'Ulupalakua Ranch, this shooting site offers a panoramic view from high above Wailea and La Perouse Bay. With more than 35 sporting clay stands for every level of shooter, it is open daily from 9:00 a.m. until dusk. Fees cover gun, shells, targets, protective gear, instruction and round-trip transportation from the Wailea area. Reservations are required.

FISHING

Recreational ocean fishing along Maui's shoreline does not require a license, and there is no freshwater fishing here. Opinions on the best fishing areas are like other fish tales-- they vary with the telling. Experienced fishermen soon learn to talk with the owners of sporting goods stores to get a fix on the best fishing spots.

With the Pacific as a playground, it is no wonder that Maui spawns numerous charter boats for hire. Some of them are simply for cruising, some for deep-sea fishing only. Still others advertise sailing and snorkeling trips, or fishing-snorkeling-picnic

sails. The boats range from serviceable dive boats to luxurious fifty-eight-foot catamarans. Many of the boats for charter also take trips to Molokini Island, the collapsed volcano that now has a sweeping half-moon bay and is a marine conservation area. Hotel desks have the latest information on the various types of charters, plus the latest fees, or you can go down to the harbors at Lahaina or Mā'alaea and check out the boats for yourself.

Although the 'Big Island' of Hawai'i is the mecca for fishermen, Maui is justly famous for its game fishing. Record-breaking *a'u* (marlin) have been pulled from local waters, and on a day-to-day basis, fishermen take on the *'ahi* (yellowfin tuna), *aku* (skipjack tuna), *mahimahi* (dolphin fish), *ono* (wahoo), and *ulua* (jack crevalle). The blue marlin can run larger than a thousand pounds and sailfish, more than 200 pounds. The *mahimahi* and the tuna are strong fighting fish, a thrill to hook.

On some fishing boats in Hawaii, it is customary for the boat captain and crew to keep the catch; others allow visitors to retain any fish they catch. Ask ahead of time which practice the boat you choose subscribes to in order to prevent any misunderstanding. It is also customary to tip the skipper and crew after a successful voyage.

Aerial Sportfishing Charters (667-9089) sails *Aerial II* and *III* out of Lahaina on fishing excursions. Also operating out of Lahaina is **Luckey Strike Charters** (661-4606) with two boats, the *Luckey Strike II* (45-foot Delta) and *Kanoa* (31-foot Uniflite). This company is experienced in seeking out deep-water fish, and offers bottom fishing as well. **Lahaina Charter Boats** (667-6672) has three boats operating out of Lahaina Harbor, accommodating groups of six to eight passengers: the *Broadbill* (36-foot Harcraft), *Judy Ann II* (43-foot Delta) and *Alohilani* (28-foot Topaz). With so many boat choices, take a stroll along the harbor in the afternoon when most boats have returned to the docks, at either Lahaina or Mā'alaea.

Trilogy Excursion's snorkel tour to Lāna'i--one of Maui's most fun adventures

SNORKELING and SAILING TOURS

One of the best ways to appreciate the beauty of Maui is to venture out on the deep blue frontier, where views of the islands and underwater life are stunning. The waters thrive with interesting sea creatures, including giant green sea turtles, bright orange clown fish, shy mottled moray eels, graceful manta rays and gentle smiling dolphins. From late November to early May, you have a good chance of spotting humpback whales which each year migrate thousands of miles from the North Pacific to Maui to frolic, breed and bear their young.

What follows is a sampling of the many local boat excursions. A wide selection of tours and cruises can be booked and tailored to satisfy one's particular interest. Visitors can either book tours directly with the boat companies or go through a tour desk or reservation service situated at a number of locations throughout Maui. Listed at the end of this section are some companies we have found to be the most knowledgeable.

Maui's oldest sailboat company is **Trilogy Excursions** (661-4743, 800-874-2666), owned and operated by the respected Coon family, experienced sailing pioneers. Their all-day "Discover Lanai" snorkel sail aboard one of three yachts, Trilogy I (a 64-foot trimaran), *Trilogy II* (a 55-foot catamaran) or *Trilogy III* (a 51-foot catamaran), is their most popular. Breakfast is served on board and features Mom Coon's hot home-made cinnamon rolls; a barbecue lunch is enjoyed at a private picnic site on the island of Lāna'i. The cost of the day-long tour is $149 for adults, and half-price for children under age twelve. A *Los Angeles Times* article once commented: "If you do one excursion on Maui, let it be this one", and if you ask around, this opinion will be confirmed. For a truly first class getaway, the Lāna'i trip can be combined with an overnight stay at Lāna'i's luxurious Manele Bay Hotel, sailing back to Maui the following day, perhaps after a round of golf at one of Lānai's two challenging courses. Another option is a half-day excursion to Molokini aboard *Trilogy IV*, a 44-foot trimaran cutter which sails out of Mā'alaea at 6:30 a.m. The cost is $75 per person (half-price for children under twelve), and includes a tasty breakfast and an all-you-can-eat lunch. On both adventures, scuba diving is available on request, suitable for any skill level, from beginner to expert. First-time divers especially appreciate the thorough and safety-conscious guidance provided by experienced instructors.

The 70-foot, three-masted schooner, *Spirit of Windjammer* (661-8600), offers daily cruises, including a two-hour sunset sail featuring all-you-can-eat barbecued chicken and prime rib dinner and authentic Hawaiian entertainment. The boat sails daily out of Slip 1 at Lahaina Harbor at 5:00 p.m. The cost is $65 per person, and half-price for children age twelve and under. At Slip 9 in Lahaina is the *Scotch Mist II* (661-0386), offering a half-day Lāna'i sail and snorkel, a snorkel cruise around West Maui, and a champagne sunset sail, among others. Prices range from $35 to $55 per person, and the boat is also available for private charters.

One of the island's most beautiful yachts is the *Lavengro* (879-8188), a 60-foot classic schooner sailing out of Mā'alaea Harbor. It sails to the islet of Molokini for a snorkel excursion, serving a tropical breakfast and deli-style lunch. The 64-foot whaling schooner, the *Silent Lady* (875-1112), also sails to Molokini out of Mā'alaea for a five-hour snorkel sail, serving a continental breakfast and deli lunch. If you would prefer a relaxing, romantic evening, the sunset sail features Hawaiian music and pupus.

A fine sailing yacht, operated by **Alihilani Yacht Charters** (667-7733), is the 65-foot *First Class*, touted as the fastest sailing yacht in Hawai'i, and capable of speeds in excess of 15 knots. A 90-minute "performance sail" is their most popular, departing from Lahaina Harbor at 2:00 p.m. Also offered is a morning snorkel sail, a sunset sail and a whale-watch excursion (seasonal).

Double-hulled canoes are a Pacific tradition that have evolved into modern-day catamarans. If you like the feel of wind in your hair, you may want to check out one of Maui's fastest catamarans, *Paragon* (244-2087), launched in late 1993 and built for speed, featuring a state-of-the-art rotating carbon fiber mast. One tour offered is a five-hour morning snorkel/sail to Molokini, with buffet lunch, and on-board hot and cold fresh water showers. The boat departs Mā'alaea Harbor at 7:30 a.m. Another option is a three-hour afternoon snorkel and speed run, which promises to be an exhilarating sailing experience, with speeds in excess of twenty knots.

The Hyatt Regency's 55-foot catamaran, the *Kiele V* (661-1234, ext. 3104), is a beautiful luxury sailing yacht which sails along the Kā'anapali coastline Tuesday through Saturday. The snorkel sail runs from 10:00 a.m. to 2:00 p.m., with a continental breakfast, deli lunch, and open bar. The 90-minute afternoon sail leaves at 3:30 p.m., and includes an open bar and appetizers.

RAFTING and KAYAKING TOURS

Inflatable rafts are another popular way of plying Maui's waters, usually accommodating up to 16 passengers each.

Ocean Riders Inc. (661-3586) offers tours of Lāna'i waters, Kaho'olawe, or the north shore of Moloka'i, depending on ocean and weather conditions. Their trips include continental breakfast, mid-morning fruit platter and a buffet lunch, as well as snorkeling equipment and instruction. **Hawaiian Rafting Adventures Inc.** (661-7333) has both half-day (morning or afternoon) and full-day expeditions to Lāna'i. Introductory scuba dives and private charters are also offered. **Ocean Rafting** (667-2191) has excursions to Lāna'i and Moloka'i. Also available are seasonal whale-watching trips (December to May), with a portion of the proceeds donated to the Honolulu-based environmental organization, Earthtrust. **Maui Rafting Expeditions** (667-5678) offers day tours of Lāna'i aboard the bright yellow *Wiki Wahine*, departing from Lahaina Harbor at 7:00 a.m. and 1:30 p.m.

For a relaxing change of pace, paddling your own kayak can be a rewarding experience, and a way to get a close-up look at some of Maui's scenic and secluded coastline areas. **Kayaking Adventures of Maui** (879-8599) offers two guided tours, a two-and-a-half-hour "Discovery" tour ($45/person) and a five-hour "Marine Trek" ($75/person). **Valley Isle Kayaking, Inc.** (874-8560) has a guided scenic tour from Mākena to La Perouse Bay, providing kayakers with beautiful views of Haleakalā. The cost of the three-hour tour is $55 per person, and kayakers must be over the age of twelve.

WHALE WATCHING

The North Pacific humpback whales have been popular attractions in our islands since 1966, but they have plied Hawaiian waters for much longer. Some scientists believe the mammals have been here for centuries, but no one knows for certain. Others say there is little evidence that they were here more than 200 years ago.

There is no doubt, however, that Hawaiian waters became dangerous territory for whales in 1819 when two whaling ships, The *Balaena* and *The Equator*, became the first of hundreds to make port here. Maui became the whaling capital of the Pacific, the place for restocking provisions, as well as seeking rest and recreation.

The whaling industry gave rise to at least five shore-based whaling stations by the late 1860s. They disappeared a decade later, the humpbacks hunted to the very edge of extinction and the industry doomed.

Today, whales still face dangers, but are showing signs of recovery. Whale watching, meanwhile, has become a growing industry in itself. Local organizations began to focus on scientific study of the migrating whales. The motivation to protect the large mammals grew appreciably. The International Whaling Commision scored an impressive victory when a moratorium on commercial whaling was passed in 1982. In 1987, the commission closed a loophole through which some whaling nations were able to take up to 1500 whales a year for 'scientific purposes'. Japan announced it would end its Southern Ocean minke whaling and its hunting of bryde's whales, and in 1988 ended its coastal sperm whaling. Still, uncounted numbers of whales, dolphins, seals and seabirds, die each year by entanglement in miles and miles of driftnets set out by foreign driftnet fleets fishing the waters of the North Pacific. Earthtrust, a Honolulu-based environmental organization, has been instrumental in drawing worldwide attention to this irresponsible fishing technology, which not only endangers sea mammals and birds, but threatens massive depletion of many other fish species.

When the whales arrive in Maui (see "The Whales" under INTRODUCTION), most of Maui's charter boats become instant whale-watching platforms. The boats simply add this recreation to their other specialties, and/or run special whale-watching expeditions. To protect the whales from harassment, though, boats are restricted on how close they can get to the whales, and are not allowed to come between a whale and her calf. Similarly, helicopters and aircraft have strict height limits so as not to disrupt these magnificent mammals while they are in the Hawaiian breeding grounds. Boat skippers know and respect the necessity of keeping a little distance and cannot be persuaded to go any closer than the regulation distance, currently 100 yards.

Photographing the whales from a distance with ordinary camera lenses is difficult, but much improved if using an 80-200 zoom lens. The whales that breach (leap almost out of the water) tend to do it more than once, affording great photo opportunities. Whale watching, enhanced greatly by using binoculars, can be done from a roadside park or a scenic point, from the air or by boat.

A fascinating and informative

book, with just about everything you ever wanted to know about humpback whales, is *Hawaii's Humpback Whales: A Complete Whale Watcher's Guide,* by Gregory D. Kaufman and Paul H. Forestall of Maui's Pacific Whale Foundation. The book is available in most bookstores in Hawai'i, as well as at the beautiful new **Pacific Whale Foundation Store** (corner of Dickenson and Luakini Street, 667-7447) in Lahaina. The store is open daily from 9:00 a.m. to 8:00 p.m. and offers a wide selection of whale-themed gifts, greeting cards, calendars, art posters, t-shirts, videos and books. If you are hooked on humpbacks, this is a store you won't want to miss.

The Pacific Whale Foundation also

Whale-watching season in Hawaii runs from December to May

operates two cruise/snorkel research boats, *Whale One* out of Māʻalaea Harbor and *Whale II* out of Lahaina Harbor, with sails to Molokini, Lānaʻi and other select snorkeling areas. Whale-watching tours are in operation from December 1 to May 1,

with guaranteed whale spotting or you get a coupon for another whale-watching tour. All profits from the tours benefit their marine research, conservation and education programs.

ACTIVITY RESERVATION SERVICES

You will not find a shortage of places through which to book your boat excursions. Listed here are a few of the more knowledgeable companies we have found on Maui.

Capt. Nemo's Ocean Emporium (661-5555) in Lahaina, aside from being a fine dive shop, can arrange for you one of a variety of cruises ranging from sailing to Lānaʻi to snorkeling, scuba diving to sunset sails. Located one-half block off Front Street at 150 Dickenson Street, Capt. Nemo's, with years of experience on Maui, has a helpful and informed staff who can match up the best excursions to suit visitors' individual needs and skill level.

Ocean Activities Center in Wailea (879-4485), **Activity Warehouse** (667-4400) located behind Lahaina's Hard Rock Cafe, and **Tom Barefoot's Cashback Tours** are three other good choices for booking activities. Tom Barefoot's Cashback Tours, located across from Kimo's Restaurant at 834 Front Street (667-5011) in Lahaina and at 2395 S. Kihei Rd. (879-4100) in Kihei's Dolphin Plaza, offers a 10% discount off regular tour prices if you pay with cash, and a 7% discount when using a credit card. Note to Hawaiʻi residents: remember, whenever booking reservations, be sure to inquire if *kamaʻaina* discounts are available. It never hurts to ask!

HEALTH CLUBS

Most local health clubs welcome visitors, and most are open seven days a week. Here are some major ones: **Lahaina Nautilus Center** (667-6100) at 180 Dickenson St., Ste. 201, Lahaina; **World Gym** (667-0422) at 845 Wainee, Lahaina; **Powerhouse Gym Maui** (879-1326) at 300 Ohukai Rd., Kihei; **A Sante Spa** with three locations - Lipoa Center in Kihei (879-5211) , 358 Papa Place in Kahului (871-7190) and Dickenson Square in Lahaina (661-5358); and **Valley Isle Fitness Center** (242-6851) in Wailuku Industrial Park. Most clubs have up-

to-date equipment, conduct fitness classes, and offer private personal training sessions. **The Aerobic Co.** (661-0444), located in the Embassy Suites Resort near Kāʻanapali, is open daily and welcomes visitors to its aerobics and step-aerobics workouts, offering water exercise and personal training as well.

In addition to the clubs noted above, many of the larger hotels and condominiums have exercise programs available to guests on a daily basis. Consult the concierge or front desk for a current schedule of classes.

108

ENTERTAINMENT

Maui's Nightlife
Lu'au
Hawaiian Music
Calendar of Events

ENTERTAINMENT & NIGHTLIFE

For an overwhelming majority of visitors, an evening spent enjoying the lovely Hawaiian ballad, the exciting hula, and the tropical lu'au feast is as much a part of a holiday in Maui as a trip to the beach during the day. A Polynesian show or a lu'au is on almost every first-time visitor's agenda, and most seek out Hawaiian music, knowing they're not likely to find it anywhere else. This section outlines the entertainment scene on Maui in general. For specifics, check the free tourist publications and newspapers, magazines and radio stations.

POLYNESIAN SHOWS

On nearly every island in the Pacific, Polynesian or not, the 'Polynesian Show' has become virtually *de rigueur* tourist entertainment. These shows stage performances based on the traditional music, dance and costumes of Hawai'i, Tahiti, Sāmoa, New Zealand and, occasionally, Tonga and the Cook Islands; sometimes, primarily Melanesian Figi is also included.

Available on Maui at all lu'au and dinner shows, these spectacles are glitzy, show-biz interpretations, and the Tahitian *tamure* almost invariably highlights the evening with its fast-paced hip-swiveling, grass skirts, tall headdresses and wildly beating drums. Another show-stopper is the Sāmoan fire dance or its close kin, the knife dance. Hawaiian hula is usually the *'auana* or 'modern' variety, though some shows include a traditional *'olapa* or *kahiko* hula as well. The Maori (New Zealand) contributions are always a *poi* dance (*poi* in Maori is the white balls on string that the women manipulate so expertly in some of their dances), and the fierce *haka* where men challenge each other (and their audience) with spears and protruding tongues.

LU'AU

Undoubtedly, the lu'au is the most famous feast on visitors' entertainment menu. This highly-civilized Polynesian custom resembles the American Thanksgiving feast, except that the lu'au can be given at any time, for any reason. One good traditional reason for a lu'au is to honor and entertain visitors, so your attendance at one is entirely appropriate. The feast is named after the taro tops *(lu'au)* that are always served. Cooked with coconut cream, they are delectably delicious and highly recommended.

Other traditional fare on such occasions includes such dishes as *laulau*, small packages of fish, pork, chicken or beef, with taro tops, wrapped in ti or banana leaves and baked; *poi*, a thick, purplish-gray paste made from the cooked and pounded base of the taro plant (the staple starch food of the Hawaiians); *kalua* pig, traditionally cooked in an underground oven *(imu)*; and *haupia*, a thick, creamy coconut pudding. The introduction of European and

Asian foods to Hawai'i has added great variety to the culinary concoctions that are now traditional at a lu'au. There is so much to choose from that the lu'au can please the palate of almost everyone.

Though the focus of the feast is food, a lu'au includes a host of entertainments to feast the eye and ear as well. Music, dance, and usually a bit of comedy enhance the festive atmosphere and add to the fun. They are staged on a grand scale, and prices at the different venues are comparable.

A great Polynesian dinner show called **Drums of the Pacific** takes place in an outdoor amphitheater at the Hyatt Regency Maui (667-4420) in Kā'anapali. Here the entertainers also take you on a tour through the exotic islands of Polynesia, in a setting of palm trees with the surf not far away. Shows are currently presented four nights a week, with lu'au seating starting at 5:30 p.m. and cocktail seating (show and cocktails only) at 6:45 p.m. The show begins at 7:00 p.m. The price is $57.30 for adults, $15.63 for children ages 6-12, and children under age 5 are admitted free of charge. For those preferring cocktails and show only (without dinner), the cost is $30.31 for adults and $10.42 for children.

In Wailea, the Maui Inter-Continental Resort (879-1922) holds **"Wailea's Finest Luau"** every Tuesday, Thursday and Friday evening on their oceanfront lawn. Cocktails begin at 5:30 p.m., followed by the Imu Ceremony and opening of the lu'au buffet at 6:15 p.m. The ancient hula *(kahiko)* starts off the show at 7:15 p.m. The fast-paced 50-minute show includes songs and dances from around the Pacific, and ends with an exciting fire dance as its grand finale. The price is $52.00 for adults, and $26.00 for children ages 6-12.

The **Maui Marriott** (661-5828) on Kā'anapali Beach offers a lu'au which has received numerous accolades, one of which is having been chosen as the "Best Lu'au" on Maui by a poll of *Maui News* readers. The lu'au is presented nightly from 5:00 to 8:00 p.m. in a lovely oceanfront garden setting. Mai tais are served all evening, along with a sumptuous buffet of traditional lu'au fare, accompanied by an exciting Polynesian revue. An interesting added touch is an exhibition of games and crafts of old Hawai'i, in which guests may participate, presented from 5:00 to 6:00 p.m. The cost is $48 for adults, $22 for children ages 6-12, and children under age 6 may attend free of charge.

An intimate and romantic lu'au which has become a Maui favorite is the **Old Lahaina Lu'au** (661-3303), situated in a lovely oceanfront plantation-style cafe, at 505 Front Street in Lahaina. The lu'au is considered one of Maui's most authentic, presented in the traditional Hawaiian style. Guests may select table seating or sit on mats on the ground. The Hawaiian show is less glitzy than some of the larger productions on the island, and has been given the "Keep it Hawaii" award from the Hawaii Visitors Bureau. The lu'au is held Tuesday through Saturday starting at 5:30 p.m., in time to watch sunset. Due do its smaller audience (maximum of 280 guests) and growing popularity, reservations are recommended. The price is $56 for adult, and $28 for children.

Please note that all prices quoted are subject to change without notice. It is best to confirm all rates and event schedules when making reservations.

The **Royal Lahaina Lu'au,** held nightly at the Royal Lahaina Resort in Kā'anapali (661-3611), features a spectacular Polynesian revue, along with a dinner buffet and open bar. The lu'au site is a garden setting, amongst palm trees and tiki torches, and the show is a definite crowd-pleaser, ending with a dramatic fire dance. The lu'au starts at 5:30 p.m. September through April, changing to 6:00 p.m. May through August. The cost is $47 for adults and $23.50 for children ages 5-12. Children under age 5 may attend free of charge. A fun lu'au/submarine excursion package is available through **Atlantis Submarines** (667-2224) at a cost of $99 for adults and $48 for children age 12 years and younger. The combination package represents a $27 per person savings over what they would cost if booked separately. The submarine dives run daily from 8:00 a.m. to 4:00 p.m. on the hour, and the duration of the excursion is two hours.

The **Sheraton Maui** at Kā'anapali, which previously offered a wonderful lu'au show, is undergoing extensive renovation, and is estimated to reopen at the beginning of 1997.

Stouffer Wailea Beach Resort's **Wailea Sunset Lu'au** (879-4900) is presented on Thursdays from 5:30 to 9:00 p.m., with the Imu Ceremony (presentation of baked pig) beginning at 6:00 p.m. The lu'au is situated in an attractive oceanside garden setting. Included in the Polynesian revue is a traditional *kahiko* hula. The cost is $51 for adults, $29 for children ages 5-12, and free of charge for children under age 5.

The Grand Wailea Resort Hotel and Spa's **Grand Ohana Lu'au** (875-1234) is held on Mondays and Wednesdays starting at 5:15 p.m. in the lobby, at which time a preview of the night's entertainment is presented. The lush lu'au grounds are located near the ocean, with entry via a thatched roof hut. A complimentary photograph of your party is included in the cost of the evening. The lighting of tiki torches is followed by an authentic Imu Ceremony at 6:15 p.m. In keeping with the lu'au tradition, the entertainment is a showcase of the food and culture of Polynesia, complete with Maori warriors, fire knife dancing, Hawaiian *kahiko* hula and a Tahitian revue. The price is $58 for adults, $30 for children ages 6-12, with free admittance for children under 6 years of age. Cocktails-only seating is offered on a space available basis, starting at 6:45 p.m. The price for cocktails and show (no dinner) is $30 for adults and $20 for children.

The **Hawaiian Country Barbeque and Revue** (244-7643) is presented Tuesday, Wednesday and Thursday evenings at Maui Tropical Plantation in Waikapu, near Wailuku. In addition to a generous all-you-can-eat barbeque-style buffet, a Hawaiian Country Revue is the featured entertainment, a blending of Polynesian song and dance with country music. Seating begins at 5:00 p.m. The price for adults is $48.25, and the price for children is $20.42. (You may want to call to verify the time and prices, as the event was in the process of being updated as of this writing.)

If a lu'au epitomizes the culinary delights of our island culture, hula captures its heartbeat. Dance was an integral part of the ritual life of the ancients, and the old hula never died. New dances derived from it became popular entertainment for visiting sailors, who paid well to witness these alterations, but Hawaiians didn't fundamentally connect this new and lucrative enterprise with their sacred dance. Reviled by missionaries as 'obscene', the old dance was taken underground and taught in secret, while the new dance thrived in places where religious reformers held no sway. Thus, there developed two distinct classes of hula, the ancient and the modern.

Hula 'ōlapa, more recently known as *hula kahiko*, the old style, is performed to the accompaniment of chanting and percussion only. Traditionally, the dance was done to accompany the chant, which was of primary importance, and it was performed on most occasions by men. Though most hula groups today have a preponderance of women, the men's hula is every bit as beautiful, and is energetic with a virile grace that seems absent from the aggressive men's dances of other Polynesian cultures. Chanting, too, is an art that is experiencing a revival, along with the upsurge of interest in the Hawaiian language, which is always used in the chants.

The women's hula is softer than the men's, but still has strength and precision. Precision is a vital element of this hula style, and while there is ample scope for the enactment of modern tales in the ancient mode, the rules are strict and strictly followed.

It is interesting to note that the most famous symbol of the hula, indeed of Hawai'i--the grass skirt--is not Hawaiian at all. The grass skirt was introduced from Micronesia by laborers from the Gilbert Islands in the early nineteenth century. Hawaiians subsequently used native materials, such as ti leaves, in a similar fashion but they were always fresh and green out of respect for the gods, a strictly Hawaiian innovation.

Prior to European visitations, their garments had been of bark cloth *(kapa)*. During the reign of King Kalakaua, when by royal decree the hula was again performed in public (earning him the nickname the "Merrie Monarch"), the European clothing of the time was worn in the dance, and hula from that era are still performed in costumes of the period.

Hula ku'i, a transitional form, which combines traditional hula movements with those of nineteenth-century European ballroom dance, arose at this time. Prior to this innovation, men and women seldom danced together; in most ancient hula performed today, they still do not.

Hula 'auana, the modern style, is much more flexible than its ancient forebear, just as modern ballet can be interpreted more freely than classical. Its costuming is limited only by the imagination and is keyed to the story being told. Modern hula is usually accompanied by both melody and lyrics as well as ukuleles, guitars and other instruments, and the songs may be in any language, though English and Hawaiian are most common.

Pa'u O Hi'iaka is among several Maui *hālau* that perform both the modern and traditional hula; this troupe specializes in the latter. **Ka Makani Wili Makaha O Kauaula** specializes in the traditional hula, and occasionally performs at Stouffer Wailea Beach Resort. **Pukalani Hula Hale** is another good *hālau* from

ENTERTAINMENT

Pukalani, in Upcountry Maui, that performs both *kahiko* and *'auana* style of dance. **Halau Hula O Ka'ula** performs Hula Kahiko O Hawai'i, "the ancient dance of Hawai'i," for free at the Kapalua Shops every Thursday morning. Maui County's late historian emeritus, Inez Ashdown, was the originator of this hula presentation, making it one of Maui's most authentic. Check tourist publications and the *Maui News* for listings of when and where *ho'olaule'a* or other community events are scheduled that feature hula, because what you see can be significantly different from what you may see in a Polynesian show, especially if you catch a good *kahiko*.

HAWAIIAN MUSIC

There is no sound more clearly associated with the tropical beauty of these islands than the lovely Hawaiian melody accompanied by the ukulele. Though neither melody nor harmony had existed in Polynesian tradition prior to European contact, the people of the islands demonstrated remarkable natural affinity with and talent for both. They also adopted enthusiastically the stringed instruments these visitors introduced, and each Polynesian group has developed a distinctive musical style during the past century or two.

The guitar is probably the instrument most commonly used by contemporary Hawaiian musicians, but its baby brother, the ukulele, is most strongly identified with Hawai'i. *'Ukulele* is, in fact, a Hawaiian word. It means 'leaping flea' and was first applied as a nickname to Edward Purvis, a popular nineteenth century player of the instrument who jumped around while he strummed. Brought to Hawai'i by Portuguese laborers in 1879, the diminutive instrument was known to them as *braquinho*.

The other stringed instrument immutably linked with Hawai'i is the steel guitar, played horizontally with a metal slide. Last, but certainly not least, is the distinctively Hawaiian 'slack key' guitar, a tuning effect achieved by loosening the strings.

Today's island music has continued to evolve and is now less stereotypical and more grounded in true expression of the feelings of island life. Within it, naturally, are varieties--and insertions from the contemporary idiom--but the unique island flavor is discernible throughout.

Most of the large resort hotels have live Hawaiian music in their cocktail lounges and sometimes in restaurants during dinner hours. A stroll through any of them around the early evening is the best way to discover by just following your ears.

COCKTAIL LOUNGES & NIGHT SPOTS

When the sun goes down after a full day of sight-seeing and tan-cultivating, many people just want to relax and have a cocktail. To others, nightfall means jumping into high gear and dancing and schmoozing until the wee hours.

As for night clubs, West Maui's major resorts always have entertainers to amuse their guests, and, since club acts come and go, the most reliable indicator of what's playing at the moment is the *Maui News* ("The Scene" section). Stroll down Front Street in Lahaina and tune in to the music floating out of various establishments. Occasionally a well-known entertainer will come to Maui from Honolulu, but these appearances are sporadic. Also, celebrities visiting Maui sometimes stop in at a club unannounced, treating lucky audiences to impromp-tu performances while enhancing the club's reputation.

For an excellent view of sunset, stop in at the Hula Grill's **Barefoot Bar** (661-3894) situated right in the sand on Kā'anapali Beach at Whaler's Village. Live Hawaiian style or soft reggae music is featured nightly from 7:00 to 9:00 p.m. The bar menu includes a variety of appetizers, sandwiches and burgers.

The Makai Bar (667-1200) at the Maui Marriott in Kā'anapali is another spot for catching a beautiful Maui sunset. It was voted "Best Pupus and Best Views" on Maui by a *Maui News* readership poll. Hawaiian and contemporary entertainment is featured nightly from 5:00 to 11:30 p.m.

The younger crowd is drawn to Lahaina's longtime popular restaurant/bar hangout, **Moose McGilly-cuddy's** (667-7758) at 844 Front Street, where rock 'n' roll is the music of choice. Live bands entertain on Thursday, Friday and Saturday starting at 9:30 p.m. **Blue Tropix Restaurant and Nightclub** (667-5309), is another popular place for dancing and dining, located upstairs at 900 Front Street, in a choice oceanfront location. The entertainment features DJ-hosted disco, as well as frequent live bands. Dinner can be enjoyed here as well, with a varied menu

selection including sushi, salads, pasta, pizza, steak, chicken and fresh fish. Here, you can dance the night away until 2:00 a.m.

Wailea's Maui Inter-Continental offers a spicy selection of dancing music in the **Inu Inu Lounge** (879-1922). Bands playing there range in musical styles from jazz to swing to Top-40, and they change frequently.

Tsunami (875-1234), the Grand Wailea's elegant night club has an attractive high-tech interior, featuring Top-40 contemporary music, and boasts a state-of-the-art sound, lighting and video system, as well as a 10,000-square-foot dance floor. Its hours are from 9:00 p.m. to 1:00 a.m. weekdays, and until 4:00 a.m. on weekends. There is a $5.00 cover charge, applicable only to non-guests of the hotel. There is no cover for guests of the hotel.

Casanova's Italian Restaurant and Deli (572-0220) in Makawao has live music on the weekends, featuring a varied range of musical styles. **Charley's** (579-9453) is a favorite restaurant and bar in Pā'ia, and has evoked impromptu performances in past years by such famous Maui visitors as Willie Nelson and Ringo Starr.

A number of additional bars and cocktail lounges exist on the island, and anyone you ask will have a favorite spot to send you off to. Sometimes the most fun is exploring and stumbling onto a place all on your own, just as long as you don't over-imbibe and stumble on the way out. You've heard it before, but here's a bit of advice again. **Don't drive a car if you've been drinking alcoholic beverages.** Even with one's full wits about them, Maui's roads can be dangerous, especially since they are not divided. When crossing the island, one should be extremely attentive to the road and to other drivers. The thing to do if you plan on drinking is to appoint a designated non-drinking driver in your group, or leave the rental car behind and travel to and from by taxi (or trolleys in the Lahaina area). It may add to the cost of a fun evening, but you and your companions can relax knowing you'll arrive back at your rooms safely.

116

THEATRE

The **Maui Community Theatre** (242-6969), also known as **Maui Onstage,** is an active Thespian group that presents approximately six productions a year. The group makes its home in the historic Iao Theater at 68 N. Market Street in Wailuku. The 60-year-old theatre closed in May of '95 for a major $500,000 renovation, which will expand its seating capacity to 400 and revamp its aging interior. Call for a current update and schedule. The $30 million state-of-the-art **Maui Arts and Cultural Center** (ticket office: 242-SHOW) opened in May of 1994, providing a much needed addition to the island's performing arts facilities.

The **Maui Academy of Performing Arts** (formerly the Maui Youth Theatre) (244-8760) is a growing organization that stages several plays and other events each year, many of which are for children's entertainment. In existence since 1974, its educational programs on creative dramatics and theatre art skills are strongly supported in the community. The **Baldwin Theatre Guild** (242-5821) is another fixture on Maui, in existence since 1964, presenting a number of theatrical productions and workshops during the year.

The *Maui News*, other local publications and hotel desks can provide the most up-to-date information about current productions.

CINEMA

Films currently showing on the U. S. mainland play at the local cinemas, which are located in Kukui Mall, Kihei; the Wharf Cinema Center and Lahaina Center, Lahaina; and Kahului Center, Kahului.

A favorite attraction is **"The Hawaii Experience" Omni Theater** (661-8314) on Front Street in Lahaina. A 40-minute film documents Hawai'i's past and present, with superb photography and excellent sound system. "Hawaii, Island of the Gods", is shown on a giant domed screen, with seating which allows 180° unobstructed panoramic views of Hawai'i's natural splendor. Shows run on the hour from 10:00 a.m. to 10:00 p.m. daily. The cost is $6.95 for adults, $3.95 for children ages 4-12.

CALENDAR OF EVENTS

JANUARY

United Airlines Hawaiian Open, PGA Tour event, Waialae Country Club, Oahu (526-1232)

FEBRUARY

Asahi Beer Kyosan Golf Tournament--professional men and women golfers from Japan and Hawai'i vie for $100,000 purse. Wailea Golf course (879-4465)

The Art Affair--annual art auction and gourmet dinner held at Monroe's, at the Grand Waikapu Country Club. Fundraiser for Hui No'eau Visual Arts Center, Makawao. (572-6560)

MARCH

Maui Marathon--annual marathon (26.2 miles) from Wailuku to Whalers Village, Kā'anapali (871-6441)

APRIL

Iao Valley 10K Run (871-6441)

Art Maui--an annual juried exhibition of works by Maui's art community, Maui Arts and Cultural Center, Kahului. (572-6660)

Maui Community College Ho'olaule'a--some of Hawai'i's best entertainers perform. Also food booths, arts and crafts, and games. Maui Community College, Wailuku (242-1260)

Maui O'Neill Invitational--first windsurfing event of U.S. Pro Tour. Features 150 competitors from sixteen countries. Ho'okipa Beach, Pā'ia

Buddha Day--flower festival pageant at temples island-wide to celebrate the birth of Buddha. Sweet tea ceremony, flower presentation, fun day for kids, lunch and bingo games at Lahaina Hongwanji Mission (661-0640).

April/May

Hula Pakahi and Lei Contest -- held at the end of April or first week in May, in honor of May Day. Maui Inter-Continental, Wailea (879-1922)

ENTERTAINMENT

117

The sun's dimming light marks the beginning of a romantic evening

MAY

May Day (May 1) is Lei Day in Hawai'i--island-wide festivities at many locations, featuring Hawaiian entertainment, lei-making events and crafts.

Kapalua Tennis Jr. Vet/Sr. Championship--men and women thirty-five years and older compete in singles, doubles and mixed doubles. Kapalua Tennis Garden (669-5677) or Kapalua Village Tennis Center (665-0112)

Hal "Aku" Lewis Golf and Tennis Tournament--Hollywood celebrities participate in this tournament for charity. Maui Inter-Continental, Wailea (879-4465)

Seabury Hall Craft Fair--arts and crafts, food booths, games and entertainment. Seabury Hall, Makawao (572-7235)

JUNE

Annual King Kamehameha Celebration--June 12--state holiday honoring Kamehameha the Great. Celebrations on all islands. Parade in Lahaina, ho'olaule'a, arts and crafts, food, lei-making. Check newspaper for current schedule of festivities.

Annual Up-country Fair--old-fashioned farm fair featuring 4-H farmers' products, a fun run, sports tournaments, entertainment and food booths. Eddie Tam Center, Makawao (572-8883)

Kapalua Music Festival--internationally acclaimed artists from all over the world assemble to perform chamber music at Kapalua Bay Hotel (669-0244)

Outrigger Canoe Racing--Maui clubs compete for county titles, June through July. Good local food and fun. Check local papers for location.

JULY

O'Bon Season July thru August. Colorful O'Bon dances and floating lantern ceremonies are held at

various locations during Buddhist memorial season. Hongwanji missions of Maui.

ENTERTAINMENT

AUGUST

Haleakalā Run to the Sun--an uphill ultra-marathon of 36.2 miles. Starts at 5:30 a.m. at Maui Mall, Kahului, and finishes at the top of Haleakalā National Park, going from sea level to 10,000 feet. (871-6441)

Maui Onion Festival--held the first weekend in August. Food booths, exhibits, demonstrations and entertainment. Maui Onion Cookoff, onion-eating contest, and other events. Whalers Village, Kā'anapali (661-4567)

Plantation Day--cultural demonstrations, entertainment, good food, keiki fishing contests. Maui Tropical Plantation, Waikapu (244-7643)

SEPTEMBER

Maui Channel Relay Swim--this 9-mile relay begins on Lāna'i and finishes in Lahaina. Six-person teams compete in various age divisions. (522-7619 - Honolulu)

Kapalua Open Tennis Tournament--top players from around the state compete in this Hawai'i Grand Prix event for one of the largest purses in open and 'B' divisions. Kapalua Tennis Garden (669-0244) or Kapalua Village Tennis Center (665-0112)

Hāna Relay--a 54-mile annual relay run by six-person teams from Kahului to Hāna, starting at 6:00 a.m. Valley Isle Road Runners (871-6441).

Aloha Week Festivals--Hawaiian pageantry, canoe races, ho'olaule'a, parades, and a variety of entertainment and stage shows statewide. Consult newspapers for dates and schedule of events on each island.

Cycle to the Sun--38 miles uphill time trial bicycle race, beginning in Pāia and climbing to the rim of Haleakalā. Ehrman Productions. (575-9151)

Hi-tech Pro-am Wavesailing Championship. Amateur windsurfers compete. Ehrman Productions. (575-9151)

Children enjoy storytelling at Ka'anapali Beach Hotel.

OCTOBER

Maui County Fair--the state's oldest fair features a grand orchid exhibition, arts and crafts, ethnic foods and a parade to kick off the four-day event. Kahului Fairgrounds (877-5343, 244-3242)

Mazda International Amateur Golf Championships--amateur golfers from around the world gather to compete for prizes. Wailea (875-5111) and Makena (879-3344) Golf Clubs.

Dracula's Dash--8 K run. Runners wear Halloween costumes. Begins at Kā'anapali Beach at 5:00 p.m. (877-5827)

Halloween in Lahaina--Front Street in Lahaina breaks out in Mardi Gras-style frivolity. A people-watching feast with plenty of outrageous costumes. The place to be on October 31!

Halloween Parade--fun for children, on Lahaina's Front Street. October 31, 4:00 p.m. Community-sponsored benefit for children. (667-6619)

Lahaina Historic Fun Run (871-6441)

Hyatt Regency Kā'anapali Classic Senior PGA Tournament (661-1885)

NOVEMBER

Aloha Classic Windsurfing World Championships--one of the biggest windsurfing contests, with 150 competitors from 16 countries participating in this 10-day event. $200,000 in prize money. Final event of Pro World Tour. Ho'okipa Beach, Pā'ia. Ehman Productions. (575-9151)

Hawai'i International Film Festival--award-winning cross-cultural films from the Asia-Pacific area, shown free at several locations.

Harbor to Harbor 10-Mile Run-- (871-6441)

Na Mele O Maui Festival--a festival of Hawaiiana through Hawai'i's arts and crafts, dances, music and a lu'au. Hotels in Kā'anapali and Lahaina. (879-4577)

Maui County Rodeo Finals--paniolos (cowboys) from Moloka'i and Maui compete. Top ten contestants take part in finals. Oskie Rice Arena, Makawao. (572-9928)

Lincoln-Mercury Kapalua International Championship Golf--top golf professionals meet at Kapalua Bay Resort for the 'Super Bowl' of golf and one of the sport's largest purses (more than $600,000). Spectator admission free. (669-0244).

Thanksgiving Fun Run (the Turkey Trot)--runners estimate completion time for 8.6 mile or 16.1 mile run. Closest guess wins a turkey. Starts at 7:00 a.m., Rice Park, Kula. (871-6441)

Kapalua/Betsy Nagelsen Tennis Invitational--select field of women professional players, as well as amateurs, in both a pro-doubles competition and pro-am doubles tournament at the Kapalua Bay Resort. Kapalua Tennis Garden (669-5677) or Kapalua Village Tennis Center (665-0112)

ENTERTAINMENT

DECEMBER

The Kirin Cup World Championship of Golf--teams representing the US PGA Tour, the PGA European Tour, the Japan Professional Golf Association Tour and the Australia/ New Zealand PGA Tour play at the Bay Course, vying for a $900,000 purse. Kirin Cup Tournament Office, Nāpili (669-4844)

Hui No'eau Christmas House-- Christmas arts and crafts featuring the work of Maui's best artists. First weekend in December. Admission charge. Hui No'eau Visual Arts Center, Makawao. (572-6560)

Bodhi Day--Buddhist temples commemorate 'Day of Enlightenment' on all islands. Contact Hawaii Buddhist Council (548-3805 - Honolulu) or Lahaina Hongwanji Mission (661-0640 - Maui).

Santa Comes to Wailea--Santa arrives attired in a red and white lava-lava by way of canoe. Maui Inter-Continental, Wailea (879-1922)

Lokahi Pacific Christmas Bazaar-- Hawaiian and other homemade Christmas decorations and baked goods for sale. Kahului Shopping Center, Kahului (877-5523)

GTE Kā'anapali Golf Classic-- Kā'anapali Senior Classic purse of $300,000. Tour purses total more than $9.5 million. Kā'anapali (247-6841-Oahu)

SHOPPING

SHOPPING

Most of Maui's visitors go shopping for *something* during their island holiday. What's available on Maui and how it is presented encompasses all shades of the shopping spectrum. Funky galleries, gift shops and boutiques in Pā'ia, Makawao, Wailuku and Lahaina, upscale resort shops at the Hyatt Regency Maui, Whalers Village, Wailea Shopping Village, and the Kapalua Shops, adjacent to the Kapalua Bay Hotel, and the urban shopping centers in the Central Valley, Kaahumanu Center and Maui Mall, offer something for everyone. This categorized listing points out some of the more notable shops. Addresses and telephone numbers of these are listed at the back of this book as an appendix.

CENTERS

One of the oldest shopping centers, the **Wharf Cinema Shops and Restaurants,** is located opposite the Banyan Tree on Front Street in Lahaina. Some fifty businesses sprawl among three stories around an open-air courtyard. The complex contains restaurants, apparel stores strong in Polynesian wear, resort- and swimwear, and other specialty shops. Parking is along Front Street, behind Burger King, behind the center itself between Waine'e and Luakini Streets, and on Dickenson Street. Resort trolleys stop here, as does the bus from the Sugarcane Train terminal.

Also in Lahaina, at the corner of Front Street and Lahainaluna Road, is **Lahaina Market Place,** with cobblestone walkways, kiosks, and shaded courtyard. Parking is along its bordering streets. **Lahaina Center,** located at 900 Front Street, offers twenty-something stores to browse through. They include specialty shops such as Hilo Hatties, Banana Republic, Arabesque and Waterwear, and restaurants such as the Hard Rock Cafe, Blue Tropix Nightclub, World Cafe and Red Lobster, as well as a newly opened four-screen movie theater. Parking here is reasonably priced.

At the eastern end of Front Street (heading the opposite direction from Kā'anapali), is the **505 Front Street** shopping complex. Its two levels house restaurants (Pacific 'O, Casa de Mateo, and Old Lahaina Cafe and Luau), retail shops and galleries. Cars park for free either in the basement of the center or in free county lots across the street. The **Lahaina Shopping Center** just off Front Street draws many residents from the Lahaina area, and its anchor store is Nagasako Super Market. Made up of several two-story buildings, it covers a large area, parking lot included. On Waine'e Street, just across from Lahaina Shopping Center, is **Lahaina Square Shopping Center,** a small wooden complex with free parking. Foodland Supermarket is its main tenant.

The **Lahaina Cannery Mall** at 1221 Honoapi'ilani Highway on the western fringe of Lahaina, is built on the site of an old pineapple cannery. The enclosed mall is air-conditioned, providing a refreshing oasis away from Lahaina's hot sun. Safeway and Longs are its anchor stores, and Compadres Bar & Grill its most popular dining spot. With about fifty stores, it is Lahaina's largest shopping complex, and parking is free.

The **Lahaina Square Shopping Center,** on Waine'e Street, across from Lahaina Shopping Center, is a small wooden complex with free parking and Foodland Supermarket as its main tenant. **Mariner's Alley** at 844 Front Street is made up of two levels with a courtyard, boutiques, and the popular watering hole Moose McGillycuddy's upstairs, and superb Avalon restaurant downstairs. In Kā'anapali, **Whalers Village** is the major attraction for shopping. Centered around the Whale Center of the Pacific, its stores include different types of art galleries (Dolphin Galleries, Lahaina Printsellers), upscale boutiques (Louis Vuitton, Chanel), jewelry shops (Tiffany, H. F. Wichman & Co.), a number of clothing shops (Maui Clothing Co., Blue Ginger Designs, Crazy Shirts), as well as restaurants (Hula Grill, Leilani's, Rusty Harpoon). Parking rates are reasonable at the adjacent lot.

Located in Kahana on Lower Honoapi'ilani Road, **Gateway Shopping Center** includes Whaler's General Store, Roy's Kahana Bar and Grill, Roy's Nicolina and other stores.

In **Kapalua Shops,** next to Kapalua Bay Hotel, you can find many stores including McInerny, Reyn's, Lahaina Galleries, Kapalua Kids, and The Market Cafe.

Kaahumanu Center, one of the Central Valley shopping centers on Ka'ahumanu Avenue in Kahului, was expanded and renovated in 1994 and has more than forty stores. Anchor stores Liberty House and Sears are its major retail establishments. Other stores include Shirokiya, Honsport, Casual Corner, Foot Locker and Waldenbooks. Eateries include China Chef and Koho Grill & Bar. Shirokiya, a Japanese department store, offers a *bento* lunch, a favorite with residents.

Just down Ka'ahumanu Avenue is the **Kahului Shopping Center,** built in he late 1940s and Maui's first shopping center. Take a stroll through **Ah Fook's Super Market** and **Noda's Market,** old time Maui grocers, and you'll feel like you've stepped into another world.

The nearby **Maui Mall,** on the same side of the street, has a number of specialty shops in its beautifully landscaped complex, with J. C. Penney being its largest occupant. The funky Sir Wilfred's (coffee, tea and tobacco shop) deserves a look-see, along with the famous natural food store, Tasaka Guri Guri Shop (which makes special local ice cream concoctions). Star Market, Longs Drugs and Waldenbooks can also be found in the mall. Maui entertainers frequently perform here.

Kukui Mall at 1819 S. Kihei Rd. has a variety of specialty shops, including a four-screen movie theater, Waldenbooks and Local Motion Inc. There is lots of free mall parking, as well. Nearby, on the same street, is **Kihei Town Center,** anchored by Foodland. Here you can find Chuck's Steak House, a bank and other stores .

Azeka Place Shopping Center at 1280 S. Kihei Road in Kihei has forty-five stores and three restaurants. Parking is ample and stores include Liberty House, O'Rourke's Tourist Trap and Paradise Swimwear. Restaurants include A Pacific Cafe, Peggy Sue's and The Coffee Store.

Between Kama'ole Beach Park I and II on South Kihei Road, you'll fid the **Kamaole Shopping Center,** with fourteen shops and three restaurants. Also in Kihei, opposite Kama'ole Beach Park, is **Rainbow Mall,** with its mixture of restaurants, clothing and specialty boutiques, among other businesses.

In Upcountry Maui, the **Pukalani Terrace Center** is easy to find alongside Haleakalā Highway (Route 37). Foodland, Ben Franklin, Pizza Hut, banks and a launderette accommodate the community's needs. A western theme throughout befits this center that Upcountry residents frequent, as do visitors en route to Haleakalā.

DEPARTMENT STORES

Two home-grown department stores with souvenir and *aloha* wear displays, **Liberty House** and **Ikeda's,** are joined by their mainland counterparts, **Sears** and **J C Penney.** **Shirokiya,** a Japanese-owned store in Kaahumanu Center, sells many items made in Japan.

ALOHA WEAR

Casual island clothing, suitable for our tropical climate, comes in the form of *aloha* shirts for men and *mu'umu'us* (long, loose dresses) for women. These can be found in a number of colorful fabrics, usually bright, flowery prints.

Such fashion is acceptable almost everywhere in the island; only a scattering of restaurants still require men to wear jackets. Even so, some men wear *aloha* shirts under their jackets and enjoy the contrast. The matching his-and-her *aloha* shirts are mostly worn by our visitors.

Many boutiques, resort shops and department stores merchandise *aloha* wear. **Liberty House** has a fine selection, as does **Hilo Hattie Fashion Center** at Lahaina Center, which shuttles visitors from Lahaina and Kā'anapali hotels. Also geared for children as well as adults, **Leilani Gift Shop** in Kihei has gift items, in addition to island clothing.

More than a dozen shops with *aloha* wear are located at the Wharf Cinema Shops and Restaurants (see 'Centers' above). Well-known local designers include Reyn's, Mamo Howell, Cooke Street and Princess Kaiulani Fashions.

T-SHIRTS

Everyone wears t-shirts, and their popularity never seems to fade. The classic success story and undisputed king of trendy tees in Hawai'i is **Crazy Shirts,** with five stores on Maui, in Kā'anapali, Kihei, and Lahaina. Hundreds of original designs are available. Their hallmark design is the delightful device of depicting on the back of the shirt a rear view of whatever is on the front. Another retail store, the highly visible **T-Shirt Factory,** has a wide selection of low-priced tees, in seven locations on the island.

MEN'S SHOPS

Men--and women buying gifts for them on Maui--tend to gravitate to **Reyn's** (four locations on the island), which produces the cloth and clothing known as Reyn Spooner, a comfortable, wrinkle-resistant fabric that makes great *aloha* and resort wear. **Kramer's** a youth-oriented men's store in Lahaina and **Panama Jack's** (Kihei and Lahaina) are other good sources for men's fashions.

WOMEN'S BOUTIQUES

The emphasis at **Silks Kaanapali Ltd.**, in Whalers Village, is on originality. Local artists design the images that are painted on silks, rayons and cotton. Each piece is done individually, with meticulous attention to the marriage of design and fabric. On the high end of the spectrum, also located at Whalers Village, is the extravagant **Chanel** boutique, a recent addition to the Village.

Arabesque in Lahaina Center is another fine shop selling glittery evening and party outfits (for both women and children), as well as stylish casual clothes and unique fashion accessories. **Perles de Tahiti** on Front Street sells attractive Balinese designs and Hawai'i-made clothes for women and children, and has a nice selection of jewelry, as well as gorgeous decorative baskets. A fun casual clothing boutique is **Sun Day,** located at the Wharf Cinema Center, offering an array of swimsuits, shorts, t-shirts and jewelry.

In Wailea Shopping Village, **Susu's Boutique** carries a superb collection of high-quality *aloha* attire and resort wear. Other noteworthy clothing stores are **Maui Clothing Company Inc.** in Whalers Village and Lahaina Shopping Center, and **Escape to Maui** in Kamaole Shopping Center (Kihei) and Lahaina Cannery. **Tropical Tantrum** in two Kihei locations, Azeka Place and Kamaole Shopping Center, features a colorful selection of tropical fashions designed on Kauai.

In three locations on Maui (Kapalua Shops, Four Seasons Resort and the Grand Wailea Resort and Spa), is **Mandalay Imports,** specializing in custom-designed imports in Thai or antique Japanese silks.

Several interesting boutiques are located in Pāia, many of which feature Balinese designs, and it's worth taking a casual stroll through town to explore these trendy stores. Drive up Baldwin Avenue from Pāia into Makawao, for another string of quaint stores. One of our favorites is **Collections,** which features not only casual ladies apparel, but also has an excellent selection of greeting cards, jewelry, gifts and accessories.

JEWELRY

Jewelry manufacturers and stores in the islands do not limit themselves to but specialize in treasures from the sea and shore, and many offer custom made designs. At several jewelry stores throughout the island, you can find a local tradition--leis, bracelets and earrings made from the rare, tiny shells painstakingly gathered from the beaches of the privately owned island of Ni'ihau. This shell stands alone as the only kind that is classified as a gem and that can be insured.

Another tradition, Hawaiian 'heirloom' jewelry, generally takes longer than a brief visit to have custom made; bracelets, pendants and rings are made of heavy gold bearing the wearer's name approximated in Hawaiian and enameled in black Victorian lettering. **Kaneshige Jewelers,** a store dating back to 1894, located at Maui Mall, sells such Hawaiian heirloom jewelry, in addition to diamonds, jade and other fine gemstones. **Royal Hawaiian Heritage Jewelry,** another established island jewelry merchant, in business since 1972, has an extensive selection of heirloom and diamond jewelry, and is located at Lahaina Cannery Mall. **Yoshimura Jewelers,** located on Front Street in Lahaina, also stocks Hawaiian gold jewelry, as well as coral, pearls, and diamonds. One more to try is **Emura Jewelers** on Market Street, in Wailuku, for Hawaiian jewelry and low-priced eelskin.

Antique netsuke--the closures on purses that were slipped over the sash of the kimono in old Japan--are rare, expensive, and available through only seven dealers in the world. However, contemporary souvenir netsuke, made in Hong Kong or Japan for the tourist trade, can be found at many gift shops around Maui.

Daring divers going to greater and greater depths in the waters off Maui bring up gold, pink and black coral stems, which are then highly polished and designed into unique pieces of jewelry. Founded by Jack Ackerman, who rediscovered coral after its 400-year disappearance, **Jack Ackerman's The Original Maui Divers** on Front Street has an extensive collection of coral Ni'ihau shells, and pearls.

The **Coral Tree** at Wharf Cinema Shops in Lahaina, **Yoshimura Jewelers** in Lahaina, and many other jewelry stores showcase unusual and beautiful coral creations.

SCRIMSHAW

The whaling ships that sailed Hawai'i's waters and docked at her ports in the 1800s introduced the craft of scrimshaw carving to the islands. The intricate carving and etching techniques were passed down through the generations and scrimshaw pieces are quite valued today. Fossilized ivory and bone, as well as non-fossilized walrus tusks are shipped to Hawai'i from Alaska, carved with special tools and then etched in black, depicting sailing ships, whaling scenes and other artistic renderings, and fashioned into a variety of art objects and gift items.

For environmental reasons, elephant ivory and whale bone are no longer used in scrimshaw. Eskimos are, however, legally allowed to hunt walrus for use in "Native American" artwork; even though they are not the actual artisans for Hawai'i's scrimshaw, they make some minuscule scratches on the tusks prior to shipping to meet government regulations.

Lahaina Scrimshaw, in Lahaina and Kā'anapali, features not only a wide selection of scrimshaw, but also Oriental carvings and jewelry. **The Whaler's Locker** on Front Street also carries scrimshaw pieces.

ART

Maui has slowly become one of the major centers of art in Hawai'i. Many artists live here either part-time or year-round, and more and more are achieving international recognition while showing a fierce loyalty to the Hawaiian Islands.

The list begins with internationally recognized nature artist and Maui resident **Robert Lyn Nelson** and his paintings of two worlds--above and below the surface of the sea. You'll pass his showroom driving from Lahaina into Kā'anapali, on the *mauka* (mountain) side of the highway. Paris-born **Guy Buffet**, an impressionistic artist in a primitive setting, has had an ongoing love affair with Hawai'i that keeps him living and working on Maui part of the year, and selling internationally. **Curtis Wilson Cost** is an accomplished traditionalist painter and Kula resident, whose detailed landscapes of Maui's lush Upcountry pastures and rural beaches may be viewed at his gallery, located at the Kula Lodge.

The list continues: **Hisashi Otsuka** does spectacular work based on classical Japanese art; **Lau Chun's** impressionist paintings are a mainstay of the Maui scene; China-born **H. Leung,** also lives and paints on Maui; **George Allan** masterfully paints Lahaina scenes with his expert use of light and color; **Chris Lassen** turns the underwater world into a fantasy paradise, and his artwork is recognized worldwide--he has three galleries on Maui; **Mark MacKay** captures Hawai'i's marine life with incredible realism and painstaking detail; **Gary Swanson,** a foremost wildlife painter, portrays cats from all over the world; and **Andrew Annenberg's** works are hung in prized collections around the world.

Well-known artist and Honolulu resident **Pegge Hopper** is famous for her colorful native Hawaiian women posing in serene settings, and exhibits on Maui. **Margaret Keane's** wide-eyed children can be found at many shops. Maui resident **Sherri Reeve,** best known for colorful tropical fish and flowers painted in her trademark "splattered" style, exhibits her work at the Dolphin Galleries. Hawai'i artist, **Wyland,** whose "Whaling Walls" and marine mammal artwork have brought him worldwide attention, has four galleries on Maui.

There are as many galleries as artists in this hub of the island art scene. **Lahaina Galleries,** one of the oldest, has several locations, including Lahaina Cannery Mall, Whalers Village, and the Grand Wailea Resort. **The Village Galleries** has three West Maui locations, at 120 Dickenson Street in Lahaina, Lahaina Cannery Mall and the Ritz-Carlton Kapalua, featuring art from both mainland and Hawai'i artists. **Dolphin Galleries** has a lovely store at Whalers Village, as well as one at the Grand Wailea. A contemporary art gallery at 505 Front Street, **New York-Paris Collectible Art** has an exciting collection of museum-authorized limited edition "artagraphs", as well as a fine gift shop.

The small **Curtis Wilson Cost Gallery** in Upcountry's Kula Lodge handles only the artist's own works. **Larry Dotson Galleries** at the Pioneer Inn in Lahaina, features the owner's sculpture and seascapes. **Coast Gallery** at the Maui Inter-Continental in Wailea handles original art by local artists.

In Wailuku, you'll find the **Jovian Gallery,** on Market Street, which features paintings, sculpture and jewelry of Hawai'i artists, as well as greeting

SHOPPING

129

cards, unique gifts and paper products. In the small town of Kahakuloa, on the less-travelled side of West Maui, between Lahaina and Wailuku, is the **Kaukini Ranch Gallery and Gift Shop.** Here, truly off the beaten path, you'll find fine art paintings by local artists, handwoven baskets, and unique gifts. (Note: The road around this western side of the island used to be rough, but has now been fully paved.)

Viewpoints fine arts gallery on Baldwin Avenue in Makawao is owned an operated by Maui artists and features a wide selection of paintings, including those of George Allan. Also located in Makawao, is the non-profit **Hui No'eau Visual Arts Center,** which occupies a lovely nine-acre estate (Kaluanui) on Baldwin Avenue, with ongoing art exhibits featuring works of both international and local artists, and a small gift shop. In Hāna, the **Hana Coast Gallery,** at the Hotel Hāna-Maui, exhibits a fine showcase of original island art, sculpture and mastercrafts.

HANDCRAFTS

Hawaiians traditionally wove and plaited the leaves of *hala,* or pandanus *(lauhala)* into all manner of useful items including floor mats and baskets; today the range has been expanded to include handbags, lamp shades, placements and much more. Similar items are made in *tapa* (bark cloth), but this is not the traditional Hawaiian *kapa,* as the art of making the fine felt-like material the Hawaiians produced (the finest in all Polynesia) was lost generations ago. The *tapa* you buy here is, however, authentic; it is produced by hand using the ancient methods in Sāmoa, Tonga and Fiji.

Another traditional craft still very much alive and thriving is the making of permanent leis. These were and are made from feathers, seeds and shells. Ni'ihau shell leis now command hefty prices (see Jewelry above), but attractive strands of other local shells are quite reasonably priced. Feather leis are a bit more expensive, but require much more time and care in the making as well as more material. Feather neck and head leis were traditionally worn by the ali'i, as were *lei niho palaoa,* hook-shaped pendants, originally made of whale ivory. Later made of wood or stone--or of walrus tusk or beef bone brought by merchant sailors--these hook-shaped pendants became so popular that virtually everyone wore them.

Woodcarving, too, has expanded far beyond its traditional application in creating *akua ki'i,* images representing gods. Indigenous woods such as koa, milo and monkeypod are carved into decorative bowls and utensils. You can also buy modern renditions of ancient gods, as well as more mundane figures such as fish and pineapples.

Most of these crafts can be found at gift stores all over Maui. On your way into Pāia, on the *makai* side of Hāna Highway, you'll find the **Maui Crafts Guild,** a co-op of Maui artisans, offering some of the best selections of woodwork, jewelry, baskets, glass items, ceramics and clothing you'll find on the island.

SOUVENIRS

In addition to hotel shops and department stores, many Hawaiian gift and souvenir items can be found at the ubiquitous **ABC Discount Stores.** They have eight locations on Maui: five in Lahaina, one each in Kīhei, Honokōwai, and Kā'anapali. In Kihei Town Center, **Hawaiian Etc** also carries the souvenirs visitors want to take home for gifts. Reasonably priced souvenirs and gift items can also be found at **Longs Drug Store** (Kīhei, Kahului, and Lahaina), and **K-Mart** (Kahului). **Whaler's General Stores** have seven locations

on Maui, in Kīhei, Lahaina, Kā'anapali and Honokōwai. Also, the various hotel lobby shops--**Leisure Sundries,** Maui Prince Hotel; **Traders** and **Whaler's Chest,** Royal Lahaina Resort; **South Pacific Gifts & Sundries,** the Westin Maui and Hyatt Regency; **W H Smith,** Stouffer Wailea Beach Resort; and **Lamont's,** Four Seasons Resort Wailea, Embassy Suites, and Ritz-Carlton Kapalua.

Another one-stop gift shop with hundreds of knickknacks to choose from is **O'Rourke's Tourist Trap,** with three locations, in Kīhei and Kahana.

SHELLS

Tropical shells are a popular souvenir item for visitors, but few are found on Maui's accessible beaches. However, numerous shops carry such shells, as well as an incredible potpourri of decorative items made

from them. **La Pre Shell & Gift Shop,** in Kihei's Azeka Place II, has decorative and specimen shells, coral and jewelry. **Jane's Shells & Craft** in Pā'ia and **Lahaina Shell Shop** are other alternatives.

FRUIT, FLOWERS and FOLIAGE

Cuttings and seeds of tropical plants provide a living reminder of a colorful Hawaiian holiday, and fresh fruits or flower leis make delightful gifts for presenting to friends back home. Shipping is easily arranged; many vendors will handle it for you. Some fruits and flowers are subject to quarantine regulations imposed by the U.S. Department of Agriculture and are prohibited entry into mainland states.

Pineapples are no problem, but the only papayas allowed are those treated, passed and sealed by agricultural inspectors. Only the frozen flesh of mangoes is allowed; the seeds are forbidden unless they are split open and inspected.

Guavas and passionfruit *(liliko'i)* are not allowed at all. Coconuts are fine and fun. Don't bother packing them; just buy them (or pick them up off the ground in an area where the trees remain untrimmed) still in the outer husk. This is excellent natural packing and has served to float coconuts for thousands of miles across open oceans to be dashed by waves, unharmed, upon foreign shores. Not only that, they survive the rough handling of the U. S. Postal Service. Just write the address on the coconut itself--unwrapped--and paste on the necessary postage stamps. The post office actually accepts these unorthodox parcels.

Airport Flower & Fruit Inc., three

minutes from Kahului Airport, sells fruit that has been treated and passed by agricultural inspectors. They will deliver them to the airport with pre-payment. **Take Home Maui, Inc.** on Dickenson Street in Lahaina, is another good source for pineapples, papayas and Maui onions, offering free airport and hotel delivery.

One of Maui's prized flowers is the protea, transplanted from Australia and South Africa and exotic in its many different shapes and colors. **Clouds Rest Protea** in Kula allows visitors to walk through the gardens, and can arrange the shipping of plants and blossoms. **The Protea Gift Shoppe** at Kula Lodge is a charming store that features dried protea wreaths, baskets, craft items and Hawaiiana gifts, and can pack and ship their lovely protea or tropical arrangements directly after harvesting. In the Wailuku area, the **Plantation Marketplace** in Maui Tropical Plantation sells many unique gift items, most of which are edible:

pineapples, papayas, macadamia nuts, and a unique blend of Maui coffee sold exclusively at that location. **Hana Gardenland,** Maui's oldest certified nursery, located in Hāna, will ship orchids, anthuriums, plants and other tropical cut flowers nationwide.

Maui Blooms, located at the Kihei Commercial Center, features handcrafted island baskets, protea wreaths and arrangements, and tropical flowers, which can be boxed up to carry on the plane or shipped direct.

Be cautious when buying leis to take home. Flowers such as roses, *maunaloa* and jade, berries such as mock orange and *mokihana*, and leaves such as *hala* and *kikuyu* are prohibited and leis containing them will be confiscated. If you're leaving the country, you can take whatever you like, but there's no guarantee of its passing quarantine inspection in your country of arrival.

BOOKS

At the back of this guide, we have listed books we recommend for more detailed information on Hawai'i. Most of these are easy to find in our local bookstores, but may be not so easy to find at home. Books are one of the surest ways to take a perma-nent remembrance of Hawai'i home with you. The huge mainland chain, **Waldenbooks,** has five shops on the island: two outlets in Kahului, one each in Kihei, Lahaina and Kā'ana-

pali. In addition to books, all stores carry a good variety of calendars, magazines, videocassettes, newspa-pers and other paper products.

Miracles Bookery Too in Maka-wao offers an excellent assortment of New Age and self-discovery books, tapes and CD's, videos, incense, cards and gifts. **The Whaler's Book Shoppe** at Wharf Cinema Shops in Lahaina has a substantial Hawaiiana book selection.

GROCERIES

Those visitors with kitchen facilities may not choose to eat out for every meal. Local supermarkets

carry most of the standard items that you're used to, and a lot more, including large sections of Oriental food items. Some visitors find a tour of the large grocery stores an amazing experience, especially in the produce department where you may see a number of things you don't recognize.

Grocery stores include: **Foodland**, with three locations (Kahului, Lahaina, and Pukalani); **Safeway**, in Kahului and Lahaina; **Star Markets**, in Kahului and Kīhei; **Pukalani** **Superette** in Pukalani; **Hāna Ranch Store** in Hāna; and **Ooka Super Market** in Wailuku. **Nagasako Super Market** in Lahaina offers a variety of local foods, as does **Ah Fook's Super Market** in Kahului. Located in Wailea Village, **Wailea Pantry** carries gift and beach items in addition to food and beverages. If you are staying in the Kahana area, the **Honokowai Food Pantry** services this area.

CONVENIENCE STORES

Operating twenty-four hours a day, the two **7-Eleven** stores on the island are located in Kīhei and Kahului. Keeping the same hours are the **Minit Stop** stores, situated in Kahului, Wailuku, Pukalani and Pā'ia.

In Lahaina, **Whalers General Stores** have five locations. **Wailea Pantry** operates out of Wailea Village, and **ABC Discount Stores** have five shops in Lahaina, plus one each in Kīhei, Honokōwai, and Kā'anapali.

HEALTH FOOD STORES

Down to Earth Natural Foods is an excellent natural foods and organic produce market, with two locations on Maui, one in Wailuku and one in Makawao. **Mana Foods** is another very good source for health-oriented products, foods, vitamins and organically grown produce, and is located on Pā'ia's Baldwin Avenue.

In Wailuku, **Herbs Etc** offers a complete line of herbs, teas and vitamins. **Hawaiian Moons Natural Foods** services the Kīhei area, and **Haiku Natural Foods**, on the corner of Kokomo and Ha'iku Road, services the Ha'iku area. **Maui Natural Foods** has a nice selection of vitamins, herbs, skin care products, organic foods and teas.

The Vegan, a small restaurant located in Pā'ia, caters to the health-conscious, featuring freshly prepared vegetarian (vegan) cuisine. Lunch and dinner are served Tuesday through Saturday, and prices are reasonable. The menu includes international hot entrees, sandwiches and salads.

DRUGSTORES

There are plenty of drugstores on Maui, enough to meet the needs of both residents and visitors. By area, they include: Lahaina--**Longs Drug Stores** at Lahaina Cannery Center, and **Lahaina Pharmacy** at Lahaina Shopping Center; Kīhei--**Kihei Professional Pharmacy** at Lipoa Center, and **Longs Drug Stores** on South Kīhei Road; Upcountry--**Paradise Pharmacy** in Makawao, and **Pukalani Drugs** in Foodland at Pukalani

Terrace Center; and Central Valley, **Valley Isle Pharmacy** at 2180 Main Street in Wailuku, and **Longs Drug Stores** at the Maui Mall in Kahului.

MISCELLANEOUS

For film processing, **Fox Photo** has one-hour processing, with locations in Lahaina, Kā'anapali, Kīhei and Wailea. **Longs Drug Stores** also has film processing and photographic equipment at their stores in Kahului, Kīhei and Lahaina. **Maui 60 Minute Color Photos** in Maui Mall, Kahului, and **One Hour Moto Photo,** at the Westin Maui in Kā'anapali, also offer one-hour film developing.

Mark's Hallmark Shop in Kaahumanu Center carries gifts and greeting cards. **Hopaco Stationers** on the Hāna Highway in Kahului also has a selection of cards, and is known for their office supplies.

One of the many colorful and exotic variations of protea

DINING

The Best Restaurants
Fast Foods
Special Foods
Island Fish Guide

FINE and FUN DINING

Maui's restaurants satisfy any taste, budget and mood. From lavishly prepared French cuisine to exotic Asian dishes to the best in Hawaii Regional cooking, the dining experience on Maui is as fine as that offered in any resort area in the world. Whether you wish to dine beachfront at Kā'anapali, join the young and young-at-heart crowd at an energetic Front Street bistro, enjoy elegant fine dining in a posh Wailea resort, or escape for a romantic meal at a cozy Upcountry establishment, it is the variety in Maui restaurants that makes dining here a joy.

THE BEST RESTAURANTS ON MAUI

A selection of choice dining establishments is listed here, arranged by regions of the island. A complete list is included as an appendix at the back of this book. Fast food restaurants are listed towards the end of this section.

The following symbols will assist you in choosing a restaurant to suit your requirements, taste and budget.

Price ranges indicated are per person and do not include drinks. Many of the restaurants on the island accept major credit cards.

B	Breakfast	$$$$	$40 +
L	Lunch	$$$	$30-$40
D	Dinner	$$	$15-$30
R	Reservations suggested	$	$10-$15
E	Entertainment	No $	Less than $10
W	Wheelchair access		

The following criteria were used in evaluating the quality of the restaurants listed in this section:

- taste, texture and presentation of food

- attentiveness and demeanor of service staff

- price in relation to food

- appropriateness of menu selections

- decor and lighting

- building and setting

- ambiance and decor

Lahaina/Kā'anapali/Kapalua Area Restaurants

Avalon $-$$$ L, D, R   667-5999

Situated in its own intimate courtyard set back from the bustle of Front Street, this casual restaurant is stylishly furnished with bright, tropical decor and original island artwork. The menu features Hawaiian Regional Cuisine, beautifully presented and prepared with the freshest of ingredients, under the meticulous direction of talented chef/owner Mark Ellman. Entrees (quite a few of which are flagged with a "healthy heart" symbol) include grilled "pina colada chicken", chili-seared salmon, Avalon's Sicilian pasta, and fresh island fish. Vegetarian dishes include grilled eggplant salad with goat cheese lau lau, Chinese tofu salad and stir-fried vegetables and tofu. The dessert menu offers such teasers as Hawaiian chocolate torte and lilikoi cheesecake. Chef Ellman's signature dessert is "caramel Miranda", a house-made caramel sauce with tropical fruits and berries served hot over macadamia nut ice cream. Open daily from 11:30 a.m. to 10:00 p.m. Non-smoking environment. Reservations suggested for dinner. *844 Front Street, Lahaina*

BJ's Chicago Pizzeria $/$$ L, D, E   661-0700

This casual restaurant and bar opened in the summer of 1994, and is part of a Southern California restaurant chain. Situated in a prime second-story location overlooking Front Street, it offers great ocean views. The decor was carefully selected to capture the ambiance of old Hawaii, with walls full of historical photos of Maui, a 46-foot-long hand-painted mural and a bar replicating an Upcountry water tank. One wall contains airplane memorabilia from the restaurant's former incarnation as The Blue Max, a popular bar/eatery that was a Lahaina fixture for years. Its deep-dish pizza, offered in three sizes with your choice of more than a dozen toppings, has received rave reviews from numerous food critics. The menu also features a selection of homemade sandwiches (grilled chicken breast, roast beef, Italian link sausage), pasta dishes (lasagne, fettucini, spaghetti), specialty salads (Caesar, antipasto, Greek) and soups. For dessert, choose a light sorbet or a decadent "pizookie 'n cream", a freshly baked cookie served with vanilla ice cream and toppings. Good selection of imported and domestic beers, as well as a small, moderately priced wine list. Open daily from 11:00 a.m. to 11:00 p.m. *730 Front St., Lahaina*

Blue Tropix Restaurant/Night Club $/$$ D, R, E   667-5309

This is a popular Lahaina dining and dancing hotspot, situated in an excellent oceanfront location, upstairs overlooking Front Street. An *a la carte* menu features tasty appetizers such as Tropix potstickers with plum wine ginger sauce, and seared ahi with lime ginger miso sauce, as well as entrees such as pan-fried lasagna, tequila roasted lamb, fresh catch-of-the- day, and grilled tenderloin of beef with roasted garlic Cabernet sauce. Gourmet pizza selections include interesting toppings such as grilled chicken, sashimi, and shiitaki mushrooms with roasted shallots. By 9:00 or 10:00 p.m., the place is usually hopping. Dinner is served nightly 7:00 p.m. til 1:00 a.m., with dancing until 2:00 a.m. Cover charge after 9:00 p.m. *900 Front Street, Lahaina*

DINING

Casa de Mateo $/$$ L,D,E   661-6700

For authentic and delicious Mexican cuisine, this place is hard to beat. Appetizers include guacamole and ceviche (marinated raw fish), prepared at the table. Entrees are made fresh, served in generous portions and include camarones al ajo (fresh shrimp sauteed in garlic butter), burritos Oaxaquenos, pescado Veracruzano (red snapper in garlic and Mexican spices) and chicken or vegetarian enchiladas. Open daily from 11:00 a.m. to 11:00 p.m. Live reggae music on Sundays and Mondays from 11:00 p.m. to 2:00 a.m. Tuesdays: DJ Latin salsa. *505 Front Street, Lahaina*

Chart House $$ D, R   661-0937

This well-established Lahaina restaurant has three locations on Maui, each serving consistently good American-style food. The Lahaina site is attractively decorated with natural woods and lava rock, and some tables offer nice ocean views, with Lāna'i and Moloka'i in the distance. Entrees include steaks, prime rib, chicken, seafood and fresh island fish, all accompanied by two kinds of warm bread (sourdough and squaw), rice, and an impressive all-you-can-eat salad bar. For dessert, try mud pie, served in slices large enough for several persons to share. A children's menu is available and reasonably priced. Other Maui locations: Kahului and Wailea. Open daily from 5:00 to 10:00 p.m. *1450 Front St., Lahaina*

Cheeseburger in Paradise $ and less   L,D,E   661-4855

This casual open-air restaurant affords great harbor and ocean views from its two-story Front Street location. Its menu is American cuisine, featuring a variety of tasty French fries, and burgers such as the signature Cheeseburger in Paradise, tofu burger, and Garden burger. Other offerings include Polynesian shrimp and fries, "ono" onion rings, calamari rings and Upcountry salad. They also serve tropical drinks and claim to have "the coldest beer in town". Live music at sunset and into the evening. Open daily, 11:00 a.m. to 11:00 p.m. *811 Front St., Lahaina*

Chez Paul $$/$$$ D, R   661-3843

The best things in life are often found where you least expect them. Tucked away next to the main highway, just five miles south of Lahaina, this unpretentious establishment has been open on Maui since 1979, and has the distinction of being Hawai'i's oldest French restaurant. Over the years, it has continued to receive recognition as one of Maui's top dining spots, and has won numerous awards. Entrees are accompanied by two vegetables, soup or salad, and French bread. The wine list is excellent, and desserts are irresistible. Two seatings are available nightly, at 6:30 and 8:30 p.m. Reservations are required. Closed Sundays from May to November. *820-B Olowalu Village*

David Paul's Lahaina Grill $$/$$$ D, R   667-5117

Voted "Best Restaurant on Maui" in 1994 by readers of *Honolulu Magazine*, this stylish restaurant is located in the cozy Lahaina Hotel just off Front Street. Chef/owner David Paul Johnson has dubbed his culinary style "New American Cuisine", and many of his dishes flaunt the spicy taste of Southwestern cooking. His menu is creative, with entrees changing regularly. Tequila shrimp is his signature dish, served with red chili-spiced firecracker rice. Other specialties include grilled fresh local seafood, Kona coffee roasted lamb, and fried maki sushi. Spicy crab cakes, made with Dungeness crab, chili peppers and capellini pasta, are a tasty appetizer. Turn-of-the-century decor and an intimate bar create an airy cafe atmosphere. Dinner served nightly from 6:00 p.m. *127 Lahainaluna Road, Lahaina*

The Garden Restaurant $$-$$$$ B, D, R   669-5656

This lovely restaurant features fine al fresco dining accompanied by meandering streams and panoramic views of the Pacific Ocean. The *a la carte* menu offers well-prepared regional, American and Continental cuisine, and varies seasonally. A sumptuous seafood buffet is featured on Fridays, and a brunch buffet is offered on Sundays. Cost-conscious diners can take advantage of the "earlybird" special on Friday nights, offered between 5:30 and 6:00 p.m. Excellent wine list and service. Open from 6:00 to 10:00 p.m. Wednesday, Thursday and Saturday, and from 5:30 to 9:30 p.m. on Friday, with brunch available on Sunday from 9:30 a.m. to 1:30 p.m. Reservations suggested. *Kapalua Bay Hotel and Villas, Kapalua*

Gerard's $$/$$$ D, E, R   661-8939

This enchanting French restaurant is unequivocally one of the top restaurants in Hawai'i. Located just a short block away from Front Street, on the first floor of the Plantation Inn, it could easily be mistaken for an intimate country cafe, perhaps in the wine country of France. Since opening on Maui in 1982, its success can primarily be attributed to chef/owner Gerard Reversade's meticulous attention to each detail of food preparation and presentation. The wine list here was honored by the *Wine Spectator* as one of the world's most outstanding. The menu offers such specialties as quail stuffed with basmati rice, grilled rack of lamb with persillade crust, and opakapaka roasted with Hawaiian peppers. Appetizers, soups and salads are equally as pleasing to the palate, all made with the freshest ingredients. For dessert, try the creme brulee, their signature dessert. Mellow guitar music sets a soothing mood. The waiters are attentive and friendly, offering superb service in the polished European tradition. Dinner served nightly from 6:00 to 10:00 p.m. Reservations recommended. *Plantation Inn, 174 Lahainaluna Road, Lahaina*

The Grill $$$/$$$$ D,R,E   669-1665

Located at the posh Ritz-Carlton Kapalua, this lovely dining spot features island cuisine on the lighter side. Chefs Patrick Callarec and Jeff Vigilla have teamed up to present one of Maui's most unique dining experiences. Menu items are accented by fresh herbs and Upcountry Maui-grown vegetables, including such dishes as ahi and kajiki tempura with spicy eggplant poki, rack of lamb with paniolo barbecue sauce, and grilled Kohala Coast lobster. Dinner served Monday through Saturday from 6:00 to 9:30 p.m. *Ritz-Carlton Kapalua, 1 Ritz-Carlton Drive*

Hard Rock Cafe $ and less   L,D   667-7400

Situated right on Front Street, this popular rock 'n' roll memorabilia-filled cafe serves up a wide and reasonably priced selection of American-style food in a high-decibel, pulsating setting. Ask for their free brochure, which identifies the rock 'n' roll artifacts gracing the walls throughout. The menu features baby rock watermelon barbecue ribs, lime barbecue chicken, Maui burgers with sauteed Maui onions, and Mexican fajitas. For dessert, try the homemade fudge brownies. Their logo T-shirts and other souvenir items are coveted by HRC visitors from near and far. Note: This place can get crowded, so either go during off-peak times or anticipate a wait. Open daily from 11:00 a.m. *Lahaina Center, 900 Front St., Lahaina*

Hula Grill $/$$ L,D,R   661-3894

This attractive oceanfront restaurant opened at Whaler's Village in June of 1994, and is situated in an exclusive Kā'anapali Beach location. An interesting assortment of authentic Hawaiian artifacts creates a casual atmosphere reminiscent of Maui in the '30s, featuring an extensive ceramic hula doll collection in lighted display cases, a 19th-century koa outrigger canoe, and framed vintage Hawaiian song sheets. Operating partner and renowned Big Island chef Peter Merriman created an excellent menu specializing in what he calls "Hawaiian Home Cooking", each dish prepared with an artful blending of spices, sauces and mostly Maui-grown ingredients. Meals begin with a delicious focaccia bread, which may be dipped in your choice of olive oil or a mild chile pepper oil. Fresh island fish grilled over a *kiawe* wood barbecue is the specialty, and includes such creations as wok charred ahi, grilled ono with pineapple and Maui onion salsa, and firecracker mahimahi. Other entrees include Hawaiian seafood gumbo, herb-grilled New York steak, and grilled free-range chicken breast. Creative appetizers, generously-sized salads, delicious desserts and gourmet coffees round out the menu. Their Barefoot Bar is right on the sand, offering a nice selection of pupus, salads and pizza, and is a great place enjoy a cool drink, and watch the sun go down. Open daily 11:00 a.m. to 12:00 midnight. Dinner from 5:00 until 10:00 p.m. Inquire about excursions aboard their own catamaran, anchored offshore. *Whalers Village, Kā'anapali*

Kapalua Bay Club $$/$$ L,D,E,R 669-5656, 669-8008

A popular tropical restaurant atop a lava rock promontory fronting Kapalua Bay, this elegant establishment offers a spectacular ocean view and relaxing atmosphere. The food is excellently prepared in the international culinary style called "nouvelle cuisine". Specialties include sauteed breast of duck, fresh fish with artichokes and shiitake mushrooms, sauteed sea scallops, and roasted veal chops. For dessert, try their chocolate, macadamia nut, and caramel flan. Lunch features a generous salad bar, as well as sandwiches and seafood dishes. Live piano music accompanies dinner. Fine wine list. Reservations suggested. *1 Bay Drive, Kapalua Bay Hotel & Villas, Kapalua*

Kapalua Grill and Bar $/$$ L,D,R 669-5653

This informal, attractively decorated Kapalua restaurant serves excellent food in a beautiful setting, with golf course and ocean views. An interesting menu features entrees with a Pacific Rim flair, such as duck with Szechuan peppercorn sauce, shrimp and scallops linguine, and fresh grilled island fish. Start your meal with J.J.'s baked artichoke, their signature appetizer, and you won't be disappointed. Hula Pie is the popular choice for dessert. Excellent wine list. Dinner reservations suggested. *Kapalua Bay Hotel & Villas, Kapalua*

Kimo's $/$$ L,D,E 661-4811

Situated right on the water on Front Street, this bar and eatery has been a Maui favorite for over sixteen years. Its consistently good food, attentive service, modest prices and superb location are the secret to its success. Lunch offers sandwiches, salads and burgers; dinner selections include fresh fish-of-the-day, prime rib, and Koloa ribs. Dinner entrees are served with Caesar salad, rice and home-baked muffins and rolls. For children, there is a *keiki* menu. Hawaiian music is featured at sunset Wednesday through Sunday, making it an ideal spot to enjoy a cocktail at sundown. Open daily, with lunch served from 11:30 a.m. to 2:30 p.m., dinner from 5:00 to 10:30 p.m. The bar closes at 1:00 a.m. *845 Front St., Lahaina*

Kobe Japanese Steak House $/$$ D,R 667-5555

The theme of this restaurant is that of a Japanese country inn, with an interesting decor which includes such authentic items as a 300-year-old fisherman's kimono, Emperor dolls and other Japanese artifacts. Teppanyaki-style cooking is the featured cuisine. Knife-wielding chefs trained in this ancient Japanese art prepare and cook the meal with great showmanship and flair on teppan (grill) tables. Your choice of fourteen entrees includes steaks, chicken and seafood dishes, each accompanied by a shrimp appetizer, miso or mushroom soup, teppan vegetables, rice and hot tea. A two-entree children's menu is also available, as well as a first-rate sushi bar. Open nightly, serving cocktails from 5:00 p.m., dinner from 5:30, with reduced-price "earlybird" specials offered between 5:30 and 6:30 p.m. *136 Dickenson St., (behind Baldwin Home) Lahaina*

La Tasca Nouveau Bistro $$ L, D, E   661-5700

Situated in Lahaina Center, this white-tiled Mediterranean-style bistro combines European cooking with healthy American cuisine. The extensive menu offers hot and cold *tapas* (appetizers), salads and unique dishes representative of France, Italy, Greece and Spain. Entrees include crispy confit of duck, paella, osso bucco, peppered steak, fresh lobster, and rack of lamb. Appetizers include pate campagne, dolmas, calamares fritas and ceviche. Lunch: Monday through Friday, 11:30 a.m. - 2:30 p.m. Dinner: Monday through Sunday, 5:30 - 10:00 p.m. Flamenco guitar music Sunday through Tuesday from 7:30 p.m. *900 Front St., Lahaina Center, Lahaina*

Lahaina Coolers $ and less   B,L,D   661-7082

This is the place to go if you want to relax and take a refreshing break from the Front Street crowds. Their motto is "...because life is too short to eat boring food!" Located just two blocks off Front Street in Dickenson Square, this is an attractive cafe with bright, fresh decor offering both indoor and al fresco dining. The decidedly "un-boring" breakfast menu features a plentiful selection of reasonably priced omelettes, four kinds of eggs Benedict dishes, pancakes, breads and fruits, with a few appetizing vegetarian dishes. For lunch and dinner, an interesting array of international selections is offered, such as Moroccan chicken spinach enchiladas, shrimp pesto linguini, 'Evil Jungle' pasta, fish tacos, curried prawn pizza and zebra ravioli with gorgonzola cream sauce. Open seven days a week. Breakfast: 7:00-11:15 a.m. (til noon on Sundays). Lunch: 11:30 a.m.-5:00 p.m. (from 12:15 p.m. on Sundays). Dinner: 5:00 p.m.-midnight. *180 Dickenson Street, Lahaina*

Leilani's $/$$ L,D   264-4495

Beachfront at Whalers Village Shopping Center, this restaurant is an ideal place to watch sunset while enjoying a nice selection of American cuisine including seafood, chicken and burgers. Their *kiawe* wood smoker ovens, roasting ovens and lava rock broilers lend interesting flavors to meat and chicken dishes. Menu items include smoked pork ribs, barbecued chicken, filet mignon, and a variety of fresh local seafood. A modestly priced children's menu offers burgers, ribs and chicken. Their "Beachside Grill" has a casual mini-menu featuring pupus, salads, burgers, sandwiches and local plate lunches. Lunch: Daily, 11:30 a.m.-4:00 p.m. Dinner: Daily 4-10:30 p.m. *Whalers Village Shopping Center, Kā'anapali*

Longhi's $/$$ B,L,D,E   667-2288

This attractive and airy restaurant has been a fixture on Maui's dining scene for more than 18 years, and features Continental and Italian fare. Entrees include shrimp Longhi, prawns Amaretto, chicken Marsala, and lobster and chicken cannelloni. Upstairs is a traditional dining room; downstairs is a bright and casual bistro-like area open to the sidewalk. Waiters recite a lengthy or *ala la carte* menu. Extensive award-winning wine list. Entertainment Friday and Saturday. *888 Front Street, Lahaina*

Old Lahaina Cafe and Luau $/$$ B,L,D,R,E   661-3303

This charming cafe is situated oceanfront in Lahaina, with a casual and refreshing ambiance that captures the spirit of the islands. Breakfast and lunch are modestly priced, with all entrees under $10. Breakfast features such savory fare as banana, macadamia nut or papaya pancakes, Portuguese or luau omelettes, Moloka'i French toast and Anahola granola (made on Kauai). The lunch menu include burgers, sandwiches, salads and local-style plate lunches such as kalua pig and teriyaki steak. Dinner continues in the local tradition, offering a Hawaiian sampler plate, Kalbi ribs, chow fun, and fresh grilled fish, among others. Their authentic beachside luau is held Tuesday through Sunday from 5:30 p.m. (see ENTERTAINMENT for further details). *505 Front St., Lahaina*

Pacific 'O   L-$ and less; D-$$ L,D,R,E   667-4341

Featuring contemporary Pacific cuisine, this stylish oceanfront restaurant offers a first-rate dining experience. Most lunch entrees are under $10, with interesting dishes such as penne pasta with smoked spicy shrimps, shrimp and goat cheese pizza, grilled chicken oriental salad, and chicken and shrimp sate. Dinner fare includes seared fish-of-the-day, lobster and papaya salad, fresh ahi tempura, Peking duck, sesame crust lamb and Hawaiian chicken Cordonbleu. For starters, try their award-winning shrimp won tons. Live jazz-by-the-sea on Thursday, Friday and Saturday. Open daily from 11:00 a.m. to 12:00 p.m. Appetizers and desserts served until midnight. *505 Front St., Lahaina*

Pineapple Hill $-$$$ D,R   669-6129

Fine dining in an old plantation house, with artifacts and antiques of Maui's bygone plantation era. The Continental menu features a wide range of selections including filet mignon, marinated rack of baby lamb, prime rib, Hawaiian lobster tail, chicken Pineapple Hill Polynesian, and prawns Tahitian. For dessert, their specialty is baked papaya Tahitian, with coconut milk. Good sunset view, with expansive vistas of Moloka'i and Lāna'i. Cocktails served from 4:30 p.m., with dinner served from 5:00 p.m. *1000 Kapalua Dr., Kapalua*

Planet Hollywood $ and less   L,D   667-7877

This high-energy Front Street eatery is the twelfth member of a popular Hollywood-inspired and celebrity-owned restaurant chain. Opened in 1994, the restaurant's trademark decor consists of movie and television memorabilia, including Tom Selleck's Hawaiian shirt from "Magnum P.I.", Patrick Swayze's surfboard from "Point Break" and a 5-foot model whale from "Free Willy". The menu features California cuisine, offering a wide selection of foods, such as turkey burgers, Hawaiian pizza, Mexican fajitas, as well as salads, pasta, grilled fresh fish and meats, sandwiches and decadent desserts. Guests can enjoy previewing up-and-coming movie trailers or watch custom-designed videos from their dining table. Their logo shop carries a full line of Planet Hollywood merchandise, including T-shirts, sweat shirts, beach towels and varsity jackets. Open daily from 11:00 a.m. until 1:00 a.m. *744 Front St., Lahaina*

The Plantation House $$/$$$ B,L,D   669-6299

Located in the Plantation Golf Course clubhouse at Kapalua, this fine restaurant has a Mediterranean influence. Chef Alex Stanislaw offers such creative dishes as honey-guava scallops, Pacific lamb salad, ahi carpaccio (a sashimi style appetizer), schicimi-crusted island snapper in black bean sauce, and pan-seared duck served with a Cabernet-citrus sauce. For dessert, try the rich *pot de creme au chocolate*. Breakfast and lunch served daily from 8:00 a.m. to 3:00 p.m. Dinner served from 6:00 to 10:00 p.m. Reservations suggested. Note: This is a good vantage point from which to watch sunset.
2000 Plantation Club Dr., Kapalua

Roy's Kahana Bar & Grill $$/$$$ D   669-6999
Roy's Nicolina Restaurant $/$$ D   669-5000

Award-winning owner/chef Roy Yamaguchi's side-by-side restaurants in Kahana offer exciting menus featuring Euro-Asian and Hawaiian Regional cuisine, with specials changing nightly. Roy's was rated the "best overall Maui restaurant" in 1992-'93 by *The Maui News,* and was listed among Hawai'i's "Top 20" restaurants from 1989 to 1992 by *Honolulu Magazine.* International specialties include grilled Szechuan-style baby-back pork ribs, Mongolian grilled pork loin, Asian vegetarian stir fry, ravioli of shiitake and spinach, and island-style potstickers with spicy miso sauce. Dishes are beautifully presented and made with the finest fresh local ingredients. *Kahana Gateway Shopping Center, 4405 Honoapiilani Hwy., Kahana*

Sound of the Falls $$-$$$$ D, R   667-2525

This lovely open-air restaurant exudes an aura of romance, offering guests stunning ocean and sunset views, complete with live flamingos and swan-filled lagoons. Located in the Westin Maui at Kā'anapali Beach, this "Pacific bistro" features island cuisine, its menu changing weekly. Creative appetizers include Dungeness crab with morel mushroom ravioli, and sesame seared ahi; unique salads such as shrimp and grilled papaya salad, and Hawaiian-style Caesar salad with wok-seared sashimi are favorites. Entree selections include vegetable-wrapped opakapaka, grilled Shutome swordfish, stuffed Hawaiian lobster and medallions of Chateaubriand with black truffle pate. Their Sunday champagne brunch is considered one of Maui's best. An excellent wine list and dessert menu are offered as well. Dinner served nightly (except for Thursday and Sunday) from 5:30 to 9:00 p.m. Reservations suggested. *Westin Maui, 2365 Kā'anapali Pkwy., Kā'anapali*

Swan Court $$$/$$$$ D, E, R   667-4420

Elegant and romantic, this open-air dining room is situated beside a lagoon graced by live swans and a rushing waterfall. Winner of numerous culinary awards, the menu is imaginative and varied. Entrees change frequently, with specialties such as sauteed onaga (red snapper) with oriental vegetables, Hunan marinated rack of lamb, Asian spiced duck confit, and filet mignon baked with shallots and herbs. Appetizers include such creations as lobster pot stickers, Scottish smoked salmon, tempura of ahi and Pacific shrimp. Exquisite salads and delightful desserts complement the *a la carte* menu. Stylish and sophisticated, this first-class operation continues to preserve its status as one of Maui's (and Hawai'i's) top restaurants. Open daily from 6:00 to 10:00 p.m. A lavish breakfast buffet is served daily from 7:00 a.m. *Hyatt Regency Maui, Kā'anapali Beach*

Kihei/Wailea Area Restaurants

A Pacific Cafe $/$$ D,R   879-0069   145

Chef Jean-Marie Josselin's second Hawai'i restaurant (Kapa'a, Kaua'i is his other location) offers some of the best food you'll find on Maui. European and Pacific Rim cuisine is featured on the *a la carte* menu, which changes daily. A variety of fresh locally-grown ingredients is used in each culinary delight, with fresh fish entrees the highlight of the menu. Sample menu items include: pepper-seared salmon and steamed Manila clams in shrimp-ginger broth, mahi mahi with garlic sesame crust and lime ginger sauce, and grilled Mongolian rack of lamb with Cabernet-hoisin sauce. Appetizers include tiger eye ahi sushi tempura with Chinese mustard sauce and grilled opaka nachos Asian style. Portions are generous and filling. Although the restaurant is situated in a busy shopping center, what it lacks in view is easily made up for in its excellent food, high quality service and stylish interior. Note: The structure itself is an architectural feast for the eyes, so be sure to take time to walk through the restaurant and observe the fabulous design elements. Open daily from 5:30 to 10:00 p.m. Reservations strongly suggested. 1279 So. Kihei Rd., *Azeka Phase II Shopping Center, Kihei*

Bistro Molikini $$ L,D   875-1234

This casual open-air bistro features creative Italian cuisine, on the "lite" side, and is situated overlooking the Grand Wailea's activity pool and the Pacific Ocean. Menu items include fresh fish, salads, chicken, seafood and thirteen pizza selections prepared in a wood-burning oven. A reasonably priced children's menu is also available. Open daily, serving lunch from 11:30 a.m. to 4:00 p.m., dinner from 6:00 to 10:00 p.m. The bar closes at 11:00 p.m. *Grand Wailea Resort & Spa, Wailea*

DINING

Carelli's on the Beach $/$$ D 875-0001

This attractive open-air Italian restaurant is situated oceanfront on Keawakapu beach and is beautifully decorated with large wall murals and imported Italian tile. One unique feature is Rocco's Mangia Bar, their "restaurant within a restaurant" which offers the same menu, but does not have the $25 per person minimum charge that the main restaurant requires, making it a better bet for the budget-conscious. Rocco's is also available for late-night snacks and cocktails after the main dining area has closed. Menu items include fusili pesto, Carelli's cioppino, seafood cannelone, shrimp Bob Longhi, homemade wood-fired pizza and fresh-seared ahi. For dessert, try the tiramisu, a delicious Italian dessert made with ladyfingers and mascarpone cheese. Note: Try to arrive in time to watch sunset! Open daily from 6:00 to 10:00 p.m. *Wailea Oceanfront Hotel, 2980 S. Kihei Road, Kihei*

Erik's Seafood Broiler $/$$ D,R 879-8400

As its name implies, Erik's specializes in seafood, but the menu also has a few non-seafood entrees such as filet mignon, rack of lamb and sauteed chicken breast. House specialties include seafood curry, cioppino, pasta-of-the-day and Hawaiian saltwater prawns. As many as nine local fresh fish entrees are available daily, depending on the season and the day's catch, prepared in a variety of delicious ways, such as spicy Cajun style, poached with wine and caper sauce, and broiled with tarragon herb butter. A choice of three "keiki" dinners is available for children under the age of twelve. Discounted "early-bird" specials are featured from 5:00 to 6:00 p.m. Open daily from 5:00 to 10:00 p.m. *Kamaole Shopping Center, 2463 S. Kihei Rd., Kihei*

Five Palms Beach Grill $/$$ B,L,D R 879-2607

This beachfront open-air restaurant is a delightful addition to Kihei's dining scene. Executive Chef Paul Wade brings impressive experience to the Five Palms' kitchen , having worked at some of Maui's top restaurants, including Carelli's, Seasons, and Haliimaile General Store. His culinary style is a mixture of Asian and American flavors. Breakfast offers such temptations as Hawaiian sweet bread French toast, macadamia nut and banana pancakes, and "Eggs Basque", a New Orleans-style crab cake served with two poached eggs and Creole Hollandaise sauce. Lunch fare ranges from gourmet fresh-ground hamburgers to open-face grilled fish tacos. Dinner entrees include fire-roasted rack of lamb, sizzling Thai snapper with curry-coconut sauce, oven-roasted prime rib of beef, and miso-garlic prawns, as well as fresh local fish. A creative pupu menu is available from 2:00 p.m. until closing. Open daily, serving breakfast from 8:00 to 11:00 a.m., lunch from 11:00 a.m. to 2:00 p.m., and dinner from 5:00 to 10:00 p.m. Note: this is a good place to watch a beautiful Maui sunset. *2960 S. Kihei Rd. (at the Mana Kai Resort), Kihei*

Grand Dining Room Maui $-$$$$ B,D   E,R   875-1234

This classic dining room, at the Grand Wailea Resort, offers a panoramic view of Molokini, Lāna'i, and the West Maui Mountains, and overlooks Wailea Beach. For dinner, guests choose from a four-course set menu or may order *a la carte* from "International Food Court" selections, featuring dishes from the Mediterranean, Mexico, and China. International entrees include penne rigate, risotto primavera, white bean stew, sweet and sour shrimp and scallops, and beef salad with avocado and chili chipotle. The set menu changes regularly, offering such gourmet entrees as braised Big Island salmon, herb-marinated venison loin, and roasted breast of pheasant. The Sunday champagne brunch is expensive and lavish, living up to the grandeur one would expect for the price, with numerous "stations" offering carved meats, made-to-order egg dishes, Japanese selections, antipasto, made-to-order pastas, salads, desserts and an assortment of hot entrees. Open daily, serving breakfast from 6:30 to 11:00 a.m., dinner from 6:00 to 10:00 p.m., and Sunday brunch from 9:00 a.m. to 2:00 p.m. *Grand Wailea Resort & Spa, Wailea*

Hula Moons $/$$ L,D,   E   879-1922

This casual oceanview restaurant is situated at pool level at the Maui Inter-Continental Resort, with seating available either outside or inside. Named after the title of a book published in 1930 by Hawai'i's Poet Laureate Don Blanding, the restaurant's decor contains period pieces and Blanding memorabilia. In recognition of its perpetuating the essence of Hawai'i, the Hawaii Visitor's Bureau presented Hula Moons with its coveted Kahili Award. Hawaiian entertainment and hula are featured nightly from 5:30 p.m., with a torch-lighting ceremony at sunset. The lunch menu offers healthy fare, including gourmet salads, sandwiches, pizza and pasta. Complimentary pupus are served from 5:30 to 6:30 p.m., their "sunset hour". Dinner features fresh island fish, lobster, lamb and steaks, and an excellent salad bar is included with dinner. Open daily, serving lunch from 11:00 a.m. to 5:00 p.m., and dinner from 6:00 to 10:00 p.m. *Maui Inter-Continental Resort, Wailea*

Humuhumunukunukuapua'a $$/$$$ D, R   875-1234

If you're looking for a refreshing tropical ambiance and excellent seafood, this "floating" restaurant at the Grand Wailea is the place, featuring contemporary Hawaiian cuisine. For family and on-a-budget dining, however, look elsewhere, as entrees here are expensive (the cheapest is "Ewa Chicken" @ $24). The restaurant is named after Hawai'i's official state fish, and consists of a grouping of attractive thatched-roof huts, hand-crafted from ohia and koa woods, perched over a picturesque saltwater lagoon. Specialties include fresh island fish, steak and King Crab legs, wok-fried mahimahi, and Maine or spiny lobster. Soups, salads and side dishes are available at an additional cost. Desserts are also expensive and include lychee flan, coconut creme brulee, and "Frozen Mochi Delight", their specialty. Open daily for dinner and cocktails from 5:30 to 10:00 p.m. *Grand Wailea Resort & Spa, Wailea*

DINING

147

Kea Lani Restaurant $$/$$$ B,D, R   875-4100

Fine Euro-Pacific cuisine is the culinary style of this elegant eatery at the Kea Lani Resort. The menu changes monthly, with fresh fish their specialty, prepared in such delicious variations as broiled with roasted papaya and green tomato relish, pan-seared with Dungeness crab and chow mein vegetables or grilled with lemon basil-caper butter sauce. Other entrees include lobster cioppino, vegetarian stir-fry, linguine seafood pesto and New York sirloin pepper steak. Their gourmet appetizer menu is equally as alluring, with offerings such as moo shu duck, Japanese style sashimi, and artichoke fritters. Open daily, serving breakfast from 6:30 to 11:00 a.m., and dinner from 5:30 to 10:00 p.m. *Kea Lani Resort, 4100 Wailea Alanui Drive, Wailea*

Kihei Prime Rib and Seafood House $$/$$$ D,E,R   879-1954

Offering oceanfront dining in the heart of Kihei, this attractive restaurant has a nice selection of American-style entrees. The menu includes prime rib, veal scallopini, rack of lamb, shrimp scampi, sauteed calamari filet, and fresh catch-of-the-day. The meal is accompanied by rice or pasta, fresh home-made bread, and your choice of soup or salad bar. Three wallet-friendly "early bird" specials are available nightly from 5:00 p.m. to 6:00 p.m. Piano entertainment. Open daily from 5:00 to 10:00 p.m. *2511 S. Kihei Rd. (Kai Nani Village), Kihei*

Kincha $$$$+   D,R   875-1234

Fine dining in the authentic Japanese style is offered at this elegant tea house restaurant, located at the Grand Wailea Resort, set amongst lush gardens and tranquil koi-filled ponds. The menu changes seasonally, with *a la carte* items including meat, seafood, sashimi, tempura, sushi, rice, noodles and soup dishes. A full four-course dinner is also available. Their most expensive meal is their traditional 14-course *kaiseki* dinner, with each course beautifully served in delicate handpainted trays, baskets and bowls. (Prices for the *kaiseki* dinner range from $150 to $500 per person.) There is also a sushi counter and tempura bar, each with limited seating, as well as three private tatami rooms for *kaiseki* dinners. A set children's menu runs $35 per child. With these astronomical prices, as you may have guessed, this place caters primarily to Japanese visitors. Open daily from 6:00 to 10:00 p.m. *Grand Wailea Resort & Spa, Wailea*

La Pastaria $/$$ and less   D,E   879-9001

You have to be looking for this place to find it in its tucked-away location about a block off Kihei Road. Its white tiled floors, high-beamed ceilings, and pastel color scheme give it the flavor of a San Fransciso-style bistro. The menu offers gourmet Italian fare, with a nice selection of appetizers, pizzas, calzones, fresh pasta entrees, salads, and specialty coffee drinks. It also has a full bar, and live jazz is featured nightly. Open daily from 4:00 p.m. until 1:00 a.m. Note: lunch service may be available at a future date, so call for a current update. *Lipoa Center, 41 E. Lipoa St., Kihei*

Le Gunji $$$$+   D, R   874-0500

This intimate teppanyaki restaurant is situated in a lovely garden setting, featuring French-style Japanese cuisine. A choice of several set menus (the mini-Diamond course is the least expensive) feature fresh fish, steak and lobster, and other specialties, each accompanied by an appetizer, salad, soup, rice and dessert. Prices range from $45 to $80 per person. Reservations are required and must be secured with a credit card. Two seatings are available nightly, at 6:00 and 7:30 p.m. Closed Wednesdays. *Diamond Resort, 555 Kaukahi St., Wailea*

Lobster Cove Wailea/Harry's Sushi Bar $$ D   879-7677

Whether you're in the mood for seafood or expertly prepared sushi and pupus, you can find either at these adjacent Wailea restaurants. Lobster Cove features seafood and fresh fish, offering such specialties as lobster cakes, seared black-and-blue ahi, Big Island salmon, fresh Dungeness crab, and Pacific spiny lobster. Harry's is popular with sushi-lovers, and is open daily from 5:30 p.m. until 1:00 a.m. Lobster Cove is open daily from 5:30 until 10:00 p.m. *100 Wailea Ike Dr., Wailea (next to the Chart House)*

Pacific Grill $/$$ B,L,D, R   874-8000

East meets West at this casual Four Seasons Resort restaurant, which offers all-day dining with both indoor or al fresco seating. Specialties are prepared in their Oriental exhibition kitchen, and include such Pacific Rim delicacies as Vietnamese spring rolls with peanut sauce, lamb T-bone steak with saffron basmati rice, charred duck breast with stir-fried vegetables, and lobster salad on sourdough toast. Lunch features sandwiches, pastas and salads. Open daily, with breakfast served from 6:00 to 11:30 a.m., lunch from 11:30 a.m. to 2:00 p.m., and dinner from 6:00 to 9:30 p.m. Reservations recommended for dinner. *Four Seasons Resort, 3900 Wailea Alanui, Wailea*

Peggy Sue's   L,D   875-8944

Wind your watch back to the "happy days" of the 50s when you step inside this nostalgic burger and malt shop. Decorated in soft shades of pink and blue, this funky eatery features table-top mini-juke boxes that play your favorite music from the era of ponytails and poodle skirts, and even an authentic 1954 Seeburg juke box. Menu items are reasonably priced and include a nice selection of burgers, hot dogs, fries (cholesterol-free), malts, banana splits and hot fudge sundaes. Open daily from 11:00 a.m. to 11:00 p.m. *Azeka Place II, 1279 S. Kihei Rd., Kihei*

Raffles' $$/$$$ D,R   879-4900

This elegant restaurant has established a fine reputation on Maui, and features Hawaiian Regional and Pacific Rim cuisine. Its menu offers a wonderful palette of flavors, making use of fresh Maui-grown ingredients. A sampling of their dishes includes grilled swordfish with cilantro butter, crisped whole fish with Thai coconut curry, roasted rack of lamb with Hunan marinade, Pacific seafood paella with saffron rice and chorizo, and marinated char-grilled New Zealand tiger prawns on ratatouille vegetables. An excellent appetizer and dessert selection rounds out the menu. Named after the Raffles Hotel in Singapore, an Asian landmark and one of the best hotels in the Orient. Open Tuesday through Saturday from 6:30 to 10:00 p.m. *Stouffer Wailea Beach Resort, Wailea*

The Sea Watch Restaurant $/$$ B,L,D   R   875-8080

Opened in Wailea in 1994, this attractive and spacious restaurant affords spectacular mountain and ocean views. Chef Richard Matsumoto, formerly of Raffles', specializes in Island Regional cuisine, combining interesting flavors in his dishes and using many Maui-grown ingredients. A sampling of his dinner menu: "fresh-from-our-waters" fish (prepared in one of four delicious styles), miso-chili glazed tiger prawns, teppan-seared scallop brochettes, kiawe-grilled rack of lamb, Szechuan barbecued chicken, Richard's potstickers with scallops and shrimp, and pan-seared filet mignon with Japanese pepper spice. For dessert, try the liliko'i cheesecake with macadamia nut crust, a specialty of the house. Open daily from 8:00 a.m. to 3:00 p.m. for breakfast/lunch, and 5:30 to 10:00 p.m. for dinner. *100 Wailea Golf Club Drive, Wailea*

Seasons $$/$$$ D,R,E   874-8000

This classy fine dining restaurant, located at the posh Four Seasons Resort, provides an exquisitely romantic oceanfront setting. The menu offers an interesting mix of Mediterranean and Asian cuisine, and features entrees such as smoked jumbo scallops with eggplant caviar, pan-fried opakapaka with lobster and leek hash, and grilled tenderloin of beef with Gorgonzola potato fritters. For dessert, try the "Lilikoi Symphony" for two, a trio of creme brulee, chiffon cake, and granite. Open daily, from 6:30 to 9:30 p.m. Live music nightly, with dancing on the terrace. Jackets optional. *Four Seasons Resort, Wailea*

Upcountry & Pā'ia Area Restaurants

Casanova Italian Restaurant and Deli $/$$ L,D,E   572-0020

This favorite Upcountry restaurant, situated in the rustic town of Makawao, has some of the finest pasta dishes you'll find in the state. Menu items include Caesar salad, baked eggplant marinara, wood-fired pizza, gnocchi, salmon-stuffed ravioli, fresh catch-of-the-day and filet mignon. The adjacent deli has an excellent selection of freshly prepared pastas, sandwiches, salads and pastries, all of which can be enjoyed on a cozy front porch or prepared for take-out. Live entertainment is featured several nights of the week. Voted "best Italian restaurant on Maui" by Maui News readers in 1992 and 1993. Open Monday through Saturday, serving lunch from 11:30 a.m. to 2:00 p.m., and dinner from 5:30 to 9:30 p.m. *1188 Makawao Avenue (at Four Corners), Makawao*

Charley's $ & less   B,L,D   E   579-9453

This restaurant in quaint Pā'ia town has been a local favorite since 1971, and is named after the late Charley P. Woofer, the owners' dog. It started out as a small rustic hole-in-the-wall, and over the years has been expanded and refurbished to the comfortable size it is today. Breakfasts are delicious, generous, and reasonably priced, consisting of omelettes, pancakes and other standard fare, served every day but Sunday. The lunch menu offers burgers, pizza, salads and soups. Dinner entrees include chicken, kiawe smoked ribs and fish. Sunday from 2:30 to 6:30 p.m. is their "Sunday Jam", featuring live music. Open daily, serving breakfast (except Sundays) from 7:00 a.m. to 2:00 p.m., lunch from 11:30 to 2:00 p.m., and dinner from 5:00 to 10:00 p.m. *142 Hāna Hwy., Pā'ia*

Crossroads Caffe   B, L,D   572-1101

For delicious and reasonably priced gourmet vegetarian and international cuisine, you'll find no better place to dine than this casual cafe situated at Makawao's main crossroads. Take a stroll over to their refrigerated display case and you'll see a tempting selection of the day's offerings, from curried vegetable turnovers to pasta salads to veggie pizzas to fresh baked pies. Daily specials are noted on a chalkboard and include international dishes, such as Indian or Italian fare, as well as hearty fresh vegetable soups, and delicious salads. If you like tea, try their tasty cinnamon spiced iced tea. A guest chef is featured each night, presenting vegetarian and vegan specials. Open Monday through Saturday from 8:00 a.m. to 9:00 p.m., and Sundays from 9:00 a.m. to 7:30 p.m. *3682 Baldwin Ave., Makawao*

Haliimaile General Store $/$$ L,D   572-2666

Executive Chef Bev Gannon and her husband, Joe, transformed this quaint 1929 general store, set in the midst of a 1,000-acre pineapple plantation, into one of Maui's top restaurants. Their menu features Hawaii Regional cuisine, with specialties which include sashimi Napoleon, paniolo ribs, rack of lamb Hunan style, Bev's boboli, lobster ragout, and Szechuan barbecued salmon. Generously sized salads and freshly made desserts round out the menu. For dessert, try the pina colada cheesecake or fresh raspberry creme brulee. Sushi served Tuesday through Saturday. Open daily, serving lunch from 11:00 a.m. to 2:30 p.m., and dinner from 5:30 to 9:30 p.m. Sunday brunch is served from 10:00 a.m. to 2:30 p.m. Smoke-free environment. *900 Hali'imaile Rd., Hali'imaile (5 miles up Hwy. 37, left at Hali'imaile cut-off sign, then 1.5 miles to restaurant)*

Kula Lodge $/$$ B,L,D   878-2517

This rustic Upcountry oasis is situated at an altitude of 3200 feet in the picturesque foothills of Haleakalā, and is a favorite among Maui residents. It features a lobby fireplace and large picture windows, which afford an expansive view of West Maui. Breakfast is their most popular meal, and includes such dishes as Kula Lodge corned beef hash, Belgian waffles, eggs Benedict and tofu scramble. Dinner offers a varied menu, featuring a nice selection of vegetarian dishes, all made with fresh Maui-grown ingredients, as well as meat and fish entrees. Open daily, serving breakfast from 6:30 to 11:30 a.m., lunch and dinner served from 11:30 a.m. until closing. *Haleakalā Hwy., Kula*

Makawao Steak House $$ D   572-8711

An attractive restaurant with a warm, pleasant ambience, and a nice lounge offering a cozy place to sit by the fire on cool Upcountry nights. Their excellent menu includes steak, chicken, seafood and fresh fish entrees, which come with soup or salad, potato or rice, and homemade breads. A children's menu is also available. Open nightly from 5:00 p.m. Try their mud pie for dessert. *3612 Baldwin Ave., Makawao*

Mama's Fish House $$/$$$ L,D,R   579-8488

This South Seas oceanside restaurant is situated at Kuau Cove, Pā'ia, on Maui's picturesque windsurfing shore, and has been in operation on the island since 1973. Although its prices are high, it continues to draw visitors year after year with its excellent seafood. The decor features mementos from French Polynesia, plus an assortment of shells, floats, fishing nets and nautical gear. Its fine reputation is mainly for its fresh seafood dishes, prepared in several delicious ways, however, the menu includes chicken and steak entrees as well. Reservations recommended. Open daily, serving lunch from 11:00 a.m. to 2:30 p.m., and dinner from 5:00 p.m. Pupus are available in the afternoon. *Just past Pā'ia, in Ku'au.*

Wunderbar $/$$ B,L,D   579-8808

Chef and owner Bernard Weber, a native of Switzerland, serves a constantly changing menu of German and Continental cuisine in this comfortable European-style eatery. The quaint patio in the rear is a nice breakfast nook. Lunch fare includes salads, pasta dishes and burgers, all priced under $10. A sampling of dinner entrees includes Hungarian goulash, wiener schnitzel, Bavarian hunter steak and fresh fish. Servings are hearty and accompanied by Maui-grown vegetables and fresh baked breads. Open daily, serving breakfast from 7:30 to 11:00 a.m., lunch from 11:00 a.m. to 2:00 p.m., and dinner from 5:00 to 10:00 p.m. *89 Hāna Hwy., Pā'ia*

Hāna Area Restaurants

Hāna Ranch Restaurant $/$$ L,D,R   248-8255

This informal dining spot offers an all-you-can-eat buffet at lunchtime, served from 11:00 a.m. to 3:00 p.m. daily, with a reduced rate for children under age twelve. Dinner is served on Friday and Saturday only, from 6:00 to 8:00 p.m. Entrees include New York steak, prime rib, baby back ribs, and fresh fish. Dinner reservations suggested. *Hāna Highway, Hāna*

Hotel Hāna-Maui $-$$$$ B,L,D,R,E   248-8211

The elegant Hotel Hāna-Maui's main dining room has the many charms of a slow-paced, earlier Hawaiian era. Its large, gracious room features beautiful local woods, views of Hāna Bay and myriad tropical blossoms and greenery. Continental cuisine is featured, and the dinner menu changes nightly, with such offerings as Hawaiian beef, lamb chops, duck and fresh island fish, prepared in a number of delicious ways. The food is beautifully presented and flavorful, and some of the best you will find on the island. Breakfast may be ordered from the menu, or you may enjoy the buffet; lunch features a selection of hot entrees, sandwiches and salads. Breakfast is served from 7:30 to 10:00 a.m., lunch from 11:30 a.m. to 2:00 p.m., and dinner from 6:00 to 9:00 p.m. Dinner reservations suggested. *Hotel Hāna-Maui, Hāna*

Wailuku/Kahului Area Restaurants

Chart House $/$$ L,D   877-2476

Situated on a quiet street with views of Kahului Harbor, this is one of three Chart House locations on the island, and less crowded than its Wailea or Lahaina counterparts. Its menu features American cuisine, with entrees which include teriyaki chicken breast, prime rib, top sirloin teriyaki steak, coconut crunchy shrimp, grilled chicken Caesar salad, and fresh fish. Entrees are accompanied by an all-you-can-eat salad bar, warm bread, and rice. For dessert, their mud pie is a specialty, and easily serves two to three. A reasonably priced children's menu also available. Lunch is served from 11:00 to 2:00 Monday through Friday only; dinner is served nightly from 5:00 to 10:00 p.m. *500 N. Puunene Ave., Kahului*

Ming Yuen $ L,D   871-7787

This restaurant serves some of the best Cantonese and Szechuan cuisine you'll find on the island, and is quite popular despite its unlikely location in Kahului Industrial Park. For appetizers, try the egg rolls or chicken and corn soup. An extensive menu includes a delicious assortment of entrees made with pork, chicken, beef, and fish, as well as a number of vegetarian dishes. Their mu shu entrees (pork, chicken or vegetarian) are a specialty, served with a tasty hoisin sauce. Good service and pleasing decor featuring authentic Chinese antiques contribute to the restaurant's appeal. Open for lunch Monday-Saturday from 11:30 a.m. to 5:00 p.m., and open for dinner nightly from 5:00 to 9:00 p.m. *162 Alamaha, Kahului*

Siam Thai Cuisine $ L,D   244-3817

A favorite of residents and tourists alike, this unpretentious but pleasant restaurant serves delicious and modestly priced Thai cuisine. Menu items include coconut-chicken soup, green papaya salad, satay dishes, curries and other traditional Thai fare. Open daily, with lunch served from 11:00 a.m to 2:30 p.m., dinner from 5:00 to 9:30 p.m. *123 N. Market St., Wailuku*

FAST FOODS

A number of fast food restaurants are scattered around the island, and, due to space restraints, we can highlight only a handful that stand out above the others, grouped by location.

Lahaina/Kā'anapali/Kapalua area:

Maui Tacos (665-0222), located in Napili Plaza and Lahaina Square, offers excellent and healthy Mexican food (dine in or take out), and is operated by the same owners as Avalon on Front Street. Moose McGilly-cuddy's (667-7758) is a favorite of locals and visitors, serving three meals a day in their prime second story Front Street location, at Mariner's Alley. It also has an energetic night scene, with loud music and lots of young people. Pikake Bakery and Cafe (661-5616) at 505 Front Street (also in Kihei) offers excellent lunch specials, as well as wonderful breads and pastries. Kirouac's (661-7299), about a block off Front Street at the corner of Dickenson and Wainee, is a good choice for a quick lunch, offering deli sandwiches and a few hot specialties, all freshly prepared. It also has a nice breakfast menu, opening at 7:30 a.m. Maui Swiss Cafe (661-6776) is a delightful place to stop in for a bite, located across from Burger King at 640 Front Street (set back from the street). Guests sit 'al fresco' under European cafe style umbrellas, while enjoying freshly prepared croissants, muffins, cookies, sandwiches, gourmet Swiss and Hawaiian coffees, juices and fruits, as well as ice cream and 52 varieties of genuine Swiss chocolate. The cafe is open Monday through Saturday from 8:00 a.m. to 8:00 p.m., and Sunday from 10:00 a.m. to 5:00 p.m.

Kihei/Wailea area:

Pair O' Dice Pizza (874-1968), at Kukui Mall in Kihei, offers an excellent menu of made-to-order pizzas, sandwiches, salads, and pasta specialties. Portions are generous; most are large enough to serve two. Eat in or take out; free delivery is available. The Coffee Store (875-4244) at Kihei's Azeka Place II serves not only numerous specialty coffee drinks, but also a good breakfast, lunch and dinner. The menu features freshly made salads, soups, pizzas, veggie burgers, Italian specials, sandwiches, quesadillas and desserts. Limited indoor or outdoor seating, or you can take out. International House of Pancakes (879-3445) at Azeka Place Shopping Center in Kihei is worth mention for its wide selection of inexpensive breakfasts. This is one of the chain's most popular locations, so anticipate a wait. Surfer Joe's Grill & Bar (879-8855) at 61 S. Kihei Road has a (you guessed it) surfer theme and is a fun place to grab a burger, sandwich or tasty tostada. Seating is indoors or on the patio.

Wiki Wiki Pizza & Deli (875-9454) at 2411 S. Kihei Road is a very good Italian fast food place, with limited seating and food to go. The menu offers New York style pizza with 14 varieties of toppings to choose from, as well as gourmet sandwiches, salads, pasta, roasted chicken and calzone. Its pizza was once voted "best on Maui". Open daily from 11:00 a.m. until 10:00 p.m.

Wailuku/Kahului area:

Mushroom (244-7117) at 2080 Vineyard Street in Wailuku, opened its doors in mid-1994, offering a good selection of local style lunches. Hours are from 10:00 a.m. to 2:00 p.m. daily. For inexpensive local and vegetarian food, try **Pupule Cafe** (242-8449) at 318 North Market Street in Wailuku, offering salads, soups, sandwiches, and hot entrees such as marinated baked chicken, lasagna and Shepherd's pie. **Maui Bakery, Bagelry and Deli** (871-4825) at 201 Dairy Road in Kahului (you'll pass it on your way from the airport to Lahaina) is a plain-looking place, but offers a nice selection of freshly made bagels, specialty breads and pastries, as well as sandwiches and salads. There are a few tables available or you can take out.

Pā'ia:

The best fast food place in Pā'ia (and perhaps all of Maui) is **Picnic's** (579-8021), located at 30 Baldwin Avenue, which features a superb menu of burgers, fries, healthy sandwiches, and salads. Try their spinach nutburger for a real treat! They'll fix a box lunch for you if you call ahead, especially nice to enjoy on your trip to Hāna or Haleakalā. **Peach's and Crumble Cafe & Bakery** (579-8612) at 2 Baldwin Avenue in Pā'ia, is a good place to pick up sandwiches and delicious baked goods. If you'd like to sample fresh island fish at a modest price for either lunch or dinner, try the **Pāia Fish Market Restaurant** (579-8030), on the corner of the Hāna Highway and Baldwin Avenue. Menu choices are listed on a big blackboard, and feature fresh fish plates, fish burgers, and seafood fajitas, and diners may enjoy their meal at large lacquered picnic tables.

SPECIAL FOODS

At the **Komoda Store and Bakery** in Makawao (572-7261), baked goods are sold the moment they're displayed, with their specialty being their incredibly delicious cream puffs, a favorite take-home item for visitors traveling inter-island.

Kitch'n Cook'd Potato Chips are sold in food stores throughout Hawai'i, and, like the Maui onion, may be the best in the world. The supply is limited to ensure quality, and the chips are eagerly sought by visitors from around the world.

The refreshing treat known as 'shave ice' unfortunately can't be packed and shipped home from Maui. Finely-shaved ice with flavored syrup poured over it, this cool thirst-quencher closely resembles what is generally known on the Mainland as 'snow cones', but it isn't the same. The texture of shave ice is much finer-- more like actual snow, and the rainbow version is a delight to behold as well as to consume. On a hot afternoon, this treat is ultra-refreshing. Some vendors will add a scoop of ice cream or sweet black beans under the mound of delicate ice shavings for an extra treat. Shave ice can be purchased from many places all over the island, including refreshment vans parked near beaches.

DINING

COOKBOOKS

Those doing their own cooking might wish to try some local recipes, taking advantage of the readily available ingredients, which can be hard to come by in some areas and climates. Many such cookbooks are sold at local bookstores and souvenir shops. Island Heritage Publishing has published three collections of local recipes which we can recommend: *Favorite Recipes from Hawaii, Tropical Drinks and Pupus from Hawaii* and *Entertaining Island Style*. All three are available in hard or soft cover.

GUIDE TO FRESH ISLAND FISH

When a waitperson in a Hawai'i restaurant rattles off a selection of island fish on the menu, do you get confused? Sometimes the names of island fish tend to blend together, so here's a guide to a few of the most popular varieties.

AHI: Also known as yellowfin tuna, this fish may weigh anywhere between 10 and 250 pounds. Its firm unfishy flesh is eaten raw, as sashimi, or broiled in thick filets.

AU: This is the familiar swordfish, which comes in many varieties that are great for eating. It has a white flesh similar to the mahimahi.

MAHIMAHI: This fish is probably the most popular on Hawaiian tables. It's known as the "dolphin fish", but it is definitely a fish and not the marine mammal known as the dolphin. Mahimahi has a flaky texture and a mild taste.

ONO: Another name for this fish is the "wahoo". It's a fast swimmer and can clip along at sixty miles per hour! To give you some idea of how it tastes, "ono" means delicious in Hawaiian.

ONAGA: Red snapper. Its white meat is used for sashimi. This pretty pink fish is sometimes used as a table ornament.

OPAKAPAKA: Another snapper, this one dwells in fairly deep water and isn't easy to catch. But its melt-in-the-mouth deliciousness makes it worth the trouble!

Fish guide provided courtesy of Kauai Beach Press

ACC●MMODATION

Resort Hotels
Condominiums
Intimate Inns
Bed & Breakfast Homes
Cabins and Campsites

ACCOMMODATION

O ne of the pleasures and challenges of traveling is finding the right place to stay. A comfortable room, suite or cottage can transform a *good* trip into a *great* one. The accommodations on Maui offer a broad spectrum of choices, from the posh resort hotels and all their amenities to the small condominiums and inns that often make up in price and charm what they may lack in grandeur. Most of the visitor accommodations are found in West Maui and along the southeast coast of Kihei and Wailea. They range in price from a high of more than $300 a day down to something more modest, around $85 a day, and sometimes less. In this section, we cover the top resort hotels on the island and major condominium units, as well as a sampling of intimate inns, bed-and-breakfast accommodations, cabins and campsites.

THE BEST HOTELS ON MAUI

The ratings below indicate the quality of selected hotels on Maui. The criteria for a good hotel are simple: comfort, courtesy and cleanliness. In a great hotel, different things make different properties outstanding; our evaluations are based on the following criteria:

- architecture, decor, grounds and view

- well-trained, responsible and caring staff

- personalized consideration from manager, concierge and maitre d', prompt room service, attention to details

- amenities and niceties such as fluffy towels, extra pillows, newspaper and wake-up coffee, flowers, beauty salons and shops

- fine dining, all-day restaurant and food service, poolside grazing

- most importantly, an indefinable, warm, pleasing ambiance

Unless you're traveling during the busy winter months (January through April; February at peak), reservations shouldn't be a problem. Room rates are seasonal, with the winter months fetching higher prices. The price ranges of the hotels and other lodging are categorized as follows:

$$$$	$200 and more (luxury class)
$$$	$100-$200
$$	$70-$100
$	$50-$70
No $	Under $50 (budget)
W	Wheelchair access

HOTELS

Diamond Resort Hawaii $$$$, W

800-800-0720
808-874-0500

Nestled in the foothills above the Wailea Golf Course on 14.5 beautifully landscaped acres, this Japanese-owned luxury resort has 72 one-bedroom units. Each room has a full kitchen, television, VCR and lanai, and affords expansive ocean and golf course views. A luxurious Japanese-style spa is available for guests' use. One unit is designed to accommodate wheelchairs. *555 Kaukahi St., Wailea , HI 96753*

Embassy Suites Resort $$$$, W

800-462-6284
808-661-2000

This popular 12-story all-suite hotel is situated on seven lush acres on Kā'anapali Beach. There are 395 one-bedroom suites, and 16 two-bedroom suites, with lovely ocean or mountain views. Amenities include a one-acre swimming pool area with 24-foot water slide, a year-round children's program, 18-hole miniature golf course, sandy swimming beach, video game room, three restaurants and two cocktail lounges. Suite rates include a daily complimentary breakfast buffet and two-hour manager's cocktail reception. An on-site health room has exercise equipment and saunas. Golf and tennis available nearby. Specially equipped suites are available for travelers with disabilities. *104 Kā'anapali Shores Place, Lahaina, HI 96761*

Four Seasons Resort-Wailea $$$$,W

800-334-6284
808-874-8000

Guests are truly pampered at this elegant 380-room oceanfront resort, recipient of the AAA Five Diamond distinction every year since its opening in 1990. In 1993, the readers of Conde Nast*Traveler* magazine named it the "Top Tropical Resort in the World." Guestrooms are decorated in comfortable and attractive rattan and wicker furnishings, and each have large luxurious bathrooms with eight-foot marble counters and double vanities. Its 40' by 80' swimming pool has a whirlpool at each end and a fountain in its center, with a separate children's pool and slide. Golf is available at the nearby Wailea Golf Club, and guests also receive special privileges at the exclusive Grand Waikapu Golf and Country Club, Maui's newest and most elaborate golf club. There are two on-site lighted tennis courts, and 14 courts at the nearby Wailea Tennis Center. Other amenities include three fine restaurants, an 'adults only' games bar, two lounges and supervised children's and teen programs. For the health- conscious, there's an on-site health club, as well as complimentary power walking, aquacise and aerobics classes. *3900 Wailea Alanui, Wailea, HI 96753*

ACCOMMODATION

159

Grand Wailea Resort Hotel & Spa $$$$, W   800-888-6100
808-875-1234

This extravagant 600-million-dollar resort is situated on forty oceanfront acres in Wailea, and has brought together the most successful features of resorts from around the world. It has 767 oceanfront rooms, including 53 suites, in a nine-story building, and features a 15,000-square-foot formal pool with inlaid mosaic tile, a 2,000-foot-long "action pool", a seaside wedding chapel, and a 50,000-square-foot health spa, one of the nation's largest hotel spas. Guest rooms are spacious, a minimum of 640 square feet each, and go up to as large as 4400 square feet in the exclusive $8,000 per night Grand Suites. The grounds are lush with immaculately maintained gardens and more than 150 varieties of plants and trees. The resort welcomes families, and has a 20,000-square-foot children's facility, Camp Grande, for children ages three to twelve, that features its own movie theater, computer learning center, outdoor playground, '50s style soda fountain, video game room, and arts and crafts center. Six restaurants include one that features country spa cuisine, and another that features traditional Japanese specialities. *3800 Wailea Alanui, Wailea, HI 96753*

Hotel Hāna-Maui $$$$, W   808-248-8211

The Hotel Hāna-Maui is a jewel of a resort, in a class all its own. Low key and luxurious--and a favorite celebrity hideaway--it is situated on a lush 66-acre site in the rural East shore ranching town of Hāna. The hotel is comprised of 97 bungalow-style guest rooms and seven Sea Ranch Cottage suites with dramatic ocean and mountain views. Rooms and cottage suites feature bleached hardwood floors, ceiling fans, stone counter tops, attractive and comfortable tropical furniture, large tiled bathrooms and private patios. Extra touches include plush terry bathrobes, and grinders and coffee makers to make up fresh pots of complimentary Kona coffee. You won't find in-room T.V.'s, and we doubt you'll miss them. Original artwork and authentic Hawaiian artifacts are displayed in the main building. This resort has two pools and a lovely private beach (Hāmoa--a short shuttle ride from the hotel) with guest facilities. Their Wellness Center affords an inspiring ocean view and offers a variety of workout equipment, exercise classes, life-style seminars and massage facilities. Guided nature walks along the Hāna coastline and horseback riding excursions through rolling green pastures of the Hāna Ranch are other popular guest activities. (For a description of their fine restaurant, see DINING.) To get to this remote hotel, guests may either fly in to the small Hāna Airport (the hotel provides pickup service) or rent a car and drive from Kahului, approximately a 2.5 hour trip on the winding and narrow Hāna Highway. *P. O. Box 8, Hāna, HI 96713*

Hyatt Regency Maui $$$$, W   800-233-1234
808-661-1234

Elegant and luxurious, this fine hotel is decorated with a $2 million Asian and Pacific art collection, and set on forty acres of beautifully landscaped grounds on Kā'anapali Beach. Notable features are its spectacular half-

A quick snorkeling lesson starts another day of activities.

acre swimming pool (with two waterfalls, 150-foot lava tube water slide and a swim-up bar), swan-filled lagoons, and attractive lobby, complete with penguin pool and live parrots. There are 815 spacious guest rooms and suites situated in three wings, as well as four restaurants--including the award-winning Swan Court (see DINING), well-equipped health spa, and nightly entertainment. Their Recreation Department can arrange scuba diving and snorkeling lessons, or other water sports, as well as an excursion on the Hyatt's own 55-foot catamaran. Special rooms are available for disabled visitors. A supervised daily activity program, Camp Hyatt, is available for guests ages 3-12, as well as a teenage program, Rock Hyatt, for guests ages 13-17, for an additional fee. *200 Nohea Kai Drive, Lahaina, HI 96761*

Ka'anapali Beach Hotel	$$$/$$$$, W	**800-262-8450** **808-661-0011**

This hotel, situated at the tony Kā'anapali Beach Resort, is one of this area's most modestly priced, and prides itself on being " Maui's Most Hawaiian Hotel," with a strong commitment to preserving Hawaiian culture. Situated oceanfront on the three-mile-long Kā'anapali Beach, it has four wings comprised of 430 air-conditioned guest rooms with excellent views. Amenities include a whale-shaped swimming pool, complimentary sunset hula shows every night, free scuba lessons, and daily Hawaiiana activities. Three restaurants are situated on property, and four inexpensive all-you-can-eat buffets are available daily at their Koffee Shop restaurant. Guests can ride the free Kā'anapali Trolley to and from nearby golf courses, Whalers Village Shopping Center, and Old Lahaina Town. The trolley operates from 9:00 a.m. to 11:00 p.m. daily. Honeymoon and golf packages, senior rates (age 50+) and returnee specials are also offered. *2525 Kā'anapali Parkway, Lahaina, HI 96761*

Kapalua Bay Hotel & Villas	$$$/$$$$, W	**800-367-8000** **808-669-5656**

This is the kind of world class resort that sets the standard for the others. It is a stunning showplace in northwest Maui, situated on 1,500 acres of rural gentility, the Kapalua Resort, and set amidst a 23,000-acre working pineapple plantation. It has an elegant 194-room hotel, individually owned one- and two-bedroom villas with their own private recreation facilities, and three-bedroom luxury vacation homes at Pineapple Hill. Amenities include three white sand beaches, two swimming pools, two award-winning tennis complexes, three 18-hole championship golf courses, general store, more than 20 boutiques and galleries, 14 fine restaurants, and nearby horseback riding. Rooms feature color television, VCR, mini-bar, refrigerator, large marble bathroom with his-and-her vanities. Villas come with fully equipped kitchens, in-room laundry facilities, living/dining room area, and cable color television with VCR. Scenic walking and jogging paths run throughout. A year-round children's program is offered, as well as babysitting services. In other words, anything you would need for a stay that is luxurious and complete is available at this top-ranked resort. *One Bay Drive, Kapalua, HI 96761*

Kea Lani Hotel	$$$$, W	800-882-4100 808-875-4100

Kea Lani means "white heaven", and this beautiful, luxurious resort comes very close to being a veritable heaven-on-earth. Opened in 1991, this ocean-front hotel is comprised of twelve Mediterranean-style white buildings, ranging from two to six stories in height, and is located on 22 manicured acres overlooking Wailea's Polo Beach, a sandy swimming beach. It has 413 one-bedroom suites and 37 two- and three-bedroom oceanfront villas. Suites measure a minimum of 840 square feet and feature separate bedroom and living areas, oversized European-style marble bathroom with deep soaking tub and separate shower, spacious lanai, two color TV's, VCR, entertainment center, and marble top wet bar, as well as other amenities. Villas offer these features as well, plus two full bathrooms, private plunge pool, full kitchen, laundry facilities and barbecue grill. Three restaurants, including one fine dining restaurant, are on site, as well as a complimentary 2400-square-foot fitness center, shopping arcade, beach activities center, three swimming pools, a 140-foot water slide, shaded poolside cabanas, two jet spas, wedding gazebo and year-round children's program (ages 5 through 12). Five championship golf courses and excellent tennis facilities are situated nearby. *4100 Wailea Alanui Drive, Wailea, HI 96753*

Maui Coast Hotel	$$$	800-426-0670 808-874-MAUI

Word is getting out as visitors discover this unpretentious two-story hotel in Kīhei, which opened its doors in 1993, and offers clean, modestly priced accommodations. It has 264 guest rooms, 114 of which are one- and two-bedroom suites, each with in-room refrigerators. Other amenities include a swimming pool, two outdoor spas, two lighted tennis courts, and free laundry facilities. Restaurants, golf, and beaches are nearby, and Kīhei Beach Parks are conveniently located directly across the street. *2259 S. Kīhei Rd., Kīhei, HI 96753*

Maui Inter-Continental Resort	$$$$, W	800-292-4532 808-879-1922

Sprawling and luxurious with gardens and the feel of the tropics, this recently upgraded hotel takes great advantage of its Wailea beachfront locale to conjure up an island paradise. The resort's 516 rooms make it one of the largest hotels on Maui, but it loses nothing in expansiveness. Each room has a private lanai, separate dressing and bath areas, cable television and mini-bar, and most have ocean views. There are three swimming pools, a spa, two restaurants, two lounges, an excellent luau, and a focus on Hawaiian arts and crafts in the decor. Their "Keiki's Club Gecko" children's program is offered three days a week and is open to children ages 5 to 13, for an extra fee. Complimentary daily events include cultural activities such as lei-making and hula lessons. Golf is available at Wailea Resort, with three championship courses, and the Wailea Tennis Club has 14 courts. *3700 Wailea Alanui, Kīhei, HI 96753*

Maui Islander Hotel $$/$$$, W
800-367-5226
808-667-9766

A good value for the budget-minded, this ten-acre hotel/condominium complex is located in historic Lahaina town, and less than a five-minute walk to Front Street. The complex consists of nine two-story buildings with 372 rooms and condo units. There are four room categories to choose from: hotel room, studio with kitchen, and one- and -two bedrooms with kitchen. Room features include air-conditioning, ceiling fans, cable color TV, telephone, and daily maid service. Other amenities include swimming pool, sun deck, barbeque and picnic areas, lighted tennis court and guest laundry. *660 Waine'e Street, Lahaina, HI 96761*

Maui Lu Resort (Aston) $$/$$$, W
800-922-7866
808-879-5881

Set back from South Kihei Road in a vast 26-acre garden setting, and situated across the street from the ocean, this resort is Kihei's first hotel. It offers 129 modestly furnished air-conditioned rooms, 50 of which are ocean-front, as well as 16 one-bedroom cottages. The main property has a swimming pool, two tennis courts and coin-operated laundry. *575 S. Kihei Rd., Kihei, HI 96753*

Maui Marriott $$$/$$$$, W
800-228-9290
808-667-1200

This luxurious Kā'anapali Beach resort, situated on 15 oceanfront acres and directly across from the Kā'anapali Golf Course, has 701 guest rooms and 19 suites, each with private lanais. The grounds are filled with waterfalls, coconut palms and koi ponds, and feature five tennis courts (three lighted), a beach recreation center, two swimming pools, two whirlpools, a children's pool, exercise room, a game room, and more than 17 shops and galleries. Four restaurants are available including an authentic Japanese steak house, as well as two bars, one of which has Karaoke and a big-screen television for watching sporting events. Their beachside luau is rated one of Maui's best. A children's program is offered to children ages 5 to 12. Golf and honeymoon packages available. *100 Nohea Kai Drive, Lahaina, HI 96761*

Maui Prince Hotel $$$$, W
800-321-MAUI
808-874-1111

The Maui Prince greets the sea with a graceful V-shaped structure in the 1800-acre Mākena Resort, on the sunny southwest coast of Maui. The meticulously maintained grounds feature koi ponds, a waterfall, and a lovely courtyard. Its 310 rooms, some of which are designed for visitors with disabilities, are beautifully furnished in creamy pastel tones, every one offering an ocean view. Other features are a long white sand beach, two pools, four restaurants, a fitness facility, the 36-hole Mākena Prince Golf Course, six plexi-pave tennis courts (two lighted), fitness par course and four jogging trails. *5400 Mākena Alanui Dr., Kihei, HI 96753*

Ritz-Carlton Kapalua $$$$, W

800-262-8440
808-669-6200

This elegant oceanfront hotel is situated on 37 acres at the 1500-acre Kapalua Resort, and surrounded by towering old Cook Pines and Ironwood trees. It offers fabulous vistas of the West Maui Mountains, the ocean and the neighboring island of Moloka'i. The accommodations include 492 rooms, and 58 suites, 80% of which have ocean views. Each guest room features a spacious lanai, color television, fully stocked bar with refrigerator, marble bathroom with separate shower and double vanities, plush terry cloth his-and-her bathrobes and twice daily maid service. The exclusive top three floors of the Nāpili Wing comprise the Ritz-Carlton Club, with its own concierge staff, private lounge and four complimentary food and beverage presentations daily. The hotel has numerous amenities, including three restaurants, a beachside snack shop, two lounges, ten tennis courts (five lighted), a three-tiered 10,000-square-foot swimming pool, two outdoor whirl-pools, a beautiful white sand beach, a 7,000-square-foot fitness center, jogging and walking trails, and three championship golf courses. A supervised daily children's program is available for children ages 4-12. Golf, tennis, family, and special occasion packages available. *One Ritz-Carlton Dr., Kapalua, HI 96761*

ACCOMMODATION

165

Many luxury class hotels on Maui offer comfort in an elegant setting.

Royal Lahaina Resort $$$/$$$$, W
800-447-6925
808-661-3611

This hotel retains all of the charm it radiated when it opened. It has 592 rooms and cottages all with the look and feel of the tropics, and is situated on 27 acres on the north end of Kā'anapali Beach. All rooms are air-conditioned and have color cable television, refrigerator, private lanai, telephone, and Hawaiian style decor. Cottages are situated in garden settings, and have oversized rooms, as well as lanais. Amenities include two 18-hole golf courses adjacent to the property, an 11-court Royal Lahaina Tennis Ranch facility, beach and boating center, three freshwater pools, one whirlpool, and shuffle-board. There are two restaurants, a poolside grill, ice cream parlor, and a superb luau and Polynesian revue (see ENTERTAINMENT). *2780 Keka'a Dr., Lahaina, 96761*

Sheraton-Maui Hotel $$$/$$$$, W
800-325-3535
808-661-0031

Currently undergoing extensive remodeling and refurbishing, the Sheraton is closed as of this writing. One of the more dramatic hotels on Maui, this hotel is adjacent to Kā'anapali Beach's most striking landmark and favorite snorkeling spots, Black Rock, and offers one of the best locations on the island for sun and water sports. Call for information on their anticipated reopening, tentatively set for November 1996. *2605 Kā'anapali Pkwy., Lahaina, HI 96761*

Stouffer Wailea Beach Resort $$$$, W
800-992-4532
808-879-4900

This AAA Five-Diamond Resort is situated on 15.5 acres in the posh resort community of Wailea, and features lush tropical gardens, waterfalls and pools. The hotel's 347 guest rooms are 500 square feet in size and quite livable, each featuring a private lanai, and decorated in warm creamy tones. Rooms are offered in five view categories, and include ten specially designed rooms for disabled guests, and 78 non-smoking rooms. There are four restaurants including Raffles' (see DINING), featuring Pacific Rim cuisine, and Hana Gion, offering authentic Japanese cooking. Other amenities include two fresh water swimming pools, two whirlpools, private beach cabanas, Camp Wailea children's program, fitness center, complimentary shuttle service to nearby golf, tennis and shopping, and an excellent luau. *3350 Wailea Alanui Dr., Wailea, HI 96753*

The Westin Maui $$$$,W
800-228-3000
808-667-2525

The Westin Maui is an oceanfront resort situated on beautifully landscaped grounds. It features a vast complex of pools, streams and waterfalls which occupy the centerpiece of this 762-room hotel. There is a 25,000-square-foot pool area with five free-form pools and two water slides, one of them 150 feet long. The hotel consists of two towers, which include three restaurants (their premier restaurant is Sound of the Falls--see DINING), five lounges, and exercise rooms and saunas. Guest rooms are also available for travelers with disabilities, and certain floors are designated non-smoking. The hotel also has an art collection valued at $2 million featuring artwork from around the world. A "Keiki Camp" activity program for children is also available. *2365 Kā'anapali Pkwy., Lahaina, HI 96761*

INTIMATE INNS

A unique way to experience the islands is to choose a more intimate setting than that offered by the large resort hotels. True, if you choose an inn located in a rural area, you may find less in the way of shops and restaurants, but perhaps you may discover more in the way of atmosphere, privacy and tranquility. The cozy inns located in Old Lahaina Town offer convenience in their prime location, and manage to create an ambiance reminiscent of Maui as it was long ago.

Heavenly Hāna Inn $$$/$$$$ 808-248-8442

This tranquil Japanese-style inn offers four two-bedroom suites, each with its own entrance, lanai, and large private Japanese bath. Non-smoking facility. Note: no charge cards or personal checks accepted. Maximum stay of two days recommended. *P. O. Box 790, Hāna, HI 96713*

Kula Lodge $$$ 800-233-1535 / 808-878-2517

Situated in the mountainside district of Kula, at the 3200-foot level of Mt. Haleakalā, this rustic lodge was once a private home, many years ago. It offers five cozy attached chalets, some with a fireplace, and each providing breathtaking views of the West Maui mountains, and Central Valley, with the ocean on either side. Amenities include a restaurant, serving three meals daily (see DINING), a small art gallery (Curtis Wilson Cost Gallery), and protea gift shop. *RR1, Box 475, Kula, HI 96790*

Lahaina Inn $$/$$$ 800-669-3444 / 808-661-0577

This restored 12-room Victorian inn is just off Front Street in Lahaina, and welcomes visitors with turn-of-the-century warmth. Authentic Victorian antiques, period fabrics and wall coverings, and beautifully chosen decor are a striking contrast to the ultra-contemporary interiors found elsewhere on the island. Nine double rooms and three parlor suites are individually decorated in keeping with the style of the late 1800s, and each have a private bath, telephone, air-conditioning , ceiling fans and private balconies. A continental breakfast is served each morning and is included with the room. Crazy Shirts founder, Rick Ralston, owns the inn and has turned it into a Lahaina landmark. Non-smoking environment. David Paul's Lahaina Grill is on street level of the inn, as is Ralston's Antiques and Collectibles. *127 Lahainaluna Rd., Lahaina, HI 96761-1502*

ACCOMMODATION

Pioneer Inn	$$-$$$$	800-457-5457 808-661-3636

Maui's oldest hotel with sections dating back to 1901, this green and white historic inn is famous and marks the center of Lahaina activity. The hotel consists of 32 rooms, located in the more modern wing built in 1965; these rooms were completely refurbished in 1995, and all have private lanais overlooking the courtyard. One long veranda overlooks Lahaina Harbor. Memorabilia fills the lobby, and the open-air bar, which stays open until 4:00 a.m. on weekends, is popular among Maui residents and visitors. The hotel also includes a restaurant and retail shops on the ground level. *658 Wharf Street, Lahaina, HI 96761*

Plantation Inn	$$$	800-433-8615 808-667-9225

This romantic turn-of-century inn, located just a block off Front Street in Lahaina, has 13 guest rooms, each air-conditioned, and individually decorated Victorian-style with beautiful antiques, brass and canopy beds, stained glass and ceiling fans. Room amenities include a refrigerator, television, VCR, and complimentary videos. Some suites have a kitchenette. A 12-foot-deep pool and spa are also available to guests. Situated on the inn's ground floor is the superb award-winning French restaurant, Gerard's (see DINING). *174 Lahainaluna Rd., Lahaina, HI 96761*

CONDOMINIUMS and APARTMENTS

A more at-home atmosphere is available in self-contained apartments. They are plentiful and very popular, particularly for vacationers and business travelers staying several weeks. Apartment sizes vary, as do amenities, furnishings and prices. The price ranges shown are the same as those for hotels; there are many more units of this type than those listed here, and are available through real estate and property management agents on Maui, listed in the Maui Yellow Pages.

Grand Champions	$$$	800-367-5246

Immediately adjacent to the Wailea Tennis Club and Wailea Blue Golf course, this two-story complex consists of 186 spacious one- and two-bedroom units. There are two pools, two whirlpool spas, and two outdoor barbecue grills. Each unit is air-conditioned, and has a private lanai and full kitchen. Three blocks to a swimming beach. Special golf rates at Wailea Resort and Mākena Resort. Daily maid service. Three-night minimum stay. 3750 Wailea Alanui, Wailea, HI 96753

Ka'anapali Alii	$$$/$$$$	800-642-6284 808-667-1400

This luxury condominium consists of 264 one- and two-bedroom apartments, with 1500- to 1800-square feet of space. Concierge, maid service,

24-hour security and front desk service are available. The complex includes a swimming pool, a wading pool, three tennis courts, two saunas, a Jacuzzi, an exercise room, a restaurant and sundries. Kitchens are completely furnished, including washer/dryer. Golf courses are nearby. *Situated on Kā'anapali Beach. 50 Nohea Kai Drive, Lahaina, HI 96761*

Kā'anapali Shores (Aston)	$$$/$$$$	800-367-2954 808-667-2211

This is a tasteful beachfront condominium with 463 studios, one- and two-bedroom apartments. The units are large with quality furnishings and full-service kitchens. Daily maid service is offered, as well as a 24-hour front desk, lounge and restaurant, swimming pool, putting green, two tennis courts, spa, and beach services. *100 Kā'anapali Shores Pl., Lahaina, HI 96761*

Kahana Sunset	$$$/$$$$	800-669-1488 808-669-8011

This two-story 90-unit complex is situated on a sandy reef-protected beach in Kahana, close to Kā'anapali Resort and just eight miles from Old Lahaina Town. One bedroom/one bath and two-bedroom/two-bath apartments are offered with garden or ocean view. There are also two bedroom/two and one-half bath executive oceanfront townhouses. Each unit has color cable TV, ceiling fans, fully equipped kitchen, washer/dryer, and private lanai. Other amenities include a 60-foot heated swimming pool, garden area barbecues, and daily maid service. Three day minimum stay. *4909 L. Honoapiilani Hwy., Lahaina, HI 96761*

Kama'ole Sands (Aston)	$$$	800-922-7866 808-879-0666

This 445-unit condominium resort in Kīhei features landscaped gardens overlooking Kama'ole Beach. One-, two- and three-bedroom suites are attractively furnished, with fully-equipped kitchens and daily maid service. Other amenities include four tennis courts, swimming pool, wading pool, two Jacuzzis, and ten barbecue areas with tables and benches. Situated just four miles away from Wailea Resort golf courses and tennis facility. *2695 S. Kīhei Rd., Kīhei, HI 96753*

Mahana at Kā'anapali (Aston)	$$$/$$$$	800-922-7866 808-661-8751

Every condominium is oceanfront at this 143-unit complex situated in the beachside town of Honokōwai, between Kā'anapali and Kapalua resorts. It offers luxury studio, one- and two-bedroom/two-bath suites. Amenities include a swimming pool, two barbecue areas, two tennis courts, and two saunas. Daily maid service provided. *110 Kā'anapali Shores Place, Lahaina, HI 96761*

Makena Surf $$$$
800-367-5246
808-879-1595

This attractive 100-unit condominium complex was recently upgraded, and is situated on ten acres just two miles past Wailea, on Paipu Beach. Its spacious one- two- and three-bedroom rental units are oceanfront or have an ocean view, and each is air-conditioned, with private lanai, fully equipped kitchen, wet bar, washer/dryer, and Jacuzzi in the master bath. The property has two swimming pools, two whirlpool spas, four tennis courts (two are lighted), putting green, barbecue areas and gated private entrance. Maid service provided daily. Concierge on duty seven days a week. *96 Mākena Alanui Rd., Mākena, HI 96753*

Mana Kai Maui $$/$$$
800-525-2025
808-879-1561

Located on a mile-long swimming beach in Kihei, this resort offers apartment and hotel-type units, all oceanfront, with free use of a car. Completely furnished kitchen, color television, telephone, daily maid service and front desk service are included. Units are not air-conditioned. Breakfast is included in the hotel-type units. The complex also has a restaurant and lounge, ocean activities center, gift shop, general store, beauty shop, swimming pool, and coin-operated laundry. Three miles from excellent golf courses. *2960 Kīhei Road, Kīhei, HI 96753*

Maui Eldorado Resort $$-$$$$
800-367-5004
808-661-0021

Overlooking Kā'anapali Golf Course, this low-rise condominium resort consists of studios, one- and two-bedroom suites and is set amidst gardens and swimming pools. Suites are spacious and air-conditioned, with full kitchen and daily maid service. The property has three fresh-water swimming pools, shuffleboard, an activity desk, laundry facilities, baby-sitting services, and its own exclusive private beach club on Kā'anapali Beach open from 9:00 a.m to 5:00 p.m. daily. The resort provides free shuttle service to the beach club. Assistance with golf tee times and snorkeling equipment rental is available through the concierge. Walking distance to Whalers Village and an assortment of fine restaurants. Weekly complimentary cocktail party provided for guests. *2661 Kekaa Drive, Lahaina, HI 96761*

Maui Hill (Aston) $$$/$$$$
800-922-7866
808-879-6321

On the Kihei Coast, just minutes from Wailea and a short walk to the beach, these 140 air-conditioned one-, two- and three-bedroom apartments are set in garden surroundings. Spacious lanais offer ocean view, and the rooms include modern kitchens complete with microwave oven, washer/dryer and daily maid service. Two tennis courts, large swimming pool and sun deck are available, and golfers may tee off at the adjacent Wailea Resort. *2881 S. Kīhei Road, Kīhei, HI 96753*

Napili Kai Beach Club $$$/$$$$, W

800-367-5030
808-669-6271

Guests return season after season to this ten-acre beachfront West Maui hotel that offers 162 comfortable ocean-view or oceanfront studios and suites. Each room has a private lanai and kitchenette, and most are air-conditioned. Amenities include four swimming pools, Hawai'i's largest Jacuzzi whirlpool, seasonal children's program, two 18-hole putting greens, shuffleboard courts, four barbecue areas, and coin-operated laundries. Tennis and golf are located just a few minutes away at Kapalua Resort. *5900 Honoapiilani Hwy., Nāpili Bay, HI 96761*

Napili Shores $$$

800-367-6046
808-669-8061

This condominium resort is a neighbor to the Kapalua Resort in West Maui. It has 152 studio and one-bedroom units overlooking Napili Bay, and amenities include daily maid service, private lanai and furnished kitchen. The property has two swimming pools, a Jacuzzi, and laundromat. Golf and tennis may be played at nearby Kapalua Bay Hotel. *5315 L. Honoapiilani Rd., Nāpili, HI 96761*

Papakea Resort $$$/$$$$

800-484-9884
808-669-9680

Situated on Honokōwai beachfront property, between Kā'anapali Resort and Kapalua Resort, this low-rise condominium includes 364 studios, and one- and two-bedroom units surrounded by pools and gardens. Lanais, full-service kitchens, ceiling fans, front desk are included. Maid service is available on request. Other features are two swimming pools and Jacuzzis, three tennis courts, four saunas, two putting greens and gas barbecue. *3543 Honoapiilani Hwy., Honokōwai, HI 96761*

Polo Beach Club $$$$

800-367-5246
808-879-1595

This luxury eight-story high-rise condominium is situated on 2.3 acres of prime oceanfront property bordering Wailea Resort and next door to the Kea Lani Hotel. The complex has 71 one- and two-bedroom air-conditioned units, each with private lanai, fully equipped kitchen, washer and dryer, ceiling fans, and daily maid service. A concierge is on duty seven days a week. The property features a sandy swimming beach, heated oceanfront pool, whirlpool spa, and barbecue area. Tennis and golf are available at neighboring Wailea and Mākena resorts. *20 Mākena Rd., Wailea, HI 96753*

Puamana $$-$$$$

800-628-6731
808-667-2551

This attractive resort was once part of a sugar plantation in the early '20s, and is conveniently located on the edge of Old Lahaina Town. It consists of one-, two- and three-bedroom townhouses set on 28 acres of well-maintained tropical vegetation at the very south end of Front Street. Every townhouse is furnished with linens, television, outdoor barbecues and complete kitchen.

The property has three swimming pools (one situated right on the ocean), tennis court, laundries and exercise room. The lovely oceanfront clubhouse features a card room, saunas, and reading parlor. Golf courses are nearby, as are Front Street shops, restaurants and movie theaters. *P. O. Box 11108, Lahaina, HI 96761*

Sands of Kahana $$$/$$$$, W   800-367-7052 / 808-669-0400

On Kahana Bay, situated between Kā'anapali and Kapalua, this oceanfront eight-story condominium contains 200 spacious, sparkling one-, two- and three-bedroom units, each with lanai, furnished kitchen, cable television (with HBO), daily maid service, and washer and dryer. Other features include a nice white sand beach, gardens, beachfront swimming pool and spa, three lighted tennis courts, putting green, beach volleyball court, recreation room, poolside restaurant and cocktail lounge, concierge, and children's activity program. Four championship golf courses are situated nearby. Less than a mile from the West Maui Airport. *4299 L. Honoapiilani Hwy., Lahaina, HI 96761*

172

Wailea Ekahi, Elua & Ekolu Village $$$/$$$$ 800-367-5246 / 808-879-1595

Three attractive condominium complexes make up the 500 luxurious units on 76 acres in Wailea. Wailea Elua is located on Ulua Beach, and has won awards in landscaping and architecture. Ekolu Village is situated right on Wailea's Blue Course; Ekahi Village overlooks Keawakapu Beach. Low-rise units include studios, and one-, two- and three-bedroom apartments with private lanais, expensive furnishings, complete kitchens, and include washer/dryer and daily maid service. The complex has eight pools, a beachfront pavilion and barbecue area, paddle tennis court, and putting green. Guests are offered special golf rates at Wailea Resort and neighboring Mākena Resort. Nearby tennis courts, shops and restaurants. *3750 Wailea Alanui Drive, Wailea, HI 96753*

The Whaler on Kaanapali Beach $$$/$$$$, W   800-367-7052 / 808-661-4861

This is the first condominium established on Kā'anapali Beach. The 12-story complex features big, oceanfront studios and one- and two-bedroom units with spacious private lanais, and both garden and ocean views. Rattan and wicker furnishing fill the rooms, which also include fully-equipped kitchens, air-conditioning, color television, VCR and marble bathrooms. Other amenities include 24-hour front desk and phone service, swimming pool, sauna, exercise room, five tennis courts, tennis pro shop, two paddle tennis courts, video game room, four barbecue areas, and lobby mini-market. Golf, shopping, and restaurants are all within walking distance. *2481 Kā'anapali Pkwy., Lahaina, HI 96761*

BED & BREAKFAST HOMES & COTTAGES

Maui has a number of bed-and-breakfast (B&B) homes and cottages available to visitors who want more cozy and intimate lodging than a hotel or condo might offer. Here we list, by area of the island and in alphabetical order, some of the B&B homes and cottages you may want to consider. Most have three-day minimum stays and discounted rates for extended stays of a week or more. An asterisk (*) on a listing designates it as a Hawaii Visitors Bureau member.

At the end of this section is a listing of the local reservation services you may want to call to make your arrangements, if you prefer someone else to do the legwork for you. The advantage to using a reservation service is that it can save you time and money spent on long distance calls making your own arrangements, and the services are familiar with the various properties and can help you find just the right one to suit your budget and vacation needs.

A continental breakfast is included with your room (unless otherwise noted), normally consisting of toast, muffins or pastries, island fruits and/or juices. Many hosts add nice personal touches to make the morning meal a special experience.

173

Lahaina/Kā'anapali Area B&Bs

Aloha Tony's, a Tourist Home $ (and less)   808-661-8040

This casual, modest bungalow is a small four-bedroom house situated at the south end of Front Street in Old Lahaina Town, away from the crowds, yet just a short walking distance to a beach, Lahaina Boat Harbor, shops, and some of Maui's best restaurants and night spots. It is truly a find for the budget-minded traveler. Host Tony Mamo, an electrician by trade, lives on property and rents out three of his four small bedrooms. Two shared bathrooms accommodate the four rooms. Common areas consist of a small kitchen, living room, dining room and back porch, and breakfast is optional, available at an additional cost. Smoking is allowed on the back porch. This B&B's budget rates and convenient location are appreciated by visitors who want to spend less on lodging and more on Maui's many attractions, nearby restaurants, and activities.

Blue Horizons $$ *
800-669-1948
808-669-1965

This beautiful B&B is located in a quiet neighborhood between Kā'anapali and Kapalua resorts, and near West Maui Airport. The two-story redwood home has three nicely furnished air-conditioned apartments, each with private bathroom, kitchen, and color TV. Guests have access to the rest of the house, including a gourmet kitchen and screened oceanview lanai, ideal for enjoying breakfast or watching sunset. A nice swimming pool is another amenity, with a gas barbecue for guests' use. Hosts Bev and Jim Spence, originally from Atlanta, epitomize warm Southern hospitality.

Garden Gate B&B $/$$ *   808-661-8800

This tranquil hideaway is conveniently located in a residential neighborhood between Old Lahaina Town and Kā'anapali. Entry is alongside a lovely
man-made waterfall and Japanese garden. Guest accommodations consist of a
475-square-foot oceanview "Garden Studio" apartment, and a one-bedroom
suite, the "Molokai Room". The air-conditioned studio sleeps up to four
guests, has a private bath, kitchen, telephone and private deck. The Molokai
Room has a private bathroom and accommodates two. A hot tub is situated in
the garden for guests' use. Three night minimum stay; children welcome.
Ron & Welmoet Glover are congenial hosts, knowledgeable about the island.

The GuestHouse $/$$ 800-621-8942 / 808-661-8085

This attractive B&B is situated in a quiet neighborhood just a few miles
south of Kā'anapali and a short drive from historic Old Lahaina Town. It
features a large and very private pool and deck area, as well as in-room
Jacuzzis or hot tubs. Scuba divers are especially welcome, and arrangements
may be made for dive tours and all levels of instruction through the owners,
experienced divers themselves. Each of four air-conditioned guest rooms is
nicely decorated and equipped with private bath, refrigerator, color TV,
private phone and ceiling fans; a fifth room has shared bath. A large family
room and living room offer plenty of space to relax. An optional dinner plan
is available, prepared by the manager, a gourmet chef. Trinity Tours, the
owners' activity company, can assist guests with car rental and tour arrangements, offering reasonable rates, most at discount. Large families and groups
have the option of renting the entire house, or may want to inquire about
another property managed by the owners called the Walkus House, a new
two-story, four-bedroom three-bath home right on Front Street, walking
distance to the beach. Non-smoking environment. Owner/hostess: Tanna
Branum.

Old Lahaina House $/$$ *   800-847-0761 / 808-667-4663

If you could wave a magic wand and create a lovely and relaxing island
B&B, this is the place you'd conjure up. Its location is ideal, situated just two
houses off Front Street in Lahaina, at the quiet south end away from the
crowds and cars, yet walking distance to Old Lahaina Town's fine restaurants,
shops and night spots. There's lodging to fit almost any budget, and all rooms
are air-conditioned. Two guest rooms have private baths, TV, telephone and
refrigerator; two less expensive rooms have twin beds, TV, phone and shared
bath. A fifth room, the least expensive, has a double bed and TV. A wonderful pool area features a luxurious 27,000-gallon soft-water pool enclosed in a
lovely tropical courtyard, where breakfast is served daily. Smoking allowed
outside only. Hosts John and Sherry Barbier create a warm and relaxing
atmosphere for their guests, and are happy to assist with car rental needs and
fill guests in on the best places to see and things to do on the island.

Kihei Area B&Bs

Aikane Ohana B&B $$ *   808-879-5454

This comfortable B&B, located in Kihei's Maui Meadows subdivision, has two nicely furnished guest quarters. One unit is a one-bedroom apartment, with kitchen and private bath. The second, a new addition to the home, is a two-bedroom two-bath unit with ocean view, full kitchen and deck area. A private swimming pool is available for guests' enjoyment, and a "welcome" fruit basket is included with the room. Hosts: Janna and Richard Hoehn

Ann & Bob Babson's Vacation Rentals $/$$ *
800-824-6409
808-874-1166

Hosts Ann and Bob Babson run an attractive B&B in their home, located directly above Wailea resort in the quiet upscale neighborhood of Maui Meadows. Guests have their choice of four stylishly furnished guest quarters. Two B & B suites have private baths, TV's and telephones, and include breakfast and free laundry service. The Molokini suite offers a 180° panoramic ocean view, as does the Hibiscus Hideaway apartment, and has a king bed and Jacuzzi tub. The apartment has a living room/dining room/ kitchenette, with queen bed, private bath, TV, telephone and own entrance. The ocean view Sunset Cottage has two bedrooms, two baths, full kitchen, living room, outdoor lanai, TV and telephone, washer/dryer, and can accommodate up to six guests.

Anuhea B&B Health Retreat $$/$$$ *
800-206-4441
808-874-1490

This New Age B&B retreat is situated in a safe Kihei residential area, and provides a relaxing, healing environment to its guests. Healthy breakfasts are served on a comfortable open-air lanai overlooking tranquil lush grounds. Optional amenities include nutritional counseling, massage, body purification programs and guided meditations. Special group rates available upon request. Hostess: Dr. Elaine Willis

Bed, Breakfast, Books & Beach $ 808-879-0097

This Kihei B&B, situated in Maui Meadows and just one mile from the beach, is run by hosts Natalie and John Tyler, who are spiritual psychotherapists. One guest room is available in this attractive two-story home, and features a brass queen-size bed, private bath, ocean and mountain views and own entrance. The house has a relaxing ambiance, and is filled with classical music, poetry, books and fine art. A healthy gourmet breakfast is included, served on a lovely screened porch, with views of Mt. Haleakalā. Optional extras include gourmet picnic basket lunches, gourmet dinners, guided trips to Lahaina and Hāna, snorkeling lessons, scuba trips, as well as relationship counseling. Non-smoking environment.

Upcountry Area B&Bs

Bloom Cottage $$ 808-878-1425

This cozy, romantic cottage is surrounded by flower and herb gardens, and situated at the 3000-foot elevation of Kula with views of the West Maui mountains and ocean. The interior is tastefully furnished and comes with its own fireplace, full kitchen, color TV, VCR, videotape library, phone and a relaxing front porch from which to view sunset. The closest beaches are thirty minutes away; Haleakalā summit is forty-five minutes away. Beautiful flower farms, restaurants, and the Tedeschi Vineyard are close by. Continental breakfast is included, stocked in the refrigerator. Two day minimum stay. Non-smoking environment. Hosts Herb and Lynne Horner reside in a separate house at the front of the property.

Country Garden Cottage $$ 808-878-2858

Situated on the Kula Highway and tucked away behind a tall hedge, this quaint cottage has its own secret garden, full of fruit trees and tropical plants. It features hardwood floors, a fireplace and full kitchen. Candles and fresh flowers decorate each room, creating a cozy ambiance. The bedroom offers mountain and rose garden views; the living room has an expansive view of the Central Valley, West Maui Mountains, and the ocean, a perfect vantage point from which to watch Maui's spectacular sunsets. Continental breakfast is included. Extra bedding is available for children or additional guests. Hostess: Barbara Wimberly

Kula Lynn Farm $$ 808-878-6176

Situated on the ground floor of a lovely home in rural Lower Kula, this exceptionally nice B&B offers 1600 square feet of living space, including two bedrooms and two baths, a fully equipped kitchen and spacious living room/ dining room area. The furnishings are done in pastel colors, and special touches include Italian marble floors in the kitchen, dining room and master bath, plush carpeting, mini-blinds and artwork from Maui artists. The unit offers spectacular views of West Maui, the Central Valley, Lāna'i, Kaho'olawe and the ocean. A covered carport adjoins the covered patio, and it has a private entrance. Hosts Jim and Lynn Coon own and operate one of Maui's most successful sailboat companies, Trilogy Excursions (see SPORTS), and are very knowledgeable about where to go and what to do on the island. Breakfast provisions are stocked in the refrigerator for guests to enjoy at their leisure. Non-smoking environment. Three-night minimum stay. Children age ten and up are welcome.

Puluke Farm $$ *   808-878-3263

This cozy Upcountry studio apartment is suitable for two guests and situated at the 3500-foot level of Haleakalā, in the flower country of Kula. From the wrap-around deck, guests have a lovely view of the West Maui Mountains and Central Valley. The clean, nicely decorated studio is complete with a kitchen, full bath, laundry facility, color TV, VCR and heater. A serve-yourself breakfast is stocked in the refrigerator. Hosts: Astrid and Bruce Lepolstat.

Ha'iku Area B&Bs

Haikuleana Bed & Breakfast $$ *   808-575-2890

Situated on one and a half acres in Ha'iku, just twelve miles from Kahului Airport and two miles from Maui's windsurfing mecca, Ho'okipa Beach, this quaint 19th-century plantation house was originally built for Maui's first doctor, who worked for the old pineapple cannery. The home is tastefully decorated in traditional B&B style, with hardwood floors, 12-foot-high ceilings, tropical period pieces and antiques. The serene surrounding area is filled with lush vegetation and even a chicken coop. Each guest room has its own private bath, and guests can enjoy the relaxed atmosphere in the bright living room, which has a T.V., or on the front porch. Breakfast is served each morning in the lovely dining room. Reduced rates available to Hawai'i residents and those staying longer than one week.

Pilialoha B&B Cottage $$ *   808-572-1440

This adorable cottage is located on two acres in a peaceful pastoral setting in Upcountry Ha'iku, near Makawao and not far from the town of Pā'ia, and windsurfing hub, Ho'okipa Beach. The one-bedroom unit has a queen bed and accommodates two comfortably, but can sleep up to five. Amenities include a full kitchen, cable TV, private phone, washer/dryer and a variety of videos and reading materials. Minimum two-night stay. Hosts Bill and Machiko Heyde reside on property. Direct bookings only.

Hāna Area B&Bs

Hāmoa Bay Bungalow $$$ 808-248-7884

If you want to relax in the gentle breezes of "heavenly" Hāna, this secluded Balinese-inspired bungalow is a good choice. The artistic flair of lifelong Hawai'i resident Jodi Baldwin and the influence of her world travels have culminated in this elegant and sensitively designed exotic hideaway. Conveniently located a short walking distance from Hāna's lovely Hāmoa Beach, it is reached by driving through a lush banana grove. From the cottage, guests catch glimpses of the surf framed in orange-blossomed African Tulip trees. Situated close to waterfalls, beaches, mountain pools and private jogging trails, this retreat offers as much or as little activity as you want. Amenities include a king-size bed, Jacuzzi bath for two, full kitchen, cable TV/VCR and telephone, as well as a tropical breakfast. Two-night minimum stay, with weekly and monthly rates available. Non-smoking environment. Hostess: Jodi Baldwin

B&B RESERVATION SERVICES

The following is a list of Hawai'i's bed-and-breakfast reservation services, which are knowledgeable about accommodations on each island, and can assist you in finding the right place to stay to fit your budget and traveling needs. If calling from the mainland, be aware of our time difference. Hawaiian Standard Time is five hours behind New York, four hours behind Chicago, three hours behind Denver and two hours behind San Francisco. Add an hour to these when Daylight Savings is in effect.

Service		
All Islands Bed & Breakfast	800-542-0344	808-263-2342
B&B Hawaiian Islands	800-258-7895	808-261-7895
Bed & Breakfast Hawaii, A Reservation Service Statewide	800-733-1632	808-822-7771
Bed & Breakfast Honolulu (Statewide)	800-288-4666	808-595-7533
Bed & Breakfast Pacific Hawaii	800-999-6026	808-486-8838
Bed & Breakfast Wailua Kauai, A Reservation Service Statewide	800-822-1176	808-822-1177
Hawaii's Best Bed & Breakfasts A Reservation Service Statewide	800-262-9912	808-885-0550
Hawaiian Islands Bed & Breakfast & Vacation Rentals	800-258-7895	808-261-7895
Volcano Reservations Statewide Accommodations	800-736-7140	808-967-7244

An informative guidebook for bed-and-breakfast accommodations, entitled *Bed & Breakfast Goes Hawaiian* (278 pages), is published by Evie Warner and Al Davis, who operate **Bed & Breakfast Hawaii.** The book lists descriptions of B&B's throughout the islands, and includes thirty-two color photographs, as well as handy tips on sight-seeing activities, beaches and restaurants. The book is available through their office (1-800-733-1632). Another handy resource is an informative 25-page pamphlet published by Barbara and Susan Campbell of **Hawai'i's Best Bed & Breakfasts,** available free when booking reservations through their office at 1-800-262-9912.

CABINS and CAMPSITES

Maui County maintains two campgrounds for tents and auto campers. One is **Baldwin Park** on the Hāna Highway near Pā'ia, a beachside park that has water, showers, restrooms, grills and tables.. The second is **Rainbow Park** on Baldwin Avenue just above Pā'ia, a more woodsy setting that has everything Baldwin Park has, minus the showers. You must get a permit to stay at either park, and the permits limit your stay to three consecutive nights. The nightly fee is three dollars for adults, fifty cents for children. Permits are ob-tained from the County's Parks and Recreation Department (243-7230), located at the War Memorial Gym, Ka'ahumanu Avenue, Wailuku 96793. The Department is open Monday through Friday, 8:00 a.m. to 4:00 p.m.

The state of Hawai'i provides two campgrounds, each with its particular charm. One is **Wai'ānapanapa** (see SIGHT-SEEING and BEACHES), a remote beach in Hāna, the second site is an isolated spot in a thick grove of hardwood trees and reachable by four-wheel drive--**Polipoli Springs.** It is located just above the 6000-foot level on the side of Haleakalā. This is a challenging place to get to, and once there, you are removed from amenities other than toilets and picnic tables, so don't forget anything essential. You will see striking views of Maui en route to Polipoli. There is no fee for camping in state parks, but permits are required and the maximum stay is five consecutive nights. For permits, contact the Division of State Parks, 54 South High Street, Wailuku, HI 96793 (243-5354).

The state of Hawai'i also manages cabins at two locations. They are bargains--good facilities at reasonable

prices. Permits are necessary from the State Parks office (above); length of stay and number of occupants are limited. Make reservations well ahead of time. **Wai'ānapanapa** has twelve cabins, which are very comfortable and well-furnished with bedding, towels, cooking and eating gear, hot water, showers, refrigerators and electric stoves. Each cabin will accommodate up to six people. **Polipoli Springs** has a single cabin, with all the furnishings of Wai'ānapanapa, with the exception of hot water and electricity. It has a gas stove and cold water shower. The cabin can lodge up to ten people.

The U.S. National Park Service provides campgrounds and cabins inside Haleakalā National Park (see SIGHT-SEEING), surely among the most spec-tacular campsites anywhere in the world. One campsite is **Hosmer Grove,** at the 7000-foot level. No permit is necessary here, and facilities are on a first-come, first-served basis. The site has shelter, parking area, grills and tables both in the shelter and outside.

Two campsites adjacent to cabins operated by the Park Service are located inside the crater. The sites are at the **Hōlua cabin,** the first one encountered when hiking or riding in the park, and at **Paliku,** the most distant cabin. Tent camping here is limited to three nights, and to twenty-five persons per camp-site.

A third campsite is at the extreme end of the park on the Hāna coast, at **'Ohe'o.** This latter site is relatively undeveloped and there is no water, but it does have picnic tables, chemical toilets and outdoor barbecues. There is no fee for camping at any of the sites, but permits are necessary from Park Head-quarters (572-9306) and/or by writing: Superintendent,

ACCOMMODATION

179

Haleakalā National Park, P. O. Box 369, Makawao, HI 96768. In addition to the Holua and Paliku cabins noted above, there is a third cabin, **Kapalaoa,** and all three are extremely popular with residents and visitors alike. Permits are necessary from Park Headquarters (see address above), which is open daily from 8:30 a.m. to 4:00 p.m. The cabins are warm and cozy, and equipped with water, toilets, wood-burning stove, firewood and cooking and eating utensils. There are mattresses but no bedding, and it is necessary to bring a warm sleeping bag. The cabins hold a minimum of three occupants and a maximum of twelve, which means most parties share the cabins with other groups. Fees for the cabins are five dollars per person per night, plus two dollars and fifty cents for firewood, for a total of seven fifty per night each.

Because cabins are in great demand, visitors are asked to write the Superintendent (address above), and give details on exact dates and cabins desired, and the number of people in your group. A lottery determines who gets to stay in the cabins; the lottery is held generally two months ahead, meaning your reservations should be in at least ninety days before your proposed adventure.

Camping, hiking or just visiting Haleakalā is an experience long to be remembered. The crater is one of the world's great scenic wonders, and was a spiritual place for Maui's original inhabitants. Visitors should respect the land by practicing good trail habits and refrain from littering.

Interestingly enough, an old Hawaiian legend about Haleakalā has almost been lost in time; even today's Hawaiian would be surprised to find that the old Polynesian settlers had, in their pantheon of gods, four sisters who were goddesses of the snows. This legend is easy to believe on some winter mornings when the park is closed due to snow. The four snow goddesses came from far over the sea and were rivals of Pele, the goddess of fire, who lived in the volcanoes. An old Hawaiian tale talks of the fierce battles between Pele and the paramount snow goddess, Poli'ahu. She always won the battles because at the end of the fiery eruptions caused by Pele, the gentle snow would still fall like a mantle over the summits of the volcanoes. The goddess who was said to live in Haleakalā was Lilinoe, and on dark, blustery nights in the crater, it is easy to believe she still watches over Haleakalā.

One of Maui's most attractive camps, and perhaps one of the island's best kept secrets is **Camp Keanae,** located cliff-top overlooking the remote and lush Ke'anae Peninsula on the road to Hāna, an hour-and-forty-five-minute drive from Kahului Airport. Here, individuals and groups have the option of pitching tents or staying in spacious cabins at the modest rate of ten dollars per person per night. Visitors should plan to bring their own food, towels and bedding (the beds have bare mattresses) and fill up the gas tank prior to leaving Kahului. Outdoor hibachi grills and community bathroom/shower facilities are the only amenities. Reservations may be booked through the YMCA office in Wailuku (242-9007). Note: This camp is adjacent to a lush rain forest and downpours are not infrequent, especially in winter months.

ET CETERA

Other Services
Island Weddings
Traveling with Children
Travelers with Disabilities
Other Islands

OTHER SERVICES

H ere we cover a miscellany of other services that did not lend themselves to appropriate inclusion in other sections of the guidebook-- some things you just might need along the way, from dry cleaning to luggage repair to specialists in the arrangement of tropical nuptials.

POST OFFICES

Maui's Post Offices are located throughout the island, but working hours vary from site to site. In general, hours are Monday through Friday 8:00 a.m.-4:30 p.m., Saturday 8:00 a.m.-12:00 noon. They are located at:

Ha'iku	(575-2773)	96708
Pā'ia	(579-9205)	96779

Hāna	(248-8258)	96713
Pukalani	(572-8235)	96788
Kahului	(871-4710)	96734
Pu'unene	(871-4744)	96784
Kihei	(879-2403)	96753
Wailuku	(244-4815)	96793
Kula	(878-1765)	96790
Lahaina, *main*	(667-6611)	96761
Makawao	(879-8895)	96768
Lahaina, *downtown*	(667-0050)	96767

PUBLICATIONS

Publications that may of interest to visitors include the *Maui News* , an afternoon newspaper that is printed every day except Saturday; *Pacific Art & Travel*, published quarterly and focusing on Hawai'i's art scene; *Real Estate Maui Style*, published monthly, *Maui Press*, and free tourist guides, such as *Maui Menu*, found in racks island-wide.

LAUNDRY and DRY CLEANING

The need for a laundromat can be urgent, especially for hikers and campers. **Snow White Linen/ Laundry** (871-0633), **Fabritek Cleaners** (877-4444), **Paia Clothes Cleaners** (579-9273), and **Valley Isle Dry Cleaning Laundry and Valet** (877-4111), offer full-service laundry services. For self-service laundries, there are **Kwik 'n Kleen** (661-7949) in Lahaina, **W&F Washerette** (877-0353) in Kahului, **Kihei's Kukui Laundromat** (879-7211) in Kihei, and **The Washtub** (572-1654) in the Pukalani Terrace Center.

LEATHER GOODS - REPAIR

If your luggage or shoes need fixing, you are limited to taking them to **Lahaina Shoe & Luggage** (661-3114) in Lahaina; they handle repairs while you wait. **Tester's Shoe Repair** (877-7140), in back of the Old Kahului Store, is convenient for Central Valley residents and visitors.

ISLAND WEDDINGS

Maui is just as popular an island for weddings or renewing vows as any other in the Hawaiian chain. A local firm specializing in making dream weddings happen here is **A Hawaiian Wedding Experience** (667-6689), with offices on three islands, and on Maui, in Lahaina. Similarly, **Weddings the Maui Way** (877-7711), **Dolphin Dream Weddings** (661-8535), as well as most of the large resort hotels, offer complete services. For additional listings, look under "Wedding" in the Maui Yellow Pages.

BUSINESS SERVICES

For those travelers requiring word processing, faxing, photocopying or notarial services, there are several secretarial services that can provide such assistance. **Shirley's Secretarial** has two locations on Maui, one in Kahului (871-7850) and one on Front Street in Lahaina (661-5531).

Other companies offering a wide range of business services are: **HQ Business Centers** (242-2828) and **Sandra's Secretarial Service** (244-0042), both in Wailuku; **Kihei Secretarial Service** (874-3122) in Kihei, and **Makawao Secretarial & Bookkeeping** (572-8837) in Makawao.

Traditional Hawaiian music instruments.

PHYSICIANS

Doctors On Call (667-7676) provides same day medical care seven days a week, with three locations serving the Lahaina, Kā'anapali and Kapalua areas. The **West Maui Healthcare Center** at 2435 Kā'anapali Parkway in Kā'anapali (667-9721) offers a full range of medical services, including immediate emergency care and X-rays, and is open daily with extended evening hours. In Kihei, the **Kihei-Wailea Medical Center,** located in Lipoa Shopping Center (874-8100), provides medical care to visitors and specializes in Family Practice and Internal Medicine, and is open daily, including holidays. **The Maui Medical Group, Inc.** has offices in both Wailuku (242-6464) and Lahaina (661-0051) and provides medical care in a number of specialized fields.

TRAVELING WITH CHILDREN

Warm and welcoming, Maui is an excellent place to bring children on vacation. The near-perfect climate allows children to spend time outdoors at the beach or in a park. In addition, most hotels offer supervised daily programs for children, such as the Hyatt Regency Kā'anapali's "Camp Hyatt" for ages three to twelve, and "Rock Hyatt" for teenagers. Activities may include a visit to Lahaina and other historic sites, a ride on the Sugarcane Train, or a catamaran excursion on the Kiele V. The Maui Inter-Continental Resort in Wailea offers a "Keiki's Club Gecko" for children ages five to thirteen, featuring cultural activities such as lei-making and hula lessons. Most of the large resort hotels feature similar programs. The concierge or hotel activities desk can arrange your child's participation.

High quality clothes suitable for Maui are available at **Baby's Choice** in Maui Mall, Kahului. **Superwhale Children's Boutique,** in Whalers Village, Lahaina Cannery and Wailea Shopping Village, **Maui Kids & Co.** in Lahaina Center, and **Kapalua Kids** in the Kapalua Shops also carry a good selection of fashions for children.

BABY-SITTING SERVICES

Sometimes couples want to take a break from their parenting duties and spend a romantic evening in paradise or go off on an adult excursion like scuba diving or a sunset dinner cruise without the kids. Several baby-sitting services operate on the island, providing service island-wide. One of the most established companies is **Babysit Services of Maui,** in operation since 1981, which has CPR and First Aid certified sitters. Their base rate is $8.00 per hour for one child, with a three-hour minimum. To book a sitter, call between 9:00 a.m. and 6:00 p.m. (661-0558). Other companies providing child care services are listed in the Maui Yellow Pages under "Baby Sitters".

TRAVELERS WITH DISABILITIES

The State's **Commission on Persons with Disabilities** publishes a useful guide for travelers with disabilities. To obtain a copy, call the Commission (243-5441), or write: Commission on Persons with Disabilities, State Department of Health, 54 High Street, Wailuku, HI 96793. We have previously noted, in the ACCOMMODATIONS section, those hotels accessible to guests in wheelchairs, with the letter **"W"** in the heading. To find out about access at condominiums, contact the condominiums directly.

TRANSPORTATION

Maui has no public transportation system, hence no system designed particularly for disabled travelers. Private taxis and car rentals are available, but the Commission notes they can accommodate only the partially disabled and the ambulatory traveler. Of the car rental companies on Maui, Avis and Hertz can install hand controls, but a request for this should be made as far in advance as possible to **Avis Rent a Car** (800-321-3712) or **Hertz Rent a Car** (800-654-3011).

SUPPORT SERVICES

Some Maui agencies offer personal care attendants, nurse aides, health aides and volunteer companions. **Maui Center for Independent Living** (242-4966) provides personal care attendants. Other helpful service organizations are **Action Medical Personnel** (875-8300), **Hale Makua** (877-7200) and **Interim Health Care** (877-2676).

MEDICAL EQUIPMENT

These firms on Maui rent out medical equipment for the physically disabled: **Gammie Homecare** at 355 Hukilike St. , #103, in Kahului (877-4032), **Lahaina Pharmacy** at Lahaina Shopping Center (661-3119), and **Wild Wheels Wentals** in Lahaina (661-4131) and Kihei (879-0220).

RECREATION & TRAVEL ARRANGEMENTS

The **Easter Seal Society of Hawaii** (877-4443) can help arrange recreational activities for disabled people, including wheelchair tennis and basketball, bowling and swim classes.

Over the Rainbow Disabled Travel Service (879-5521) on Maui caters to disabled travelers, and assists visitors with hotel reservations, transportation, excursions, sports activities and even weddings. A Honolulu-based travel agency, **Access Aloha Travel Inc.,** provides travel arrangements for visitors with disabilities, including booking reservations for sight-seeing tours. On O'ahu, call 545-1143 or dial 800-480-1143 from neighbor islands.

ACCESS

Most major shopping malls and major dining establishments provide handicapped parking stalls, wheelchair access, adapted restrooms and lowered telephone booths. The Commission on Persons with Disabilities suggests checking with such places in advance. Additionally, there are several hotels that have specially designed rooms to served physically disabled travelers.

The notation **'W'** used in the ACCOMMODATION section of this book denotes those hotels that have wheelchair access. To find out about access at condominiums, contact the condominium directly or the Commission.

OTHER ISLANDS

Each of the main Hawaiian islands has its own special magic, and *The Essential Guide to O'ahu, The Essential Guide to Kaua'i* and *The Essential Guide to Hawai'i, the Big Island* provide the same in-depth coverage of those islands as does this guidebook. We hope you can visit all of our islands and discover for yourself the unique charm of each.

Visitors occasionally are surprised to find that the county of Maui consists of four islands: Maui, Moloka'i, Lāna'i and Kaho'olawe. The county, the second largest in the state, consists of 1174 square miles (3042 sq. km) of land and about 113,000 people (1994 estimate).

MOLOKA'I

The Pailolo Channel separates Moloka'i from Maui. Moloka'i and her people embody much of the traditional Hawaiian spirit, and prefer to keep the tradition of the old ways as much as possible. This sleepy island has a handful of hotels and remains uncrowded. The northwestern coast contains the peninsula where, in the 1860s, those suffering from leprosy were forced ashore in isolation. Today this settlement, Kalaupapa, is still the home of a dwindling number of those afflicted with Hansen's disease. Remote, wind-swept and quiet, Kalaupapa receives an occasional visitor, who must be accompanied by a guide. To make a ground tour of Kalaupapa, contact Richard Marks of Father Damien Tours (567-6171), who will arrange for a visitor's permit. Children under the age of sixteen are not permitted in the settlement. Visitors may make flight arrangements to Moloka'i through two commuter airlines--Air Molokai (877-0026) or Island Air (800-652-6541). Kalaupapa contains a memorial to the Belgian priest, Father Damien, who died a martyr serving the lepers on this peninsula.

LANA'I

Only nine miles from Moloka'i and seven miles off the western coast of Maui is the rural island of **Lāna'i,** mostly owned by Castle and Cooke. Pineapple was the only major industry for years until the opening of two resort hotels, The Lodge at Koele, opened in 1990, and The Manele Bay Hotel, opened in 1991. Both are elegant luxury hotels, the former being styled after an English country manor and set on twenty-one acres in the central uplands skirting Lā'nai City, and the latter a splendid beachfront resort on the cliffs overlooking Hulopo'e Bay.

The Lodge at Koele has 102 richly decorated rooms and is situated at an elevation of 1600 feet and nestled amongst towering Norfolk pines and breathtakingly beautiful, meticulously manicured grounds. The large lobby area, or "Great Hall" has 35-foot beamed ceilings, natural stone fireplaces and large comfortable couches and chairs ideal for enjoying leisurely evenings. Excellent cuisine is offered in either the octagonal formal dining room or on the casual terrace, each providing superb service and overlooking lovely hillside gardens. A Greg Norman designed championship golf course, "The Experience at Koele", is adjacent to the Lodge, in a forested setting surrounded by tall pines and lush mountain vegetation. Readers of Conde Nast's Traveler magazine rated The Lodge at Koele the number one tropical resort for 1994.

The cliff-top Manele Bay Hotel overlooks Hulopo'e Bay and has a lovely white sand beach and lavish Hawaiian, Japanese and Chinese gardens all around. There are 250 luxuriously appointed guest rooms and suites in the two-story hotel, whose architecture is a blend of traditional Hawaiian and Mediterranean styles. An excellent spa facility offers customized workouts, low-impact exercise classes, beauty treatments and personal fitness training. Several dining facilities are on property. The romantic Kailani

Terrace serves afternoon tea, and cocktails are served in the evening, accompanied by live entertainment for guests' listening and dancing pleasure. The Mediterranean-theme Hulopo'e Court is the main dining room, and the Ihilani dining room offers classic Island gourmet cuisine with a French flair. The Pool Grill, situated pool-side, offers a nice selection of sandwiches, burgers, gourmet hot entrees, large and delicious main course salads and desserts. Surrounding the hotel is the Jack Nicklaus designed 18-hole golf course, which opened on Christmas Day of 1993, called "The Challenge at Manele". The course is built on 350 acres atop natural lava outcroppings and set amongst native kiawe and ilima trees. Its signature hole (no. 12) plays from atop a cliff rising 150 feet above the sea, and requires a 200-yard tee shot across the ocean.

Reservations for either hotel may be booked through Rockresorts central reservations at 800-223-7637 or through your travel agent. Although rental cars are available on the island, the resorts provide regular complimentary shuttle service be-tween the two hotels, the boat harbor, Lā'nai City and the airport.

The Hotel Lanai, in sleepy Lā'nai City, is a charming, cozy inn built in 1923 to house guests of Jim Dole, visionary and pineapple czar, who purchased the island in 1921. From its veranda, you can relax on white wicker furniture and look out at towering Norfolk pines surrounding the hotel. Brightly decorated rooms have natural wood floors, old style fixtures and pedestal sinks from another era, and rates are quite reasonable. Ideal for families, an adjacent plantation-style cottage is also available, featuring period furnishings and a four-poster canopy bed. Reservations may be booked by calling 800-321-4666 or 808-565-4700.

A privately owned passenger ferry boat, Expeditions (661-3756), runs five trips daily between Maui's Lahaina Harbor and Lā'nai's Manele Bay; the crossing time is about fifty minutes one way. They also offer a daytime golf excursion and a golf/stay-over package tour to the island.

O'AHU

Beyond the county of Maui lies the island of O'ahu, seat of government, capital of the state of Hawai'i, and called, with reason, 'the Gathering Place'. Some seventy percent of the state's population (or approximately 874,000) is found on O'ahu. Combining a modern, urban atmosphere with a beautiful tropical setting; Honolulu is as cosmopolitan as any other leading city in the world. Among its most popular sites are Pearl Harbor, Diamond Head, Waikiki Beach, and Punch Bowl cemetery.

KAUA'I

One hundred miles northwest of O'ahu is the oldest inhabited island in the chain, Kaua'i. Known as 'the Garden Isle', Kaua'i is an island of flowers, pristine beaches and slow ways, but highly experienced in handling masses of visitors while protecting this breathtaking paradise.

Hanalei is one of the world's most beautiful valleys, and is located at the north of the island. The spectacular Waimea Canyon tends to dwarf everything else on the island. Sometimes referred to as the 'Grand Canyon of the Pacific', it is not quite as large as its namesake, but is every bit as stunning.

NI'IHAU

The island of Ni'ihau is privately owned. Seventeen miles from Kaua'i, it has been removed from mainstream Hawai'i for decades. The Robinson family of Kaua'i has kept the island as a place where Hawaiians, if they chose, could live a traditional life-style. Most residents never leave the island. The spoken language is Hawaiian. The only authorized visits to the island are those by a few state government leaders who go to assure themselves that educational funds and other state monies are being properly dispensed and utilized. Scenic helicopter flights over the island are provided by one helicopter company, flying out of Kaua'i and landing for a short stopover on a secluded beach. No contact with residents, however, is allowed.

HAWAI'I

The remaining inhabited island is located nearly thirty miles southeast of Maui, across the 'Alenuihāhā Channel--the island of **Hawai'i** referred to as **'the Big Island'**. Youngest in the island chain, the Big

Reflections of grandeur at The Lodge at Koele, Island of Lāna'i

Island is so massive that all the other islands would fit into its borders, with room to spare. Five major volcanoes built the island of Hawai'i, and one of them, Kilauea on the flanks of Mauna Loa, continues an eruptive cycle that is still building the coastline. This island is a place of great variety, from the sleepy plantation town atmosphere of East Hawai'i to the tropical bustling West side. In the center of the island are the two highest peaks in the Pacific, Mauna Kea and Mauna Loa, each rising to almost 14,000 feet. Here too is the enormous and privately owned Parker Ranch, more than 200,000 acres dotted with beautiful, healthy cattle. The Big Island was the birthplace of the conqueror, Kamehameha the Great, who united the islands into one kingdom. The monarch died in Kona, and his remains are hidden forever, as was the custom for great leaders in Hawai'i.

MORE ISLANDS

There are other islands in the Hawaiian archipelago, but the average visitor is not likely to see them. They comprise the more than one hundred shoals, sand bars and islets that stretch from the Big Island northwest to tiny Kure Atoll, above Midway, more than 1500 miles away. Parts of them are wildlife sanctuaries.

Uncharted reefs have ripped out the bottoms of unsuspecting ships. One such island complex is French Frigate Shoals, for years a U.S. installation for navigation and weather reporting.

A million or so years from now, the visitor here is likely to find a new Hawaiian island. If the underwater eruption south of the Big Island keeps going at its present rate, another island will be created. Scientists who have seen the undersea eruption with its sea mount beginning to form have given it a name--Lo'ihi--a word which means "long" or "tall" or "prolonged in time."

INTERISLAND TRAVEL

Hawai'i's residents as well as its visitors travel between our islands often, and the high volume of traffic makes interisland air transportation economical and efficient. Flights are short, the longest taking approximately half an hour. Many interisland flights connect in Honolulu, but some fly directly between islands other than O'ahu. Aloha, Aloha Island Air, Hawaiian, and Mahalo are the main interisland carriers. Air Molokai offers service between Moloka'i and the neighbor islands of Maui, Lāna'i and O'ahu. An interisland ferry also transports passengers traveling between Maui and Moloka'i. Another passenger ferry runs daily between Maui's Lahaina Harbor and Lā'nai's Manele Bay, a fifty minute trip one-way.

APPENDIX

Address & Phone Numbers
Word Lists
Recommended Reading
Index

VEHICLE RENTALS

AUTOMOBILES

Alamo Rent A Car - Kahului Airport 871-6235;   Toll-free 800-327-9633
Avis Rent A Car - Kahului Airport 871-7575;   Toll-free 800-321-3712

Budget Rent A Car - Kahului Airport 244-4721;   Toll-free 800-451-3600

Dollar Rent A Car - Kahului Airport 877-2731;   Toll-free 800-800-4000

Hertz Rent A Car - Kahului Airport 877-5167;   Toll-free 800-654-3011

Maui Rent A Jeep - 190 Papa Pl.   Toll-free 800-701-JEEP
                   Kahului 877-6626

National Car Rental - Kahului Airport 871-8851;   Toll-free 800-227-7368

Word of Mouth Rent A Used Car - 150 Hana Hwy.   Toll-free 800-533-5929
                                877-2436

BICYCLES & MOPEDS

A&B Moped Rentals 3481 L. Honoapiilani Hwy., Lahaina   669-0027
Kukui Activity Center 1819 S. Kihei Rd., Kihei   875-1151
South Maui Bicycles 1913-C S. Kihei Rd., Kihei   874-0068
West Maui Cycles 4310 L. Honoapiilani Hwy., Lahaina   669-1169

MOTORCYCLES

Island Riders   1794 S. Kihei Rd., Kihei   874-0311
                   126 Hinau, Lahaina   661-9966

LIMOUSINE SERVICE

Arthur's Limousine Service   871-5555
                                                   800-345-4667
Kapalua Executive Limousine Service   667-7770
Wailea Limousine Service   875-4114

TAXICAB SERVICE

Alii Cab Co.   661-3688
Classy Taxi   661-3044
Jake's Taxi   877-6139
Kaanapali Taxi   661-5285

APPENDIX

Kapalua Executive Cab Service	667-7770
Kihei Taxi	879-3000
La Bella Taxi	242-8011
Royal Sedan & Taxi Service	874-6900
Wailea Taxi & Tours	874-5000
Yellow Cab of Maui	877-7000

WATER SPORTS:
EQUIPMENT & INSTRUCTION

PARASAILING

Island Watersports	Lahaina	667-0536
Lahaina Para-Sail	Lahaina	661-4887
Parasail Kaanapali	Lahaina	669-6555
UFO Parasailing	Lahaina	661-7836
West Maui Para-Sail	Lahaina	661-4060

SCUBA DIVING & SNORKELNG

Capt. Nemo's	Lahaina	661-5555
Central Pacific Divers	Lahaina	667-7647
Dive Maui	Lahaina	667-2080
Dive & Sea Center	Kihei	874-1952
Ed Robinson's Diving	Kihei	879-3584
Extended Horizons	Lahaina	667-0611
Hawaiian Reef Divers	Lahaina	667-7647
Lahaina Divers	Lahaina	667-7496
Makena Coast Charters	Kihei	874-1273
Maui Dive Shop	Kahana	669-3800
	Kihei	879-3388
	Lahaina	661-5388
	Wailea	879-3166
Mike Severns Diving	Kihei	879-6596
Molokini Divers	Kihei	879-0055
ProDive Maui	Kihei	875-4004

SURFING

Alan Cadiz's HST	Kahului	871-5423
Andrea Thomas Surfing School		875-0625
Hawaiian Island Windsurfing	Kahului	871-4981
Hi-Tech Surf Sports	Kahului	877-2111
Local Motion	Lahaina: 661-7873; Kihei: 879-7873	
Nancy Emerson School of Surfing	Lahaina	244-7873
Second Wind Sail & Surf	Kahului	877-7467
West Maui Surfing Academy	Lahaina	661-7337

WIND SURFING

Alan Cadiz's HST	Kahului	871-5423
Hawaiian Island Windsurfing	Kahului	871-4981
Kaanapali Windsurfing School	Lahaina	667-1964
Maui Sailing Center	Kihei	879-5935
Maui Windsurf Co.	Kahului	877-4816
Maui Windsurfari	Kahului	871-7766
Nancy Emerson School of Surfing	Lahaina	244-7873
New Waves Windsurfing School	Kihei	875-4045
Ocean Activities Center	Kihei	879-4485
Second Wind	Kahului	877-7467
Windrigger Maui	Kahului	871-7753
Windsurfing West Maui	Kahului	871-8733

BOATING & WATER TOURS

FISHING TOURS

Aerial Sportfishing Charters	667-9089
Lahaina Charter Boats	667-6672
Luckey Strike Charters	661-4606

INTERISLAND CRUISES

American Hawaii Cruises	800-765-7000

KAYAKING, RAFTING

Hawaiian Rafting Adventures, Inc.	661-7333
Kayaking Adventures of Maui	879-8599
Maui Rafting Expeditions	667-5678
Ocean Rafting	667-2191
Ocean Riders Inc.	661-3586
Valley Isle Kayaking, Inc.	874-8560

SNORKELING/SAILING TOURS

First Class (Alihilani Yacht Charters)	667-7733
Kiele V	661-1234, ext. 3104
Lavengro	879-8188
Paragon	244-2087
Scotch Mist II	661-0386
Silent Lady	875-1112
Spirit of Windjammer	661-8600
Trilogy Excursions	661-4743, 800-874-2666
Whale One	667-7447

AIR TOURS

Big Island Air	808-303-8868
Biplane Barnstormers	878-2860
Paragon Air	244-3356

HELICOPTER TOURS

Alexair Helicopters	877-4354
Blue Hawaiian Helicopters	871-8844
Cardinal Helicopters	877-2400
Hawaii Helicopters Inc.	877-3900
Incredible Journey! (simulated tour-Hyatt Regency Maui)	661-0092
Sunshine Helicopters	871-0711
Temptation Tours	878-2911

GUIDED LAND TOURS

Arthur's Limousine Service	871-5555
Barefoot's Cashback Tours	661-8889
Ekahi Tours	877-9775
Gray Line Maui	877-5509
Roberts Hawaii Tours	871-6226
Temptation Tours	877-8888
Trans Hawaiian Maui	877-7308

SPORTING ACTIVITIES

BICYCLING TOURS

Chris' Bike Adventures	871-BIKE
Makawao Mountain Bike	572-2200
Maui Downhill	871-2155
Maui Mountain Cruisers	871-6014
Mountain Riders Bike Tours	242-9739

FITNESS CENTERS & SPAS

A Sante Spa	Lipoa Center, Kihei	879-5211
	358 Papa Place, Kahului	871-7190
	Dickenson Square, Lahaina	661-5358
The Aerobic Co.	Embassy Suites Resort, Kā'anapali	661-0444
Lahaina Nautilus Center	180 Dickenson St., Lahaina	667-6100
Powerhouse Gym Maui	300 Ohukai Rd., Kihei	879-1326
Valley Isle Fitness Center	Wailuku Industrial Park	242-6851
World Gym	845 Wainee St., Lahaina	667-0422

GOLF

Grand Waikapu Country Club	Waikapu	244-7888
Kaanapali Golf Courses	Kā'anapali	661-3691
Kapalua Golf Club	Kapalua	669-8044
Makena Golf Club	Mākena	879-3344
Maui Country Club	Spreckelsville	877-0616
Pukalani Country Club	Pukalani	572-1314
Sandalwood Golf Course	Lahaina	242-4653
Silversword Golf Club	Waikapu	874-0777
The Challenge at Manele	Island of Lāna'i	565-2222
The Experience at Koele	Island of Lāna'i	565-4600
Waiehu Municipal Golf Course	Wailuku	243-7400
Wailea Golf Club	Wailea	875-5111

HIKING

Crater Bound		878-1743
Hawaii Geographic Society	(O'ahu)	538-3952
Hike Maui		879-5270
Sierra Club	(O'ahu)	538-6616

HORSEBACK RIDING

Adventures on Horseback	Ha'iku	242-7445, 572-6211
Hana Ranch	Hāna	248-7238
Ironwood Ranch Riding Stables	Nāpili	669-4991
Makena Stables	Mākena	879-0244
Maukalani Riding School	Makawao	572-0606
Mendes Ranch	Northeast Maui	871-5222
'O'heo Stables	Kipahulu	667-2222
Piiholo Riding Club	Olinda	672-1789
Pony Express Tours	Kula	667-2200
Seahorse Ranch	Northeast Maui	244-9862
Thompson Ranch Riding Stables	Kula	878-1910

HUNTING

Div. of Conservation and Resources Enforcement (O'ahu)	587-0077
Div. of Land & Natural Resources	243-5352
Hunting Adventures of Maui, Ha'iku	572-8214
Hunting Seasons Hotline (O'ahu)	587-0171
Papakea Sporting Clays, 'Ulupalakua Ranch	879-5649

TENNIS

Hyatt Regency Maui	Kā'anapali	661-1234
Kapalua Tennis Club	Kapalua	669-5677
Makena Tennis Club	Mākena	879-8777
Maui Marriott Resort	Kā'anapali	667-1200
Royal Lahaina Tennis Ranch	Kā'anapali	661-3611

| Village Tennis Center | Kapalua | 665-0112 |
| Wailea Tennis Club | Wailea | 879-1958 |

RESTAURANTS

LAHAINA/KĀANAPALI/KAPALUA AREA

Avalon	844 Front St., Lahaina	667-5999
BJ's Chicago Pizzaria	730 Front St., Lahaina	661-0700
Blue Tropix Night Club	900 Front St., Lahaina	667-5309
Chart House	1450 Front St., Lahaina	661-0937
Cheeseburger in Paradise	811 Front St., Lahaina	661-4855
Chez Paul	820-B Olowalu Village, Lahaina	661-3843
David Paul's Lahaina Grill	127 Lahainaluna Rd., Lahaina	667-5117
The Garden Restaurant	Kapalua Bay Hotel & Villas	669-5656
Gerard's	174 Lahainaluna Rd., Lahaina	661-8939
The Grill	Ritz-Carlton Kapalua	669-1665
Hard Rock Cafe	900 Front St., Lahaina	667-7400
Hula Grill	Whalers Village, Kā'anapali	661-3894
Kapalua Bay Club	1 Bay Drive, Kapalua	669-5656
Kapalua Grill & Bar	Kapalua Bay Hotel & Villas	669-5653
Kimo's	845 Front St., Lahaina	661-4811
Kobe Japanese Steak House	136 Dickenson St., Lahaina	667-5555
La Tasca Nouveau Bistro	900 Front St., Lahaina	661-5700
Lahaina Coolers	180 Dickenson St., Lahaina	661-7082
Leilani's	Whalers Village, Kā'anapali	264-4495
Longhi's	888 Front St., Lahaina	667-2288
Old Lahaina Cafe & Luau	505 Front St., Lahaina	661-3303
Pacific 'O	505 Front St., Lahaina	667-4341
Pineapple Hill	1000 Kapalua Dr., Kapalua	669-6129
Planet Hollywood	744 Front St., Lahaina	667-7877
The Plantation House	2000 Plantation Club Dr., Kapalua	669-6299
Roy's Kahana Bar & Grill	Kahana Gateway Shopping Ctr.	669-6999
Roy's Nicolina Restaurant	Kahana Gateway Shopping Ctr.	669-5000
Sound of the Falls	Westin Maui, Kā'anapali	667-2525
Swan Court	Hyatt Regency Maui, Kā'anapali	667-4420

KIHEI/WAILEA AREA

A Pacific Cafe	1279 S. Kihei Rd., Kihei	879-0069
Bistro Molikini	Grand Wailea Resort & Spa	875-1234
Carelli's on the Beach	2980 S. Kihei Rd., Kihei	875-0001
Erik's Seafood Broiler	2463 S. Kihei Rd., Kihei	879-8400
Five Palms Beach Grill	2960 S. Kihei Rd., Kihei	879-2607

KIHEI/WAILEA AREA (Continued)

Grand Dining Room Maui	Grand Wailea Resort & Spa	875-1234
Hula Moons	Maui Inter-Continental Resort	879-1922
Humuhumunukunuku-apua'a	Grand Wailea Resort & Spa	875-1234
Kea Lani Restaurant	Kea Lani Resort, Wailea	875-4100
Kihei Prime Rib and Seafood House	2511 S. Kihei Rd., Kihei	879-1954
Kincha	Grand Wailea Resort & Spa	875-1234
La Pastaria	41 E. Lipoa St., Kihei	879-9001
Le Gunji	Diamond Resort, Wailea	874-0500
Lobster Cove/Harry's Sushi Bar	100 Wailea Ike Dr., Wailea	879-7677
Pacific Grill	Four Seasons Resort, Wailea	874-8000
Peggy Sue's	1279 S. Kihei Rd., Kihei	875-8944
Raffles	Stouffer Wailea Beach Resort	879-4900
The Sea Watch Restaurant	100 Wailea Golf Club Dr., Wailea	875-8080
Seasons	Four Seasons Resort, Wailea	874-8000

UPCOUNTRY/PĀ'IA AREA

Casanova Italian Restaurant & Deli	1188 Makawao Ave., Makawao	572-0020
Charley's	142 Hāna Hwy., Pā'ia	579-9453
Crossroads Caffe	3682 Baldwin Ave., Makawao	572-1101
Haliimaile General Store	900 Haliimaile Rd., Haliimaile	572-2666
Kula Lodge	Haleakalā Hwy., Kula	878-2517
Makawao Steak House	3612 Baldwin Ave., Makawao	572-8711
Mama's Fish House	799 Poho Pl., Kuau	579-8488
Wunderbar	89 Hāna Hwy., Pā'ia	579-8808

HĀNA AREA

Hana Ranch Restaurant	Hāna Hwy., Hāna	248-8255
Hotel Hana-Maui	Hāna Hwy., Hāna	248-8211

WAILUKU/KAHULUI AREA

Chart House	500 N. Puunene Ave., Kahului	877-2476
Ming Yuen	162 Alamada, Kahului	871-7787
Siam Thai Cuisine	123 N. Market St., Wailuku	244-3817

LU'AU

Atlantis Submarines	(luau/submarine combo pkg.)	667-2224
Drums of the Pacific	Hyatt Regency Maui, Kā'anapali	667-4420
Grand Ohana Luau	Grand Wailea Resort & Spa	875-1234
Hawaiian Country		
Barbecue & Revue	Maui Tropical Plantation, Waikapu	244-7643
Maui Marriott Luau	Maui Marriott, Kā'anapali	661-5828
Old Lahaina Luau	505 Front St., Lahaina	661-3303
Royal Lahaina Luau	Royal Lahaina Resort, Kā'anapali	661-3611
Wailea's Finest Luau	Maui Inter-Continental, Wailea	879-1922
Wailea Sunset Luau	Stouffer Wailea Beach Resort	879-4900

FAST FOODS

The Coffee Store	Azeka Place II, Kihei	875-4244
International House of		
Pancakes	Azeka Place Shopping Ctr., Kihei	879-3445
Kirouac's	Dickenson & Wainee, Lahaina	661-7299
Maui Bakery, Bagelry		
& Deli	201 Dairy Rd., Kahului	871-4825
Maui Swiss Cafe	640 Front St., Lahaina	661-6776
Maui Tacos	Nāpili Plaza & Lahaina Square	665-0222
Moose McGillycuddy's	844 Front St., Lahaina	667-7758
Mushroom	2080 Vineyard St., Wailuku	244-7117
Paia Fish Market	Hāna Hwy. at Balwin Ave., Pā'ia	579-8030
Pair O' Dice Pizza	Kukui Mall, Kihei	874-1968
Peach's and Crumble		
Cafe & Bakery	2 Baldwin Ave., Pā'ia	579-8612
Picnic's	30 Baldwin Ave., Pā'ia	579-8021
Pikake Bakery & Cafe	505 Front St., Lahaina	661-5616
Pupule Cafe	318 N. Market St., Wailuku	242-8449
Surfer Joe's Grill & Bar	61 S. Kihei Rd., Kihei	879-8855
Wiki Wiki Pizza & Deli	2411 S. Kihei Rd., Kihei	879-9454

COCKTAIL LOUNGES & NIGHT SPOTS

Barefoot Bar (Hula Grill)	Whalers Village, Kā'anapali	661-3894
Blue Tropix Nightclub	900 Front St., Lahaina	667-5309
Casanova Italian		
Restaurant & Deli	1188 Makawao Ave., Makawao	572-0220
Charley's	142 Hāna Hwy., Paia	579-9453
Inu Inu Lounge	Maui Inter-Continental, Wailea	879-1922
The Makai Bar	Maui Marriott, Kā'anapali	667-1200
Moose McGillycuddy's	844 Front St., Lahaina	667-7758
Tsunami	Grand Wailea Resort & Spa	875-1234

SHOPS

ABC Discount Stores	724 Front St., Lahaina	667-9558
	Whalers Village, Kā'anapali	667-9700
	3511 Honoapiilani Hwy., Nāpili	669-0271
	Lahaina Cannery Mall, Lahaina	661-5370
	888 Front St., Lahaina	661-5324
	2349 S. Kihei Rd., Kihei	879-6305
	Lahaina Center, Lahaina	667-5733
	666 Front St., Lahaina	667-2623
Ah Fook's Super Market	Kahului Shopping Center	877-3308
Airport Flowers & Fruit	460 Dairy Rd., Kahului	871-7056
Arabesque	900 Front St., Lahaina Center	667-5337
Clouds Rest Protea	Upper Kimo Drive, Kula	878-2544
Coast Gallery Wailea	Maui Inter-Continental, Wailea	879-2301
Collections	Baldwin Ave., Makawao	572-0781
Coral Tree	Wharf Cinema Shops, Lahaina	667-2870
Cost, Curtis Wilson		
Gallery	Kula Lodge, Kula	878-6544
Crazy Shirts	Whalers Village, Kā'anapali	661-0117
	865 Front St., Lahaina	661-4775
	Wharf Cinema Shops, Lahaina	661-4712
	Azeka Pl. Shopping Ctr., Kihei	879-8577
	Lahaina Cannery Mall	661-4788
Dolphin Galleries Inc.	Whalers Village, Kā'anapali	661-3223
Dotson, Larry Galleries	Pioneer Inn, Lahaina	661-7197
Down To Earth Natural	1910 Vineyard, Wailuku	242-6821
Foods	1169 Makawao Ave., Makawao	572-1488
Emura Jewelry & Gifts	49 Market St., Wailuku	244-0674
Escape to Maui	Kamaole Shopping Ctr., Kihei	879-5545
	Lahaina Cannery Mall, Lahaina	661-3344
Food Pantry Honokōwai	3636 L. Honoapiilani Rd.	669-6208
Foodland Super Market	Kaahumanu Ctr., Kahului	877-2808
	Kihei Town Center, Kihei	879-9350
	Lahaina Square Shopping Ctr.	661-0975
	Pukalani Terrace Ctr., Pukalani	572-0674
Fox Photo 1-hr Labs	139 Lahainaluna Rd., Lahaina	667-6255
	Lahaina Cannery Mall, Lahaina	661-7681
	820 Front St., Lahaina	661-8895
	Whalers Village, Kā'anapali	667-5494
	Pioneer Inn, Lahaina	667-0710
	Azeka Pl. Shopping Ctr., Kihei	879-6351
	Wailea Shopping Village, Wailea	879-7577
Haiku Natural Foods	100 Ha'iku Rd., Ha'iku	575-2401
Hale Kohola	Whalers Village, Kā'anapali	661-9918
Hana Coast Gallery	Hotel Hāna-Maui, Hāna	248-8636
Hana Gardenland	Hāna	248-8975
Hana Ranch Store	Hāna	248-8261
Hawaiian Etc.	Kihei Town Center	879-2214

Hawaiian Moons		
Natural Foods	Kihei	875-4356
Herbs Etc.	58 Central Ave., Wailuku	244-0420
Hilo Hattie Fashion Ctr.	Lahaina Center, Lahaina	667-7911
Hui No'eau Visual		
Arts Center	2841 Baldwin Ave., Makawao	572-6560
Ikeda's	81 Market St., Wailuku	244-5459
	Lahaina Shopping Ctr., Lahaina	661-3146
J C Penney Co.	Maui Mall, Kahului	871-7186
Jack Ackerman's The		
Original Maui Divers	640 Front St., Lahaina	661-0988
Jane's Shells & Crafts	40 Baldwin Ave., Pā'ia	579-9288
Jovian Gallery	7 N. Market St., Wailuku	244-3660
Kaneshige Jewelers	Maui Mall, Kahului	877-0116
Kihei Professional		
Pharmacy	41 E. Lipoa, Kihei	879-8499
K mart Stores	424 Dairy Rd., Kahului	871-8553
Kramer's Men's Wear	Lahaina Cannery Mall, Lahaina	661-5377
La Pre Shell & Gift Shop	1279 S. Kihei Rd., Kihei	879-7400
Lahaina Galleries	728 Front St., Lahaina	667-2152
	123 Bay Dr., Kapalua	669-0202
	370 Wailea Alanui, Wailea	879-8850
Lahaina Pharmacy	Lahaina Shopping Center	661-3119
Lahaina Printsellers	Whalers Village, Kā'anapali	667-7617
	Lahaina Cannery Mall, Lahaina	667-7843
	Grand Wailea Resort & Spa	874-9310
Lahaina Scrimshaw	845-A Front St., Lahaina	661-8820
	Whalers Village, Kā'anapali	661-4034
Lahaina Shell Shop	3481 L. Honoapiilani Rd., Lahaina	669-6464
Lamont's Gift & Sundry	Hāna	248-7323
	1 Ritz-Carlton Dr., Kapalua	669-8538
	104 Kā'anapali Shrs. Pl., Kā'anapali	667-6097
	3900 Wailea Alanui, Wailea	874-9522
	4100 Wailea Alanui, Wailea	874-1844
Leilani Gift Shop	Azeka Pl. Shopping Ctr., Kihei	879-7506
Leisure Sundries	Maui Prince Hotel, Mākena	879-9305
Liberty House	Kaahumanu Ctr., Kahului	877-3361
	Azeka Pl. II Shopping Ctr., Kihei	879-7448
	Embassy Suites Resort, Kā'anapali	661-5811
	Lahaina Center	661-4451
Longs Drug Stores	Maui Mall, Kahului	877-0041
	1215 S. Kihei Rd., Kihei	879-2259
	Lahaina Cannery Mall, Lahaina	667-4384
Mana Foods	49 Baldwin Ave., Pā'ia	579-8078
Mandalay Imports	Kapalua Shops	669-6170
	Four Seasons Resort-Wailea	874-5111
	Grand Wailea Resort & Spa	879-8874
Mark's Hallmark Shop	Kaahumanu Ctr., Kahului	877-6113

Maui 60 Minute Color Photos	Maui Mall, Kahului	871-7098
Maui Blooms	300 Ohukai Rd., Kihei	874-0875
Maui Clothing Co.	Lahaina Shopping Center	667-6090
	Whalers Village, Kā'anapali	661-8483
Maui Craft's Guild	43 Hāna Hwy., Pā'ia	579-9697
Maui Natural Foods	Maui Mall, Kahului	877-3018
Miracles Bookery Too	3682 Baldwin Ave., Makawao	572-2317
Nelson, Robert Lyn	802 Front St., Lahaina	667-2100
Studios	910 Honoapiilani Hwy., Lahaina	661-1150
	New York-Paris	
Collectible Art	505 Front St., Lahaina	667-0727
O'Rourke's Tourist Trap	Azeka Pl. Shopping Ctr., Kihei	879-7055
	Kamaole Shopping Ctr., Kihei	879-0405
	Kahana Gateway, Kahana	669-1406
One Hour Moto Photo	The Westin Maui, Kā'anapali	667-5788
Ooka Super Market Ltd.	1870 Main, Wailuku	244-3931
Panama Jack's	Kamaole Shopping Ctr., Kihei	879-5545
	Lahaina Cannery Mall, Lahaina	661-3344
Paradise Pharmacy	81-21 Makawao Ave., Makawao	572-1266
Perles de Tahiti	608 Front St., Lahaina	661-8833
Plantation Marketplace	Maui Tropical Plantation	244-7643
Protea Gift Shoppe	Kula Lodge, Haleakalā Hwy.	878-6048
Pukalani Drugs	Foodland, Pukalani Terrace Ctr.	572-8266
Pukalani Superette	Pukalani (Upcountry)	572-7616
Reyn's	Kapalua Bay Hotel	669-5260
	Lahaina Cannery Mall, Lahaina	661-5356
	Hyatt Regency Maui, Kā'anapali	661-0215
	Whalers Village, Kā'anapali	661-9032
Royal Hawaiian Heritage Jewelry	Lahaina Cannery Mall, Lahaina	661-7678
Safeway Stores	170 E. Kam Ave., Kahului	877-3377
	1221 Honoapiilani Hwy., Lahaina	667-4392
Sears Roebuck & Co.	Kaahumanu Center, Kahului	877-2207
Shirokiya	Kaahumanu Center, Kahului	877-5551
Silks Kaanapali Ltd.	Whalers Village, Kā'anapali	667-7133
South Pacific Gifts & Sundries	Westin Maui, Kā'anapali	661-0234
	Hyatt Regency Maui, Kā'anapali	661-3388
	Hyatt Regency Maui, Kā'anapali	661-3006
Star Markets Ltd.	Maui Mall, Kahului	877-3341
	1310 S. Kihei Rd., Kihei	879-5871
Sun Day	Wharf Cinema Shops, Lahaina	667-1888
Su-su's Boutique	Wailea Shopping Village	879-2623
T-Shirt Factory	90 Hāna Hwy., Kahului	579-8688
	Maui Mall, Kahului	877-0552
	Rainbow Mall, Kihei	879-8066
	Wailea Shopping Village	879-7005
	730 Front St., Lahaina	667-2123
	Pioneer Inn, Lahaina	661-4440

Take Home Maui Inc.	121 Dickenson, Lahaina	661-8067
Traders	Royal Lahaina Resort, Kā'anapali	667-6016
Tropical Tantrum	Azeka Place Shopping Ctr., Kihei	874-3835
	Kamaole Shopping Ctr., Kihei	875-4433
Valley Isle Pharmacy	2180 Main, Wailuku	244-7252
	130 Prison, Lahaina	661-4747
Viewpoints Gallery	3620 Baldwin Ave., Makawao	572-5979
Village Gallery, The	120 Dickenson, Lahaina	661-4402
	Lahaina Cannery Mall, Lahaina	661-3280
	Ritz-Carlton Kapalua	669-1800
W. H. Smith	3850 Wailea Alanui, Wailea	874-1134
Wailea Pantry	Wailea Shopping Village	879-3044
Waldenbooks	Whalers Village, Kā'anapali	661-8638
	Kaahumanu Ctr., Kahului	871-6112
	Kukui Mall, Kihei	874-3688
	Lahaina Cannery Mall, Lahaina	667-6172
	Maui Mall, Kahului	877-0181
Whaler's Chest	Royal Lahaina Resort, Kā'anapali	667-9180
Whaler's Locker Inc.	780 Front St., Lahaina	661-3775
Whalers Book Shoppe	658 Front St., Lahaina	667-9544
Whalers General Store	4405 L. Honoapiilani Rd., Kahana	669-3700
	505 Front St., Lahaina	661-3504
	180 Dickenson St., Lahaina	661-4663
	2463 S. Kihei Rd., Kihei	879-8670
	5425D L. Honoapiilani Rd., Nāpili	669-6773
	Wharf Cinema Shops, Lahaina	661-8871
	1819 S. Kihei Rd., Kihei	879-7499
Wyland Galleries Hawaii	136 Dickenson, Lahaina	661-0590
	697 Front St., Lahaina	661-7099
	711 Front St., Lahaina	667-2285
	Whalers Village, Kā'anapali	661-8255
Yoshimura Jewelers	706 Front St., Lahaina	661-0156

SHOPPING CENTERS

Azeka Place	1280 S. Kihei Rd., Kihei	874-8400
Dolphin Shopping Plaza	2395 S. Kihei Rd., Kihei	875-4845
505 Front Street	505 Front St., Lahaina	667-2514
Gateway Shopping Ctr.	Lower Honoapiilani Rd., Kahana	
Kaahumanu Shopping Ctr.	Ka'ahumanu Ave., Kahului	877-3369
Kahului Shopping Ctr.	Ka'ahumanu Ave., Kahului	877-3369
Kamaole Shopping Ctr.	S. Kihei Rd., Kihei	877-7700
Kapalua Shops	900 Kapalua Dr., Kapalua	669-1029
Kihei Town Center	1881 S. Kihei Rd., Kihei	
Kukui Mall	1819 S. Kihei Rd., Kihei	244-8735
Lahaina Cannery Mall	1221 Honoapiilani Hwy., Lahaina	661-5304
Lahaina Center	900 Front St., Lahaina	667-9216

SHOPPING CENTERS (Continued)

Lahaina Market Place	Lahaina	667-2636
Lahaina Shopping Ctr.	845 Waine'e St., Lahaina	661-5518
Lahaina Square Shopping Center	2145 Wells St., Lahaina	242-4400
Maui Mall	Ka'ahumanu Ave., Kahului	877-5523
Mariner's Alley	844 Front St., Lahaina	661-8351
Pukalani Terrace Center	Haleakalā Hwy., Pukalani	572-7900
Rainbow Mall	2439 S. Kihei Rd., Kihei	244-8735
Wailea Shopping Village	3750 Wailea Alanui Dr., Wailea	879-4474
Whalers Village	Kā'anapali Pkwy., Kā'anapali	661-4567
Wharf Cinema Shops & Restaurants	658 Front St., Lahaina	661-8748

PLACES OF INTEREST

LAHAINA/KĀANAPALI

Baldwin Home Museum	688 Front St., Lahaina	661-3262
Banyan Tree	by Hotel St., Lahaina	
Black Rock	by Sheraton Maui, Kā'anapali	
Brick Palace	near Hauola Stone, Lahaina Library	
The Carthaginian	across from Pioneer Inn, Lahaina	
Coral Miracle Church	see St. Gabriel's Church	
Coral Stone House	see Richards, William, home of	
Hale Pa'i, the Printing House	adjacent to Lahainaluna High	661-8384
Hale Pa'ahao	Waine'e St., Lahaina	
Hauola Stone	north of The Carthaginian, Lahaina	
Lahaina Hongwanji Mission	551 Waine'e St., Lahaina	661-0640
Lahaina Jodo Mission	12 Ala Moana, near Māla Wharf	661-4304
Lahaina Restoration Fdn.	Lahaina	661-3262
Lahainaluna High School	980 Lahainaluna Rd., Lahaina	661-0313
Malu'uluoLele Park	corner Front and Shaw Sts.	
Masters' Reading Room	Front St. between Dickenson and Paelekane Sts., Lahaina	
Mt. Ball	above Lahainaluna High School	
Old Fort	next to Old Lahaina Courthouse	
Old Lahaina Courthouse	Wharf St., Lahaina	661-0970
Pioneer Inn	behind The Carthaginian, Lahaina	661-3636
Richards, Wm., home of	near Masters' Reading Room	244-3326
Rotten Row	end of Wharf St., Lahaina	
Shingon Temple	Luakini St., Lahaina	
Waine'e Cemetery	535 Waine'e St., Lahaina	
Waiola Church	535 Waine'e St., Lahaina	661-4349
Whale Ctr. of the Pacific	Whalers Village, Kā'anapali	661-5992

KIHEI/WAILEA

'Ahihi-Kina'u Natural Area Reserve	Mākena
Bellstone	by Nākālele Pt.
La Perouse Bay	South of 'Ahihi-Kina'u Natural Area Reserve

HĀNA

Hale Waiwai O Hāna	see Hāna Cultural Center	
Hāna Cultural Center	near turnoff to Hāna Bay	248-8622
Hasegawa General Store	Hāna Hwy.	248-8231
Helani Gardens	Hāna Hwy.	248-8274
Ka'uiki Head	area in Hāna	
Ke'anae Arboretum	above Hwy. 36, Ke'anae	248-8592
Ke'anae Valley Lookout	Hwy. 36	
Kuialoha Church	Hwy. 36, Kaupō	
Mantokuji Buddhist Temple	Pā'ia	
Palapala Ho'omau Church	by Kipahulu Ranch	
Pi'ilanihale Heiau	Alaino Rd.	
St. Gabriel's Church	Wailua	
Seven Pools	road past Hāna	
Wānanalua Church	corner Hāna Hwy. and Hauoli St.	248-8040

UPCOUNTRY

Church of the Holy Ghost	hillside above Waiakoa	
Haleakalā National Park	Visitor Center	572-7749
Kula Botanical Gardens	Upper Kula Rd., Kula	878-1715
Leleiwi Overlook	9000-ft. level of Haleakalā	
Pā'ia Sugar Mill	Baldwin Ave., Pā'ia	
Tedeschi Vineyards, Ltd.	Hwy. 37, 'Ulupalakua	878-6058
'Ulupalakua Ranch	Hwy. 37 near Keokea	878-1202

WAILUKU/KIAHULUI

Bailey House Museum	2375-A Main St., Wailuku	244-3326
Haleki'i Heiau	Kuhio Place.	
Ka'ahumanu Church	103 S. High St., Wailuku	244-5189
Kalana O Maui, County Building	High St., Wailuku	244-7711
Kanahā Pond	between Kahului Airport & Wailuku	
Kepaniwai Heritage Gardens	road to 'Iao Valley	244-3656
Maui Historical Society Museum	2375-A Main St., Wailuku	244-3326
Maui Tropical Plantation	Hwy. 30, Waikapu	244-7643
Pali 'Ele'ele	'Iao Valley State Park	
Sugar Plant	by Kahului Harbor	
Wailuku Library	251 High St., Wailuku	244-3945

HAWAIIAN WORD LIST

These words are likely to be seen or heard by anyone visiting these islands. Some may be seen without the markings that alter pronunciation (and meaning), as explained in the INTRODUCTION. In the pronunciation guides given here, typical English syllables which most closely approximate the Hawaiian vowel sounds are used; a precise rendition would require long and complex explanations. The *'okina* (glottal stop) has been retained to show where adjacent vowels should not slide from one to the other. The *kahakō* (macron) shows where they are especially joined, almost as English diphthongs; syllables with elongated vowels are written twice and linked with the same mark. Stress is indicated by capitalization.

a'ā (AH-'AH) a rough, crumbly type of lava
aikāne (aye-KAH-neh) friend
akamai (ah-kah-my-ee) smart, wise, on the ball
ali'i (ah-LEE-'ee) chief, nobility
aloha a nui loa (ah-LO-ha ah NOO-ee LO-ah) much love
auē, auwē (ah-oo-EH-EH) alas!, oh dear!, too bad!, goodness!
'awa (AH-vah) traditional Polynesian drink wrung from the roots of the pepper plant (kava)
hana hou (hah-nah HO-oo) encore! do it again!
hanohano (hah-no-HAH-no) distinguished, magnificent
haole (HAH-oh-leh) originally foreigner; now Caucasian
hapa (HAH-pa) half, part
hapa-haole (HAH-pa HAH-oh-leh) half Caucasian
Hau'oli Makahiki Hou (ha-oo-'oh-lee mah-ka-hee-kee ho-oo) Hawaiian translation of Happy New Year (now used, but not traditional greeting)
haupia (ha-oo-PEE-ah) coconut pudding
heiau (HEH-ee-ah-oo) ancient Hawaiian place of worship
hele (HEH-leh) go, walk around
holoholo (ho-lo-HO-lo) to visit about, make the rounds
ho'olaule'a (ho-'oh-lah-oo-LAY-ah) celebration
hui (HOO-ee) club, association
hukilau (HOO-kee-lah-oo) community net-fishing party
hula (HOO-lah) Hawaiian dance
huli (HOO-lee) turn over, turn around
humuhumunukunukuāpua'a (hoo-moo-hoo-moo-noo-koo-noo-koo-ah-poo-AH-'ah) Hawai'i's State fish; a small triggerfish famous for its long name
iki (EE-kee) little (size)
imu (EE-moo) ground oven
imua (ee-MOO-ah) forward, onward
kāhili (kah-ah-HEE-lee) a royal feathered standard
kahuna (kah-HOO-nah) priest, expert
kai (KY-ee) sea, sea water
kālā (KAH-lah) money (literally dollar)
kama'āina (kah-mah-AYE-nah) native born, longtime Hawai'i resident, old established family

kanaka (ka-NAH-kah) originally 'man' or person; now a native Hawaiian
kāne (KAH-neh) boy, man, husband
kapa (KAH-pah) tapa cloth (made from mulberry bark)
kapakahi (kah-pah-KAH-hee) crooked, lopsided
kapu (KAH-poo) forbidden, sacred, taboo, keep out
kaukau (KAH-oo-kah-oo) food
keiki (KAY-kee) child
kiawe (kee-AH-vay) mesquite tree
kōkua (ko-KOO-ah) help, assistance, aid
kona (KO-nah) winds 'that blow against the trades', lee side of an island
kukui (koo-KOO-ee) candlenut tree
kumu (KOO-moo) teacher
lānai (lah-NY-ee) porch, terrace, veranda
lani (LAH-nee) heaven, heavenly, sky
lauhala (lah-oo-HAH-lah) leaf of the pandanus tree (for weaving)
laulau (LAH-oo-lah-oo) bundled food in ti leaves
lei (LAY-ee) garland of flowers, shells or feathers, wreath
liliko'i (lee-lee-KOH-ee) passion fruit
loa (LO-ah) long
lomi (LO-mee) rub, press, massage, type of raw salmon (usually lomilomi)
lua (LOO-ah) toilet, restroom
lū'au (LOO-'ah-oo) feast, party, taro leaf
mahalo (mah-HAH-loh) thank you
mahimahi (mah-hee-MAH-hee) dorado or dolphin fish
māhū (MAH-hoo) gay, homosexual
makai (mah-KY-ee) toward the sea
make (MAH-keh) dead
makule (mah-KOO-leh) elderly, old (of people)
malihini (mah-lee-HEE-nee) newcomer, visitor
malo (MAH-lo) man's loincloth
mauka (MAH-oo-ka) toward the mountains, inland
mauna (MAH-oo-nah) mountain
Mele Kalikimaka (meh-leh kah-lee-kee-MAH-ka) Merry Christmas
Menehune (meh-neh-HOO-neh) legendary race of dwarfs
moemoe (mo-eh-MO-eh) sleep
mu'umu'u (moo-'oo-moo-'oo) long or short loose-fitting dress
nui (NOO-ee) big
'ohana (oh-HAH-nah) family, extended family
'ōkole (oh-oh-KO-lay) buttocks, bottom, rear
'ōkole maluna (oh-oh-ko-lay-mah-LOO-nah) Hawaiian translation of
'bottoms up' (a bit crude)
'ono (OH-no) delicious
'ōpu (OH-OH-POO-OO) abdomen, stomach
pakalōlō (pah-kah-LO-lo) marijuana
Pākē (PAH-keh) Chinese
pali (PAH-lee) cliff, precipice; the Pali= Nu'uanu Pali
paniolo (pah-nee-OH-lo) cowboy
pau (PA-oo) finished, done
pau hana (pa-oo HAH-nah) finish work

pāhoehoe (pah-ho-eh-HO-eh) type of lava with smooth or ropy surface
pīkake (pee-KAH-keh) jasmine flower, named after 'peacock'
poi (POY) pasty food made from pounded taro, a staple starch of the Hawaiian diet
puka (POO-kah) hole, door
pūpū (POO-poo) hors d'oeuvres (literally 'shells')
tūtū (TOO-TOO) grandmother, affectionate term for old people--relatives or friends--of grandparents' generation (according to the rules of language set down by the missionaries, there is no 't' in the Hawaiian language, but hardly anyone ever says kūkū)
'uku (OO-koo) fleas, head lice
'ukulele (oo-koo-LAY-leh) small, stringed instrument from Portugal
wahine (va-HEE-neh, wah-HEE-neh) girl, woman, wife
wikiwiki (wee-kee-WEE-kee) fast, in a hurry, quickly

PIDGIN ENGLISH WORDS

The pronunciation of pidgin is self-evident, and its spelling is phonic rather than fixed. In most cases, the derivation is also obvious. The lilt that is peculiar to this local lingo cannot be adequately described; it must be heard. This list is given as a guide to listening only. Trying to speak pidgin involves the risk of inadvertently saying something offensive or insulting. Everyone who speaks pidgin also understands correctly spoken English.

an den? So? What next? What else? (and then)
any kine anything (any kind)
ass right you are correct (that's right)
bambucha big
bambula big
blalah heavy-set Hawaiian man, may be looking for a fight
bradah friend (brother)
brah short for bradah
buggah guy, friend, pest
bumbye after a while (by and by)
bummahs too bad, disappointed expression (bummer)
cockaroach rip off, steal, confiscate
cool head main ting keep calm, relax
da the
da kine anything being discussed, used as either noun or verb when the speaker can't think of the right word
dat that
dem them, guys, folks
eh? you know, do you understand?; also used at the beginning of a statement

garans guaranteed, for sure
geevum go for it! (give them)
grind eat
grinds food
had it destroyed, wrecked
hele on go, leave, 'with it', 'hip'
high mucka mucka arrogant, conceited, elite
ho! exclamation used before a strong statement
how you figga? how do you figure that, makes no sense
howzit hi, hello, how are you doing, what's happening (how is it)
junk lousy, terrible
kay den okay then, fine
li'dat like that, shortcut for lengthy explanation
li'dis like this
humbug trouble, bother
make 'A' make a fool of yourself (make ass)
make house make yourself at home, act like you own the place
mama-san local Japanese equivalent of 'mom' at 'mom and 'pop' stores
Maui wowie potent marijuana from Maui
minors no big thing, minor
mo' more
mo' bettah better, good stuff
moke heavy-set Hawaiian male, often looking for a fight
nah just kidding (often **nah, nah, nah**)
no can cannot, I can't do it
o' wot? (added on to most questions, usually when the speaker is fed up -- or what?)
poi dog mutt, person made up of many ethnic mixtures
shahkbait white-skinned, pale (shark bait)
shaka all right, great, well done, perfect, okay, right on
sleepahs flip-flops, thongs (slippers)
stink eye dirty look, evil eye
talk story rap, shoot the breeze, gossip
tanks, eh? thank you
tita heavy-set Hawaiian woman, may be looking for a fight (sister)
try used at beginning of a command
we go let's leave
yeah? added on to the end of sentences
yeah yeah yeah yeah yes, all right, shut up

RECOMMENDED READING

T here are countless books detailing the many aspects of Hawaiian history and culture, both ancient and modern. It has been impossible to detail these fascinating areas in a guidebook small enough to be handy. We recommend the following:

Atlas of Hawaii, by the Dept. of Geography, University of Hawai'i, University of Hawai'i Press, 1983. This book provides text on Hawai'i's natural environment, culture and economy along with maps.

The Beaches of Maui County, by John R. K. Clark, University of Hawai'i Press, 1980. A complete guide to the beaches of Maui County, with maps, photographs, safety rules, local history and beach lore.

Bird Life in Hawaii, by Andrew J. Berger, Island Heritage, 1987. The story of the bird life in Hawai'i, including exotic birds and species which have become rare and endangered, each illustrated in full color accompanied by text written by the world's leading authority on Hawaiian birds.

Discovery, The Hawaiian Odyssey, Bishop Museum Press, 1993. This exquisitely designed coffee table book chronicles the dramatic saga of Polynesian exploration, celebrating the genius of ancient navigators and the triumph of Hawaiian civilization.

Entertaining Island Style, by Lavonne Tollerud and Barbara Gray, Island Heritage, 1987. Menu planning is made simple in this colorful book. From lu'aus and beach parties to elegant Hawaiian suppers, there are many creative ideas for entertaining.

Favorite Recipes from Hawaii, by Lavonne Tollerud and Barbara Gray, Island Heritage, 1987. A collection of Hawai'i's most popular recipes. It includes Hawaiian cocktails, hors d'oeuvres, soups, salads, breads, main dishes, condiments, rice and noodles, vegetables and desserts.

Flowers of Hawaii, photography by Allan Seiden and Loye Gutherie, Island Heritage, 1987. A beautifully photographed guide to Hawai'i's colorful flowers, such as hibiscus, orchids and lilies, and their origins.

A Guide to Hawaiian Marine Life, by Les Matsuura, Island Heritage, 1987. Written by a marine educator at the Waikiki Aquarium, this guide highlights the marine life in Hawai'i through description and color photographs.

Hawai'i, by Moana Tregaskis, Compass American Guides, 1992. Explore Hawai'i with *New York Times* travel writer Moana Tregaskis, who blends the insights of a native with the perspective of a sophisticated international traveler. Detailed facts of every aspect of island culture, history and places of interest, complete with superb color photographs.

Hawaii, by James Michener, Random, 1959. A novel about Hawai'i from its geological birth to the present, by this renowned author.

Hawaii: A History, by Ralph S. Kuykendall, Prentice, 1961. A good overall history of Hawai'i from the first Polynesian voyages to statehood.

Hawaii: The Aloha State, by Allan Seiden, Island Heritage, 1987. Visit exciting Waikīkī, colorful Lahaina, majestic Waimea Canyon, historic Kona-- all the Hawaiian Islands are brought to life in this beautifully photographed book.

Hawaii Below: Favorites, Tips and Secrets of the Diving Pros, written and photographed by Rod Canham. Touted by Hawai'i's diving community as the ultimate resource for diving Hawai'i's waters, this island-by-island guide is a wealth of inside information drawn from the author's own experiences and those of numerous diving pros.

Hawaiian Dictionary, by Mary Kawena Pukui and Samuel H. Elbert, University of Hawai'i Press, 1986. Hawaiian-English, English-Hawaiian dictionary, regarded as the definitive reference for Hawaiian vocabulary. It contains folklore, poetry and ethnology compiled by the leading authorities of Hawaiiana and Polynesian languages.

Hawaii's Humpback Whales: A Complete Whalewatchers Guide, by Gregory D. Kaufman and Paul H. Forestall, Pacific Whale Foundation. Everything you ever wanted to know about humpback whales is provided in this fascinating book.

Hiking Maui, by Robert Smith, Wilderness Press, 1984. This accurate guidebook lists hiking trails on Maui, all personally trod by the author, with descriptions of the route, highlights, rating of difficulty, driving instructions, distance and average hiking time.

The Illustrated Atlas of Hawaii, by Gavan Daws, O. A. Bushnell & Andrew Berger, Island Heritage, 1987. Illustrations of the Hawaiian island chain, native plants, birds and fish by Joseph Feher with a concise history.

The Island of Lanai: A Survey of Native Culture, by Kenneth P. Emory, Bishop Museum Press, 1969. The only writing of its kind, this book focuses on archaeology and anthropology of Lā'nai, and the history, customs, traditions and original genealogy of the first inhabitants of the island. Sketches and photos of *heiaus* also are included.

The Journal of Prince Alexander Liholiho, Jacob Adler, ed., University of Hawai'i Press, 1967. Young Alexander Liholiho and his brother Lot visited the United States, England and France on a diplomatic mission with Dr. Judd. This diary records the impressions of the future king.

APPENDIX

212

Ka Po'e Kahiko: The People of the Old, by **Samuel K. Kamakau,** Bishop Museum Press, 1987. This book and its companion, *The Works of the People of Old: Na Hana a ka Po'e Kahiko,* are based on a series of articles written for the Hawaiian language newspaper Ke Au 'Oko'a in 1868 and 1870.

Ka'ahumanu: Molder of Change, by **Jane Silverman,** Friends of the Judiciary History Center of Hawaii, 1987. A biography of the most powerful woman in Hawaiian history and the vast changes she wrought in the social and political life of the kingdom she ruled.

Kahuna La'au Lapa'au (The Practice of Hawaiian Herbal Medicine), by **June Gutmanis,** Island Heritage, 1987. Authoritative and definitive work on Hawaiian herbs and the secrets of Hawaiian herbal medicine, with colorful illustrations.

Kalakaua: Hawaii's Last King, **by Kristin Zambucka,** Mana Publishing Co. and Marvin/Richard Enterprises, Inc., 1983. This pictorial biography with more than 180 old photos recounts the reign of Hawai'i's last king.

Maui, The Valley Isle, **by Allan Seiden,** Island Heritage, 1986. This work contains photographs, history, tales and other information about Maui and its people.

Māui: The Demigod, **by Steven Goldsberry,** Poseidon Press, 1984. This work about a universal figure in Polynesian folktales is remarkable for its utter originality and beauty of its language. The story is wise and funny, erotic and terrifying, and filled with humanity, folly and fate.

Molokai, by **Oswald Bushnell,** World Publishing Company, 1963. A novel about a group of people sent to a leper colony on Moloka'i and the shocking details of their lives.

Myths and Legends of Hawaii, by **W. A. Westervelt,** Mutual Publishing Co., 1987. A broadly inclusive one-volume collection of folklore by this leading authority, including the great prehistoric Māui, Hina, Pele and her fiery family, and a dozen other heroic beings, human or ghostly.

Na Pule Kahiko: Ancient Hawaiian Prayers, by **June Gutmanis,** Editions Limited, 1983. This collection of traditional Hawaiian prayers, in both Hawaiian and English, is annotated with fascinating detail about the contexts in which these prayers, and prayers in general, were used in the lives of ancient Hawaiians.

Niihau Shell Leis, by **Linda Paik Moriarty,** University of Hawai'i Press, 1986. An expert documentation of the traditions of this unique art form, richly illustrated with color photographs of the many varieties of this rare and precious, gem-quality shell, and based on personal interviews with Ni'ihau women who are actively engaged in this ancient craft.

An Ocean in Mind, by Will Kyselka, University of Hawai'i Press, 1987. The extraordinary story of a 6000-mile trip from Hawai'i to Tahiti and back, the 1980 voyage of the Hokule'a, without the use of modern navigational aid. Navigator Nainoa Thompson, of Hawaiian descent, studied the stars, winds and currents to explore his Polynesian past.

The Peopling of Hawaii, by Eleanor C. Nordyke, University of Hawaii Press, 1977. A review of Hawai'i's people and the effects of population growth on an island community.

Place Names of Hawaii, by Mary Kawena Pukui, Samuel H. Elbert & Esther T. Mookini, University of Hawai'i Press, 1974. Place names listed with pronunciation and translation where known. Includes names of valleys, streams, mountains, land sections, surfing areas, towns, villages and Honolulu streets and buildings.

Princess Kaiulani: The Last Hope of Hawai'i's Monarchy, by Kristin Zambucka, Mana Publishing Co., 1982. Pictorial biography of Hawai'i's beautiful and tragic princess. Niece of Queen Lili'uokalani, Hawai'i's last reigning monarch, Princess Ka'iulani was next in the line of succession to the throne.

Pua Nani, by Jeri Bostwick, photographs by Douglas Peebles, Mutual Publishing, 1987. Stunning color photography of the myriad blossoms--both native and introduced--that festoon these islands with their glorious hues and intricate structures.

The Return of Lono, by Oswald Bushnell, University of Hawai'i Press, 1971. A fictional reconstruction of the discovery of the Hawaiian Island by Captain Cook.

Shoal of Time, by Gavan Daws, University of Hawai'i Press, 1974. An excellent and authoritative history of Hawai'i from earliest times to statehood, 1959.

Sweet Voices of Lahaina, The Story of Maui's Fabulous Farden Family, by Mary C. Richards, Island Heritage, 1990. A warm, charming and informative biography of Hawai'i's first family of music.

Tropical Drinks and Pupus from Hawaii, by Lavonne Tollerud and Barbara Gray, Island Heritage, 1987. Delicious island cocktails and fruit drinks are complemented with a wide range of Hawaiian style hors d'oeuvres.

Under a Maui Sun, A Celebration of the Island of Maui, by Penny Pence Smith, Island Heritage, 1989. An extraordinarily beautiful photographic exploration of today's Maui. More than 200 images from Hawai'i's finest photographers, accompanied by an essay on the history and culture of the island.

INDEX

PHOTOGRAPHERS

All photos by Scott Rutherford
except the following:

Title Page	Peter French	68	Bob Abraham
12	Island Heritage	70	Ron Dahlquist
	Photo Library	95	Jeffrey Asher
18	Bob Abraham	103	Ron Dahlquist
27	Courtesy of	107	Michael S. Nolan
	American Hawaii	120	Courtesy of
	Cruises		Ka'anapali Beach Hotel
29	Island Heritage	135	Island Heritage
	Photo Library		Photo Library
33	Courtesy of	157	Courtesy of Ritz Carlton
	Cruiser Bob's		Kapalua
35	Ron Dahlquist	161	Ron Dahlquist
40	Peter French	165	Courtesy of Ritz Carlton
44	Bob Abraham		Kapalua
45	Peter French	183	Island Heritage
50	Bob Abraham		Photo Library
60	Ron Dahlquist	189	Arnold Savrann
66	Ron Dahlquist	191	R. Coryell

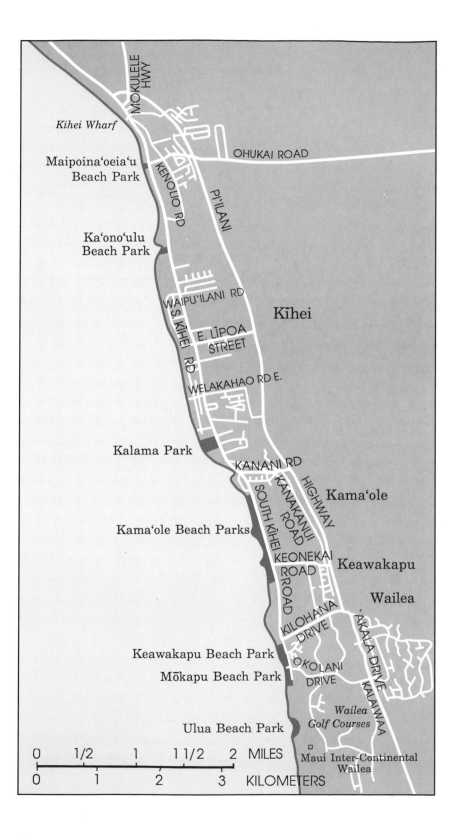

MOKULELE HWY

Kihei Wharf

Maipoina'oeia'u
Beach Park

KENOLIO RD

PI'ILANI

OHUKAI ROAD

Ka'ono'ulu
Beach Park

WAIPU'ILANI RD

S. KIHEI RD

E. LĪPOA
STREET

Kīhei

WELAKAHAO RD E.

Kalama Park

KANANI RD

HIGHWAY

KANAKANUI ROAD

SOUTH KIHEI

Kama'ole

Kama'ole Beach Parks

KEONEKAI
ROAD

SOUTH KIHEI ROAD

Keawakapu

Wailea

KILOHANA DRIVE

'AKALA DRIVE

Keawakapu Beach Park

Mōkapu Beach Park

'O'KOLANI
DRIVE

KALAI'WAA

*Wailea
Golf Courses*

Ulua Beach Park

0	1/2	1	1 1/2	2	MILES
0		1	2	3	KILOMETERS

Maui Inter-Continental
Wailea

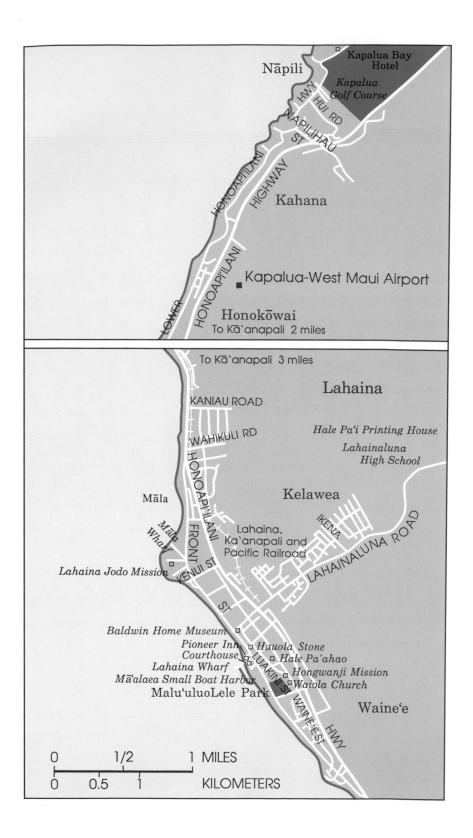